S0-AVY-687

Creating
Special Events

Second Edition

Lee J. deLisle

SAGAMORE
PUBLISHING

©2014 Sagamore Publishing LLC
All rights reserved.

Publishers: Joseph J. Bannon and Peter L. Bannon
Director of Sales and Marketing: William A. Anderson
Sales Manager: Misti Gilles
Director of Development and Production: Susan M. Davis
Production Coordinator: Amy S. Dagit
Graphic Designer: Julie Schechter

ISBN print edition: 978-1-57167-730-3
ISBN ebook: 978-1-57167- 731-0
Library of Congress Control Number: 2014942719

Sagamore Publishing
1807 N. Federal Dr.
Urbana, IL 61801
www.sagamorepublishing.com

This book is dedicated to my loving wife, Rhonda Larson.

You make every day a special event!

Contents

Section Four: Physical Resources

Section Five: Toward a Positive Future

Acknowledgments

This project was conceived at the SPRE Teaching Institute at Oklahoma State University in 2006. The first edition, which took a little longer than I imagined, was published in 2009. Working with the staff at Sagamore Publishing for that edition and the current one has been a pleasure!

Just a few short weeks ago, I saw a Facebook post from a former student from Western Michigan University who landed her first job as an event planner. She was one of the first students to begin the event management minor at Western. The program now has over fifty students from various majors across campus, all seeing the benefits of enhancing their skill set with the event management minor.

I left that program in 2012 in the very capable hands of Ms. Deb Droppers, owner of the Event Company LLC in Kalamazoo, Michigan and a dedicated adjunct instructor who continues to bring energy, wit, wisdom, and innovation to her fortunate students. I thank her for the continued positive role model she offers to the students.

The fall of 2014 will mark the beginning of a new minor in event management at my current university, Southern Connecticut State University, in New Haven, CT. During the past two years, I have witnessed students' positive response to our event management class and their interest in learning more about the profession. I look forward to sharing the challenges and rewards of offering this new program to our students and serving the university community in their efforts to create meaningful events for our students.

This second edition includes a new chapter on career development and professional opportunities in event management. It is an important part of the responsibilities of an instructor to provide not only the tools for success but also a roadmap that may lead to professional fulfillment. I hope that this new chapter will help in that work.

The technology chapter has been updated as we continue to attempt to keep pace with the rapid developments in technology that both aid our daily efforts and challenge us to remain relevant to a new generation.

Research findings have been updated where appropriate and new pictures have been added.

And so, I invite you to enjoy this second edition of *Creating Special Events*!

Lee J. deLisle

About the Author

Lee J. deLisle

Dr. Lee J. deLisle is a professor and the graduate coordinator in the Department of Recreation and Leisure Studies at Southern Connecticut State University in New Haven, Ct. He teaches courses in recreation administration, event management, and sport and entertainment management.

Dr. deLisle received his PhD in Social Science of Sport and Leisure from the University of Connecticut, in 2002. He also worked as a director of parks and recreation in Connecticut. Dr. deLisle has contributed articles to the *World Leisure Journal, Annals of Leisure Research, Journal of Park and Recreation Administration, SCHOLE,* and publications for the National Recreation and Parks Association and the Michigan Recreation and Parks Association. He co-authored the text, *The Story of Leisure in 1998.*

He currently serves as the chair of the NRPA Education Network, is a member of the Academy of Leisure Science, the World Leisure Association, the Association of Performing Arts Presenters, the North American Performing Arts Managers and Agents, the Midwest Arts Council, and the Connecticut Recreation and Parks Association.

Section One

Positioning Festivals in Community Life

This section emphasizes the importance of festivals and special events in the development and progress of human culture. Given the significant role events play in contemporary societies, it is critical that we understand the need for strategic event planning.

Chapter One
A Short, but Interesting, History of Festivals, Fairs, and Special Events

Chapter Two
Special Events = Community Benefits

Chapter Three
Strategic Planning

1

A Short, but Interesting, History of Festivals, Fairs, and Special Events

 But the gods, taking pity on human beings—a race born to labor—
gave them regularly recurring divine festivals, as a means of
refreshment from their fatigue.

Plato, *Republic* 653.d.

Introduction

While the history of festivals and events spans the breadth of recorded history, during the last thirty years, special events and festivals have grown in number and significance in communities large and small. What was once a volunteer-driven, laypersons' effort at providing a diversion from the normal demands of living, is now considered to be of paramount importance to the identity and well-being of organizations, businesses, communities, and governmental agencies from the local to the international level. Event management has become a bona fide profession with courses of study, certifications, and an increasing number of opportunities for professional development and career advancement. This evolution comes as no surprise as the service sector and the emerging creative sector both seek new and innovative ways to contribute to the cultural capital of our communities in an environment of fiscal responsibility and sustainability. The International Festival and Events Association estimates that the global special events industry includes over one million regularly re-occurring events.[1]

Beginning in the early 1990s, a concerted effort to formalize the teaching and administration of event management was initiated. One may turn to university programs such as those found at Napier University in Edinburgh, Scotland, the Event Management Program at The George Washington University, and the Purdue University Certified Festival Executive Certification program as evidence of the growing importance of this field. Over 250 colleges and universities provide curricula in event and festival management and have collaborated with working professionals to publish numerous texts and articles in support of this highly specialized aspect of management. Industry-specific organizations, such as the International Festivals and Events Association, the International Special Events Society, the International Associations of Fairs and Expositions, and others provide professionals with additional resources to expand their information base and improve their management skills with a particular emphasis on new and emerging technologies.

For the majority of recreational service professionals, event management is one of many responsibilities that require time and expertise during the course of the year. Some agencies are fortunate to have a marketing department or even a special events division, with full- and part-time employees, whose job it is to promote events and activities that serve residents and guests. Others may contract for professional services to manage single-use or annual events. Many, however, must allocate precious limited resources toward the success of such events while managing many other equally important priorities.

Organization of the Book

This book is written to provide the busy professional with an organized and systematic approach to festival and event management. Students seeking a career in event management or who wish to enhance their academic experience in this particular area of programming will also benefit from the contents of this book.

The book is designed to allow the reader to choose a topic or chapter without regard to the order of the chapters as they are presented. For example, if your main concern is managing contractual services, you may skip to that chapter in order to gain additional information. It should be pointed out, however, that the chapter order presented attempts to prioritize issues that, when taken in total, will help to assure the successful planning and implementation of the event-management process. The newest chapter on the event profession and career opportunities is at the end of the book but may be presented earlier to students in order to help them to explore career paths.

The book presents event management as the means of planning, organizing, directing, and controlling limited resources in order to achieve specific goals and objectives that are in concert with the mission of your organization. For each organization, the goals might vary greatly, but all projects of this nature will in some way address the need to provide goods and services and most importantly, experiences, in an effective, efficient, and pleasing manner.

What remains constant in this specialized area of management is the resource pool. That is to say, the management of projects, including festivals and special events, involves three categories of resources: fiscal/financial resources, human resources, and physical/material resources. Acknowledging the universality of this principal, the book is organized by way of these three resource areas. Many aspects of event management require the interplay of these resources at varying levels and are so noted in the text. Whenever possible, current and useful references are provided that allow for greater analysis of a particular element of the planning and implementation process.

It is readily acknowledged that the information contained in the following chapters is but one approach to the multitude of challenges presented by a festival or special event. You are encouraged to combine your existing knowledge with whatever useful information found in the text, and to seek out additional resources, to help you to achieve the greatest level of success in this rewarding area of professional service. With this in mind, an extensive bibliography of texts and online resources is provided. It is also evident that one text cannot address all the particularities of event management as these activities can range in scope from a birthday party, a professional conference, to the Olympic Games.

This text analyzes and presents event management from the perspective of an outdoor event with entertainment, concessions, and merchandise made available to the visitors. It is intended for service providers and students who may devote a portion of their time to special event management. The tasks associated with this type of effort are representative of many types of events that one may encounter in a professional career.

Let the Reader Beware!

The remainder of this chapter offers a look at the philosophical, historical, and anthropological significance of festivals and special events. If you are only looking for a how-to approach to an upcoming event that you need to manage, skip to Chapter 2! If, on the other hand, you would like to enhance your understanding of the historical and cultural significance of special events and would like to understand your event's place in the history of civilization—read on!

Some Philosophical Perspectives on Festive Activity

From the earliest moments of reflective human existence, our ancestors attempted to understand the unknown causes of natural, physical experience. They likewise tried to influence these experiences through their own limited powers. Science, in later times, attempted to do the same through a more in-depth and systematic analysis of the underlying principles of the natural order. In this broad sense, not much has really changed over the millennia. We continue to participate in many rituals—religious, social, and otherwise in order to deepen our understanding of human existence. We also continue to explore our understanding of reality through the sciences. In the face of staggering scientific and technological advances, we may also seek to retreat to a simpler, less threatening time, one that can be captured through ritual, embodied in special events and festivals. Recreational pursuits, now more than ever, provide a necessary haven for the wearied travelers of the 21st century.

Central to the human desire to create meaning is the development and expansion of ritualistic behaviors. Ritual, as a form of symbolic language, sought to physically express the aspirations, fears, and longings of the human condition. Ritual also seeks to reach out to others, be they the unseen forces of the universe or peripheral members of the existing social structure. With the evolution of ritual came an order to the world that was previously unknown. According to Rappaport (1999), language, both spoken and through symbolic gesture, allowed humans to "explore the realms of the desirable, the moral, the proper, the possible, the fortuitous, the imaginary, the general, and their negatives, the undesirable, the immoral and the impossible."[2] Ritual events, as much as the control of fire or applied use of the wheel, were critical to the evolution of humanity. Human culture is, in effect, the result of many forms of language. Ritual and ceremony and other symbolic behaviors, often

Food festivals are very popular with all ages.
Photo Credit: Deb Droppers Event Company

expressed through special events and festivals, are another form of language central to our understanding of humanity.

The basis of culture is said to originate in the human experience we call leisure. Furthermore, according to Josef Pieper, the genuine significance of leisure is rooted in both contemplation and celebration (Pieper, 1952).[3] While the earliest forms of celebration might have been seen as requisite for survival, the continuance and codification of these events surely suggests a significant and appropriate use of leisure. Celebration can be experienced individually, but it is realized more profoundly in significant social settings. At the heart of celebration are social group interactions commonly experienced through festivals and special events.

The concept of festivity arises from its inherent divergence from daily life activities. Festivals marked special times in the ancient lunar calendar, times that were sacred, (*sacro*-set apart), from the rest of the year. Some festivals annually commemorated past events, oftentimes agriculturally based religious celebrations, providing a link between the natural, cyclical character of the seasons and a human interpretation of time. This created enormous advances in ancient culture. What makes these festival times special is the cessation of normal daily activities in order to allow for access to something extraordinary, superstitious, and even otherworldly.[4]

Celebrating a festival, as we know, involves a great deal of planning and coordination that may actually exceed the rigors of one's usual, daily, work-related responsibilities. What differentiates this type of work is that it is planned and accomplished for its own sake. The activity is staged for its own intrinsic meaning rather than as a means to some greater end. While there might be benefits that extend far beyond the timeframe of the event, economic impact certainly comes to mind, the focus of all effort is toward the meaning and experience of the event itself. Pieper (1999, p.15), suggests that the celebration of a festival encompasses the "fulfillment of human life and the form in which the fulfillment is to take place."[5] This effort toward fulfillment requires sacrifice, the sacrifice of time away from more useful or pressing activities.

The Romans saw festivals as a time set aside for exclusive use by the gods. Renouncing labor and potential profit suggests that festivals celebrate the "existential richness" of humanity in the face of the constant demands of material existence.[6]

Festivals are deeply rooted in the history of humankind, defining communities and relationships to their environment. The next few pages illustrate a few examples from ancient times that help to position our present-day experiences in the course of history.

Anthropological Foundations

The special events of antiquity provide us with a unique insight into the values, mores, and recreational interests of past generations. To study celebration is to understand the basic needs and aspirations of a civilization. Celebrations defined what people considered beautiful or attractive as well as what was forbidden or taboo. Celebration exalts the colors, textures, tastes, and odors of daily life. Celebrations highlighted traditions, heritage, beliefs, and fears. Festivals and special events were primary outlets for both the rich and poor to avail themselves of experiences outside the norms of daily living.

These events included such dire activities as human sacrifice and the bloody appeasement of the forces of evil, yet also celebrated human excellence through competitive games, music, dance, and artistic endeavors. Accounts of these events are often found to be fascinating because they provide both a link to our past as well as a more profound connection to our most human elements. Ritualistic behaviors, including those expressed in special events, are said to be *the* social act that is basic to humanity.[7]

One may go as far to say that these special events, as a communication and further development of culture, are deeply connected to, and an extension of, the original act of creation. In this sense, creating a festival is analogous to the creation of the world. This proposition is not to be taken lightly, as it certainly elevates the primordial importance and cosmic connectivity of such events. *Ritual and festal activity seek to bring traditions of the past forward to present and future generations.* They provide critical and irreplaceable links to the past, not merely as reflections, but as living recreations of events, people, and ideologies that come to have equal significance in the present.

Our understanding of the earliest forms of festival must start with the spiritual intentions of ritualistic or symbolic behavior. Humans sought to symbolically "control" their environments by appeasing the gods or other perceived forces of nature. Events and concepts such as rain, fertility, harvest, successful hunts, war, death, and the celebration of significant events in the communal life of a group all became the object of ritual, or festive behavior. Repeating these behaviors shaped time and human experience, adding depth to short and sometimes difficult lives. Festive behavior was often co-opted by those in power, adding political weight to the otherwise religious designs of these special days. Critical to the establishment of the nuances of power in the festival environment was an understanding and manipulation of the roles played by both participants and observers.

Ancient religious practices are remembered in contemporary festivals.
Photo Credit: deLisle

Ritual vs. Performance

Celebrations have performers and audiences with different roles affecting different outcomes. Some forms of celebration attempt to blur the lines between performer and audience, bringing each group to a level of shared participation. Audiences can become congregations, as community may be a primary goal of the activity. By identifying the role of individuals in relation to the activity, we can differentiate between ritual and performance. Ritual describes an attempt to prescribe behaviors with intended results such as conformity or adherence to an accepted way of thinking or behaving. The accurate repetition of the ritual evoked power and security, familiarity and mystery. Ritual seeks to bring about a sense of unity through symbolic or actual participation.[8]

Festivals and other special events, while sometimes ritualistic, often were intended to maintain the dichotomy between performer and audience, between athletes and fans, based on the performance activity of the former group versus the passive involvement of the latter. The spectator is drawn to the event partially by the sense of uncertainty as the outcome of an artistic performance or athletic event is not predetermined. The spectator's level of identification with the performer creates a bond, a loyalty, determined to some degree by the unpredictable nature of the event. Spirits rose and fell with the success of an athlete, the performance of an actor, or the successful completion of a symbolic task by one with whom the spectator was vicariously joined. This *psychic income* remains an important factor in the mass appeal of public staged performances and events.

Festivals, fairs, and similar events were central to the development and maintenance of culture throughout the course of recorded history. There are many specialized texts that describe the festivals of past civilizations in minute detail. These works provide great insight into the role of festivals in ancient times and lend a sense of relevancy to our contemporary efforts at celebration. We will, in the next few pages, take a brief look at the role of festivals and celebration in several familiar social contexts of ancient times.

Ancient Egypt

Ancient Egypt is perhaps the best known of the ancient civilizations having a profound impact on Western civilization. Ancient Egyptian history begins around 3150 BCE and continued until approximately the fourth century CE. Egypt contributed advancements in agriculture as well as systems for construction, mathematics, religion, and communal celebration. The many festivals of ancient Egypt were designed to celebrate and honor the numerous gods that were a part of this highly evolved culture. These events appealed to the special powers of a god to influence a fertile planting season, a successful harvest, the actions of the pharaoh, or the emergence of a new year. The cultural pervasiveness of death was addressed through the honoring of dead relatives or the gods of the underworld. Other celebrations were strictly political in nature, serving to advance the agenda of the pharaoh by recounting an important victory or the special bond between the pharaoh and a particular deity. Taken together these festivals contributed to a full calendar of annual festivals during the Dynastic Period.

The Festival of Opet
This annual festival, held during the second calendar month, lasted twenty-seven days. It celebrated the link between the pharaoh and the god Amun. Amun evolved into the highest god amongst many in this polytheistic cosmology. The festival honored Amun but also acknowledged the renewed transfer of power from this god to the reigning pharaoh. Amun was envisioned as the physical father of the pharaoh, intervening in the activities of the pharaoh, including being able to impregnate the pharaoh's wife to ensure the continuation of the dynasty. This deific impregnation scenario is later found in the Christian tradition of the immaculate conception of Jesus by Mary.

The festival coincided with the annual flooding of the Nile River, which rendered agricultural tasks all but impossible at that time each year. The festival began with a procession commencing at the Temple of Amun and ending at the Luxor Temple, one and a half miles away. A statue of the god was adorned with jewelry and precious gems and placed on a shrine that was then fixed to a ceremonial boat. This forerunner to the parade float was then carried through the crowded streets by eager government officials who vied for the honor of being closely associated with this ultimate symbol of power. The practice of political hopefuls clamoring for highly visible positions in community events and parades continues in many locales to this day! The procession was accompanied by the nonstop rhythm of the military drummers, dancing Nubians, and singing priests all performing in the haze of incensed air. The pharaoh greeted the entourage at the reviewing stand outside the Temple of Luxor. Due to this symbolic act suggesting acceptance and renewal, the citizens were obliged to forgive any missteps committed by the pharaoh during the previous year. Perhaps a few were heard shouting "four more years" as they welcomed their leader. The pharaoh responded with unparalleled generosity. Records indicate that during one

The pageantry of the Festival of Opet is depicted on an ancient papyrus.
Photo Credit: www.touregypt.net/feature-stories/festival.htm
w.touregypt

festival in the 12th century, BCE temple officials distributed 11,341 loaves of bread and 385 jars of beer to the enthusiastic citizens. The Egyptians were fastidious record keepers, providing us with the first indications of event management strategies. Ancient festival calendars often included detailed lists of the endowments or offerings necessary for the appeasement of the deities. Further lists, such as those found at Medinet Habu, offer detailed accounts of the exact quantity of breads, cakes, beer containers, meat, fowl, incense, charcoal, and other resources necessary for the event. These manifests also included the amount and types of grain necessary for specific breads or blends of beer. From this data, one can ascertain the relative fiscal status of an event based on the allocation of resources that were associated with its staging. The records were also the basis for budgeting for the subsequent years of the festival.[9]

Concurrent with the mighty pageants of the Egyptians were less ostentatious but equally significant celebrations held by small agricultural communities and great city states throughout the Mediterranean basin and beyond.

Greece

Plato (Laws 653d2) referred to a festival as *anapaula*, a breathing time, a break from the necessary work of survival. The foundation of all Greek festivals was the desire to honor the gods. In the ancient Greek cosmology there were many gods available for festive worship. This pantheistic approach to religion created a calendar that was full of festivals and events dedicated to the honor of the gods through the efforts of man. In an attempt to emulate the gods who took on human forms and characteristics, the citizens strove to master particular activities or events motivated by a sense of *arête* or excellence.

The study of these festivals, *heortology*, provides us with great detail concerning the motivations and administration of these events. Accounts of festivals and their social significance are found in the writings of philosophers such as Plato, Aristotle, as well as many of the historians of that period. In addition, festal activities are depicted on thousands of works of art ranging from simple clay pottery to elaborate sculpture, all displaying activities associated with festival life.

While festivals were celebrated year round, the most significant included not only the requisite animal sacrifices and processional elements but also the opportunity for men and young boys to display their prowess in a series of skill events.

The Sacred Games of Olympia

Around 800 BCE, Greece emerged from a difficult time, their own Dark Ages (1100 – 800 BCE). Coinciding with this evolution was the initiation of a festival dedicated to Zeus, featuring competition of various sorts. In 776 BCE, the games of Olympia were first celebrated. The participants competed for the *athlon* or prize, in the form of a victory crown, shields, money, or for some, meals provided for the rest of their earthly lives. The competitors competed *gymnos*, in the nude. Our understanding of a gymnasium as a place to participate in sport and athletics is derived from this practice. The gymnikos athlon or naked competitions were performed in front of the assembly or *agon*. The *agonia* referred to the struggle for victory performed in public, and is the source of our word agony immortalized in the *Wide World of Sports* visual description of the "thrill of victory and the agony of defeat."

This religious sports festival included footraces, boxing, archery, the pentathlon, and acrobatics. Adding to the diversity and colorful nature of the festival, the competitions were accompanied by dancing, singing, and other musical skills, poetry, and equestrian events. Athletic festivals addressed the Greeks' need to honor their deities, celebrate excellence, mark a special event such as a funeral, and to provide respite from the daily routines of work or war. Due to the renaissance effort by Pierre de Coubertin in 1896, we are fortunate to be able to witness a continuation of the Olympic Games in modern times. While the magnitude of the games has grown and the number of events has been greatly expanded, including full competition for women, the underlying themes of competition and excellence remain. The logistical and political efforts required to stage the modern Olympics are enormous but also find their roots in a very detailed strategy that originated in the ancient games of Greece.

By the year 573 BCE, the Olympic games had combined with the Pythian Games, the Nemean Games, and the Isthmian Games to comprise the *stephanitic* or crown games of Greece. Miller (2004) tells us that the Olympic Games rose to the forefront as the names of the winners of the *stadion*, or 200-meter foot race, were used to identify specific years. For example, the year 490 BCE was commonly referred to as the third year of the Olympiad in which Tisikrates won the stadion for the second time.[10]

The administration of these all-important games was well planned and controlled down to the smallest details. Preparation for the games took place in the nearby town of Elis, 40 kilometers, about 25 miles, away from Olympus. The judges elected to supervise the upcoming games would move to the *Hellanodikaion*, the judges building, approximately ten months before the games. Also present was the Olympic Council of approximately fifty individuals who were the final arbiters of any disputes associated with training, eligibility, or athletes. Subcommittees were formed to coordinate and oversee the various athletic competitions. A nationwide truce, or *ekecheiria*, was arranged in order to ensure the safe travel of athletes and spectators to the game site. Envoys were sent throughout Greece to announce the truce and to instruct local representatives in the administration of the days of peace. These regional leaders served as the local representatives for the games, creating a very well organized support and marketing system for the games.

Athletes were instructed to appear at a predesignated time for training and were fined or flogged if they were late. The athletes spent several months in training and evaluation prior to admission to the games. Wrestlers were matched according to size and weight, boxers sparred, and runners trained at their selected distances. All athletes trained with, and often against, their competitors prior to the games. The best athletes were selected from this protracted training period to participate in the games. This is similar to our contemporary practice of Olympic trials in participating countries. With the arrival of the athletes came family, friends, trainers, and other spectators who spent weeks prior to the games watching the athletes in a spring training atmosphere.

Besides the preparation of the athletes, there was a permanent staff that attended to the grounds and facilities and services. Miller (2004) describes a staff that included priests, flutists, a libation pourer, dancers, a woodsman, butchers, cooks, bailiffs to ensure order, and a host of groundskeepers. Site management included the renovation of buildings and sanitary facilities, the track surface was turned and regularly wetted down, the jumping pits were prepared, and running lanes were marked with white lime. The hippodrome was made ready for the equestrian events, and the vast campground area designated for overnight guests was prepared. A parade, beginning in Elis and lasting two days, would bring the athletes and many spectators to the sacred site of the games. The number of parade participants is said to have numbered in the thousands.[11]

It was also the case that poets, musicians, painters, and sculptors would be in attendance, seeing the opportunity to sell their talents and wares to the large crowd of visitors. These commercial activities were kept away from the religious center of activity housed in the Sanctuary of Zeus.

The Olympic judges made final determinations of eligibility, and the athletes recited the sacred oath. The first day of the games featured very little competition, as the athletes prepared for the days to come. The crowd was summoned by the trumpeters for the initiation of the competitions of the second day of the games, which included chariot races and horseback riding followed by the footraces held in the stadion. The pentathlon was the featured event of the day followed by an evening of celebration for the victors. Religious ceremonies were held day and night during these high days of the festival. Great processions to the altars of the gods and animal sacrifices were the order of the day. The competition for the younger males was held on the third day, as the adults rested from the previous night of partying. The adult athletic competition resumed in full on the fourth day. The judges were on guard against bribery, corruption, and cheating, all of which took place during the games on a fairly regular basis. Those who committed fouls were whipped, while others were fined significant sums, which contributed to the upkeep of the festival grounds. The final day of the festival was marked by extravagant ceremony, with each winner receiving a crown of olive leaves cut with a golden scythe by a young boy whose parents were both alive. Those athletes fortunate to be winners were welcomed in their hometowns with parades and continued celebration, and were often the recipients of special honors, such as guaranteed meals for the rest of their lives, statues, and their names included in the official records of the town.

The Olympic site and the many administrators of the games were faced with traffic congestion, sanitary issues, wear and tear of grounds and facilities, and the need to begin the process for the next games, a mere four years away. The living conditions for the visitors were not as comfortable as their daily environs. The experience of attending the games seemed to outweigh the inconvenience of the setting. The writer/philosopher Epictetus (Miller 2004, p.120), made the following observation:

> There are unpleasant and difficult things in life. But don't they happen at the Olympia? Don't you suffer from the heat? Aren't you cramped for space? Don't you bathe badly? Don't you get soaked whenever it rains? Don't you get your fill of shouting and other annoyances? But I suspect that you compare all this to the value of the show and endure it.[12]

The highest ideals of the Greek games, directed toward religious worship and honoring the ideals of *arête* and amateurism, slowly gave way to professionalism. This evolution, reminiscent of our own experience of sport in the latter half of the 20th century, had become politically expedient for those who sought to use the games for personal gain, a development not lost on the Roman occupiers of the time.

Ludi Romani

The Roman Games, or *Ludi Magni* (Great Games), were considered the major religious festival of ancient Rome. Part of the genius of the Roman Empire was its ability to incorporate traditions and cultural practices from conquered nations into its ever-expanding military and social sphere. Initially, the Romans did not find the Olympic-style competitions of Greece particularly interesting; they did, however, note the fervor and loyalty that the games produced in the residents. The Romans sought to support the concept of citizenship and subsequently adopted the structure of the games from the conquered Greeks, as well as adding practices of the Etruscans who inhabited areas of central and southern Italy.

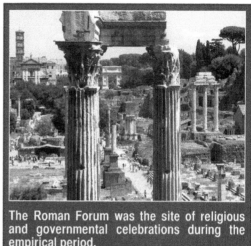

The Roman Forum was the site of religious and governmental celebrations during the empirical period.
Photo Credit: deLisle

The later Roman emperors embraced the Greek Olympic competition, often personally competing in events such as chariot racing, exemplified by the efforts of Nero. These games, established solely for entertainment and propaganda purposes, were often rigged to ensure victory to favored individuals. Ancient lore claims that the Emperor Nero was awarded a prize for a chariot race that he did not even finish due to falling out of his chariot. Nonetheless, athletic competition in the Olympic style became a mainstay of the Roman festival calendar.

At the time of the games, the center of Rome, the *Forae Romanum*, was the focus of religious, governmental, and commercial activity for residents, and a place that inspired awe and respect on the part of the many visitors who passed through the gates of Rome. The existence of countless perfectly proportioned buildings, arches, and manicured roadways all set the stage for the expression of Roman prowess and excess that were characteristic of their games and celebrations.

The great autumn festival games in Rome included a procession of significant local and national leaders marching from the Capitol to the Circus Maximus, a feat that would today require dodging quite a bit of city traffic. The government officials who led the parade were generally followed by horsemen, charioteers, athletes, dancers and impersonators, and musicians. These groups preceded the bearers of religious icons, statues, vessels, and material offerings, lending a religious tone to the procession. Finally came the animals intended for slaughter in honor of the many gods, both domestic and imported, that were included in Roman cosmology. Ritualistic bathing and the purification of priests and animals preceded the slaughter of the animals. The blood and the smoke of the burning meat was thought to have a cleansing effect on the participants and spectators.

The Circus Maximus was the site for chariot races, battle reenactments, and the martyrdom of many Christians.
Photo Credit: deLisle

The Circus Maximus, still visible in a very rough form today, had a seating capacity of 150,000 and was frequently at capacity for those who enjoyed the thrill of chariot racing. Spectators could eat and drink freely, mix with the opposite sex to whatever level pleased them, and place bets on their favorite teams of horse and driver. Between the major racing events, entertainers would take to the circle to offer music, dance, juggling, acrobatics, and athletic events, such as foot races, wrestling, and boxing. Other sites around the city of Rome, such as the Circus of Domitian and the Circus Vaticanus, held similar events. Concurrent with these games were the spectacles offered the public in the amphitheater of Flavius, which is usually referred to as the Coliseum. Sophisticated stages were erected for events as diverse as gladiatorial combat, military reenactments including naval battles, and a host of shows dedicated to the destruction of human and animal combatants. The Coliseum featured a retractable roof fashioned after the mechanics of the human iris and using the rigging technology of early sailing ships. The floor was also removable, allowing for the flooding of the area to accommodate scale models of ships for the naval battles. The coliseum represented a prototype of the multiuse indoor arenas that are present in many modern cities.

Festival after festival was added to the calendar in an effort to win the favor of the people, ensuring the longevity of political careers. The glory of Rome was offered to the citizens through brutal "blood sports," with

The amphitheater of Flavius, known commonly as the Colosseum of Rome, was a multipurpose arena allowing for the flooding of the floor for mock sea battles, racing, gladiatorial battles, and all forms of entertainment.
Photo Credit: deLisle

food and entertainment, the "bread and circuses," that filled over 120 days of the Roman calendar. The logistical demands of such event management indicate advanced methods of planning and administration of large numbers of people, animals, and props that served the goals of the Roman leaders. Pacifying and engaging the populace in various forms of less than wholesome entertainment was central to the political well-being of the ruling class. While chaos may have been the order of the day for the spectators, the rulers and organizers were generally pleased with their ability to provide such festivals and events.

Early Christianity: A Period of Transition

The rise of the religious sect that came to be known as Christianity would have profound effects on the festival culture of the latter Roman period and the subsequent period of the Holy Roman Empire. The practice of *agape*, love for others and respect for life, prevented the Christians from embracing the festival culture of the Romans. Christians refused to participate in the popular forms of entertainment, including activities at the circuses, the amphitheaters, and the public baths. Asceticism and the anticipated second coming, or *Parousia*, of their savior caused early Christian communities to live focused on the promise of salvation with a general disdain for the baser practices of roman culture. With the ascension of Constantine to the role of Emperor and the declaration of Sunday as the Christian Sabbath in 324 AD, Christian beliefs and rituals became, in principle, the norm in the civilized western world. With this came additional acculturation throughout the empire. As Christianity spread and became catholic, or universal, the cultural practices of diverse groups found their way into the Christian lexicon of practice and belief. For example, the celebration of Christmas on December 25 is more the result of the pre-existence of nature-based celebrations, such as the winter solstice, than on the historical accuracy of the early Church in determining the actual birthday of Jesus.

Festivals held an important place in the life of the Church with its increasing number of followers. Agriculturally based societies maintained their connection to the land through celebrations based on the seasons and the bounty of the earth. Planting festivals coincided with the theology of new life afforded by the Easter season. May Day, the secular paschal precursor, celebrated the end of the work of planting and the expectations and hopes for a fertile growing season. These days were marked by dancing, singing, and licentious behavior. Harvest time required hard labor and the opportunity to enjoy the fruits of that labor; wine festivals, olive festivals, beer making, and great feasts marked the completion of this important cycle of life. Harsh winters were softened by the celebration of Christmas and the revelry of the New Year, each allowing some respite from the realities of everyday living.

Societies were distinctively hierarchical, with the noble class controlling both the economic and ritual activities of the working-class peasants. It was through the beneficence of the nobility and the rulings of the Church that days were set aside to commemorate the lives of the saints, the victories of the lords, and the unending toil of the citizenry.

Carnivale!

With its roots in the Roman festivals devoted to the gods Bacchus and Saturn, Carnivale has flourished over the past 600 years, gradually accepted by both religious and communal authorities. The ancient Roman festival included the wearing of masks, feasting, and the inversion of societal roles. Slaves became masters, and nobles mixed with the commoners in the street. The people elected a King of the Feast, later termed the King of the Fools, who reigned over the festivities. It was a time of enthusiastic overindulgence. With the inversion of normal societal roles associated with the carnival season, the concept of misrule became the norm. An illiterate commoner might temporarily become the ruling bishop, a farmer would assume the role of governor, and the poor of the land took on aristocratic airs. This abandonment of tradition was a great enticement for rich and poor, as all enjoyed the suspension of the normal order of living. This is perhaps why Carnivale retains such an appeal to contemporary revelers and is celebrated with particular intensity in places such as Venice, Rio de Janeiro, and New Orleans. The Catholic Church wrestled with this and other pagan feasts, frequently incorporating them into the liturgical calendar. During the Middle Ages, after many un-

The Carnivale in Venice is a time for outlandish costumes and behavior.
Photo Credit: www.leics.gov.uk/venice_carnival_beaks.jpg

successful attempts to eradicate pagan festivals completely, the Church finally assimilated Carnivale into the Christian calendar, associating it with the Lenten season. The Roman celebrations to the gods became a period of free-spirited revelry that took place between the Feast of Epiphany, January 6, and the beginning of Lent, forty days before the celebration of Easter.

Lent was a period of enforced sacrifice, a time of fasting, abstinence, penance, and repentance, and a renunciation of the flesh. Carnivale, *carne vale*, literally, farewell to meat, was the last opportunity to enjoy the things of the flesh, including the last reserves of meat that were stored over the winter prior to the austere time of Lent. Easter welcomed spring, the renewal of life, and would be celebrated with the preparation of a new lamb for the paschal feast.

During the Middle Ages, particularly in Venice, masks became central to the celebration of Carnivale. Masks allowed for anonymity and a sense of freedom, creating a surrealistic atmosphere of excesses. The behaviors of these masked revelers became so outrageous that mask wearing was prohibited outside the weeks of Carnivale in order to return to

The Battle Between Carnivale and Lent by Brueghel depicts the excesses of Carnivale on the left and the austerity of Lent on the right.

some sense of moral order. The mask was a great social equalizer allowing for the mixing of the very distinct social classes and a license for moral misbehavior that included drinking, gambling, and sexual escapades. As Venice lost its position as a political power, it became known as the pleasure capital of Europe, mainly for the liberal delights of the pre-Lenten carnival.

Current research into the politics of Carnivale describes this type of event as both a safety valve for social pressures and popular energies, and as a source for social change in the repressive climate of the Middle Ages.[13] Festival making continues to represent a means of positive recreation, bringing together people from all strata of society in a sense of celebration, freedom, and equality. Festivals also create an environment for change and can be a catalyst for growth.

The Renaissance Feast

The Renaissance is considered the golden era of celebration in western culture as the wealthy nobility sought to recapture the glory of the Classical wonders of ancient Greece and Rome through the elevation of the arts and the exaltation of heraldry. Parades and other communal celebrations became the means of reconnecting to these ancient traditions, as well as providing the masses with unique opportunities to experience events outside the realm of normal life. Jousting tournaments were at their height of popularity in the 15th century, celebrating physical prowess and the ideals of chivalry.

Feasts were a significant means of celebration that preserved the hierarchical structure of society. These lavish events included detailed job descriptions for twenty or more specific responsibilities related to the service and entertainment of the guests. These positions included those directly related to food service, including that of the *Butler*, who protected and mixed the wines, the *Cup Bearer*, who served wine to the honored guests, the *Saucer*, who made sauces and glazes, the *Quistron*, who turned the spit to roast the meat, and the *Dresser*, who carefully arranged the food on platters. Others served ceremonial or entertainment functions. The *Laverer* saw to the ceremonial hand washing, and the *Almoner* collected alms and food for the poor who typically waited outside the banquet hall. Oftentimes the poor were given the cold shoulder, the portion of the roast that was least desirable for consumption by the honored guests and would otherwise be thrown away. Jugglers, mimes, minstrels, musicians, pages, and others were supervised by the *Surveyor of Ceremonies,* who directed all the feast activities. Strict social order was demonstrated by the seating and serving order of guests. Important attendees were seated at a higher table, literally head and shoulders above the rest of the guests. The *Pantler*, or bread server, was sure to give the finest portions of the bread, the upper crust, to the honored guests.[14] The feast was both a celebration of the largesse of the nobility as well as the honoring of the traditions of hierarchical lifestyles. Dining traditions have certainly evolved over the centuries, with a real feast of medieval proportions only found in specialty restaurants, yet we still understand the connotations of "cold shoulder," "upper crust," and being "head and shoulders" above the crowd.

The most anticipated event of any celebration, however, was the fireworks display that often punctuated the closing night of a festival. It was here that the local rulers could display a sense of theater, power, and awe that inspired the crowds and solidified their affection and loyalty.

Festivals and the Commercial Economy

Merchants realized the monetary potential of these events as audiences were drawn from far afield to the town or city square. Food and drink were in demand as was the longing to experience things that could not be found in more rural settings. In an environment of increasing wealth and a growing middle class, there was the desire for exotic foods and imported, one-of-a-kind items, in addition to the necessary staples of life. The evolution of the fair or festival as a trading event and cultural exchange was greatly expanded during this period. The local lords and rulers sponsored these events, exacted a tax from each vendor, and reaped great benefits from this nascent marketplace. The lords provided protection for safe passage for both the vendors and the populace, ensuring the success of these events. Trade fairs attracted all types of buyers and sellers and, over time, vendors elected to remain in areas that provided the most financial reward, contributing to the growth of towns and smaller cities. In addition to the goods offered for sale, one might encounter dancing bears, wrestling contests, musical and stage shows, and the occasional hanging or other form of public punishment that added to the spectacle of the event. The Leipzig Trade Fair, officially sanctioned by Kaiser Maximilian I, in 1497, and further supported by the decree of Pope Leo X in 1514, continues today in a new trade fair exhibition center constructed and dedicated on the 500th anniversary of the original founding of the fair. [15]

The economic rise of the local community was accompanied by the growth of a more independent-minded middle class, resulting in the demise of the feudal system and the initial efforts toward self-rule, individual freedom, and democracy. The guild system became the cornerstone of social and recreational life in many towns. Guilds bonded merchants and craftsmen who supported local, centralized authority, embraced the emerging work ethic associated with the new forms of Christianity, and sought a stable, capitalist environment contributing to their desire for a better life. Guild members staged special events, athletic competitions, and other celebrations to the benefit of their membership and the general population. These events, combined with more traditional agricultural events and the remnant religious holidays, provided communities many opportunities for celebration and the associated economic benefits.

Those who grew rich from the commercial activities of fairs and local commerce built schools and churches, became patrons of the arts, collected manuscripts, commissioned musicians and painters, and invested their wealth in the emerging banking system to the benefit of their posterity. Post-medieval civilization flourished due to the commercial success of the fairs and festivals. Societies experienced a marked revolution in societal norms as the hierarchical structure of the first millennium gave way to a more secular, rational, horizontal, and enlightened approach to living. Just as the Church sought to accommodate the nature-based rituals of non-Christian communities, the Holy Days of the Middle Ages were either dropped from the calendar or were transformed into the holidays of modern Europe. While maintaining a sense of tradition, the world sought new experiences through trade and travel that would eventually bring them to the shores of the new world.[16]

Celebration in the New World

Colonial America was a new beginning for the first groups to venture to this *terra incognita*. While the reasons for coming ranged from religious piety to commercial gain, the newly arrived brought with them traditions and celebrations from their homelands.

The colonists also saw the opportunity to cast off the ideas of the old order and establish a unique tradition of celebration representative of their new home. Some sought to abolish traditional celebrations such as Christmas, while others even suggested changing the names of the months of the year.[17] Between the hardships of the voyage, the demands of survival, and the natural evolution of a new culture, festive behavior adapted to new priorities.

In a continued effort to reject the old order, the colonists loyal to the Crown and Church of England retained the celebration of November 5, a day of anti-catholic demonstration. Guy Fawkes Day, or Bonfire Night, was an English anti-popish event that took the form of large bonfires set throughout the countryside to capture the sense of vigilance against the perceived threats posed by the papacy of the Roman Catholic Church. For the early Americans, this recurring reminder of the rejection of the dominance of the Church eventually became associated with the celebration of Election Day, which has traditionally fallen on or about November 5.

Much public activity in the colonies was of either a religious or political nature. The masking tradition of Europe became a method of expressing symbolic disdain toward the enemies of the new cultural order and a means of political resistance.[18] Wearing the mask of an opponent or enemy gave license for heightened forms of ridicule and derision. Parades, processions, protests, and riots marked the calendar of the colonial period. New traditions were being formed that celebrated the process of cultural and political revolution resulting in a new order, new holidays, and a distinctly new way of life.

Forefather's Day, celebrated on December 21, was first observed in the colonies in 1769. This day commemorates the landing of the Pilgrims in 1620 on Plymouth Rock and is generally observed in New England. George Washington, who was born on February 22, 1732, was honored with a commemorative day first officially celebrated in 1782. Its observance took the place of the customary birthday celebrations of the various sovereigns of Great Britain. Patriot's Day, the third Monday of April, commemorates the first battle of the Revolutionary War on April 19, 1775. Also known as the Battles of Lexington and Concord Day, the celebration is a state holiday in Massachusetts, known as Patriot's Day, and is the traditional date of the Boston Marathon.

The American experiment included the commercialization of what had otherwise been religious events. With pressure from Reform Christians to limit religious holidays in deference to the Sabbath, it was the merchant sector of society that saw the potential benefit of the traditional religious holy days. It was the merchants who rediscovered the holy days, transforming the religious communities through the commercial marketing of feasts such as Christmas, St. Valentine's Day, and Easter. This pattern continues today as businesses as diverse as car dealerships and furniture stores "celebrate" Christmas, Easter, St. Patrick's Day, Presidents' Day, and more. Few if any national holidays have escaped the designs of the commercial sector!

Summary

The history of human culture can be documented and analyzed through an understanding of the basic need for ritual, celebration, and festivity. A sense and ordering of time, the declaration of values, the realization of relationship, and the expression of faith are made present in feast and festival, in self-denial, and in self-indulgence.

Pieper (1999, p. 35), again provides us with an interesting perspective on the celebrative nature of societies. "What really matters is not the mere preservation and conservation, but a constant succession of new, creative re-shapings, which give contemporaneity to the content of festivals."[19] Pieper is suggesting that human nature, in addition to honoring the past, seeks to move forward with new and more meaningful forms of behavior that capture current desires, longings, and achievements. We are inventive by nature and this creative impulse will continue to find expression in the many events, festivals, and personal forms of celebration that we undertake throughout our communal and individual existence.

As those charged with providing this important source of meaning in the lives of so many, we better serve ourselves and our communities by attaining a thorough understanding of both the cultural significance and the professional challenges of festival and event management.

The following chapters provide a systematic approach to event management that specifically addresses the particular demands of this critical element of service that so profoundly impacts the quality and meaning of contemporary life. Thankfully, much research has been accomplished in the past few decades that directly impacts the effectiveness of modern event management. These findings are incorporated into the procedures and practices presented in this text.

Discussion Questions

1. Why did ancient civilizations celebrate festivals?
2. What role did symbolism play in ancient celebration?
3. What were the dynamics between performer and audience in ancient celebrations?
4. Which ancient civilization kept precise records of their festival resources?
5. To what extent did the Ludi Romani emulate the games of the Greeks?
6. How did fairs and festivals exert an economic and political impact during the Middle Ages and Renaissance periods?
7. Describe Pieper's understanding of the role of festivals and leisure.
8. What became of religious holidays in modern Europe?
9. Why were masks so important to medieval celebrations?
10. What is meant by "giving someone the cold shoulder" in historical and modern terms?

1. www.ifea.com downloaded from the worldwide web February 18, 2006.
2. Rappaport, Roy. (1999). *Ritual and religion in the making of humanity.* Cambridge, UK : Cambridge University Press. p.5
3. Pieper, Josef. (1952). *Leisure: The basis of culture.* New York: Pantheon Books.
4. Pieper, Josef. (1999). *In tune with the world: A theory of festivity.* South Bend, Indiana: St. Augustine Press. p.7
5. IBID p. 15
6. IBID p. 19
7. Rappaport. Op cit. p. 31.
8. Rappaport. IBID p. 45.
9. www.touregypt.net/featurestories/festival.htm downloaded from the worldwide web June 2005.
10. Miller, Stephen. (2004). *Ancient Greek athletics.* New Haven: Yale University Press. p.118.
11. IBID. p. 119.
12. IBID p. 120.
13. Humphrey, Chris. (2001). *The politics of carnival; festive misrule in Medieval England.* Manchester UK: Manchester University Press. p. 23.
14. Cosman, Madeleine. (1981). *Medieval holidays and festivals: A calendar of celebrations.* New York: Scribner. p. 11.
15. Shivers, J., & deLisle, L. (1997). *The story of leisure.* Champaign, IL: Human Kinetics. p. 59.
16. IBID. p.77
17. deLisle, L. (2002). *Leisure and theology: An analysis of the impact of the Protestant Reformation on the perception and use of leisure.* Storrs, CT :University of Connecticut: Unpublished doctoral dissertation.

2

Special Events = Community Benefits

> " At our core is a commitment to the belief that
> festivals, events and civic celebrations are at the foundation of
> characteristics that distinguish human communities and interaction.
> Civic events promote civic pride, culture, heritage and community.
> The future development of our communities and world depend in part
> on the existence of these celebratory events. "
>
> International Festival and Events Association

Chapter Objectives

- Explain how an agency mission acts to govern the activities of a group in new and existing projects
- Understand the value of festivals and special events for communities
- Identify the effects of a special event on individuals and communities from ethical, social, and economic perspectives
- Discuss several definitions of a project
- Understand the concept of project management
- Understand the relationship between goals, objectives, policies, procedures, action items, evaluation, and renovation
- Identify event stakeholders and determine how they impact an event
- Implement a pre-event feasibility study

Projects such as festivals and special events are undertaken due to the perception that there is something of value to be gained by the effort dedicated to this type of activity. The added value that can result from holding a special event may include the realization of cultural, environmental, social, political, physical, and tourism goals for a particular group or community (Derrett, 2003; Dwyer et al., 2001).[1] More specific benefits can be realized by an organization or region if the desired results are identified at the onset of the process and are included in every aspect of the event design plan. The relative short-term impact of an event can, over a period of years, be expanded exponentially through its continued success and improved reputation that the event brings to an area. There are many instances whereby an event with a limited scope has evolved into a major signature event for a community. The *Festival dei Due Mundi*, or Festival of Two Worlds, begun in 1958 in the small Umbrian town of Spoleto, has taken on international significance and has spawned similar events in other countries including the Spoleto Festival in Charleston, South Carolina, held each spring. The festival approach to artistic presentation has proven to be a very successful strategy in bringing even the most sophisticated work to larger audiences.

Additional long-term benefits that can be attributed to an event are the result of strategies that emphasize sustainability and durability. This type of success cannot be guaranteed but can certainly be envisioned and worked toward if included in the initial feasibility and planning stages of the event design effort.

Case Study: The Festival as the Soul of a Community

There exists a small mountain village in central Italy, in the Sabina mountains, that understands the importance of festival and celebration to their own sense of identity and the sustainability of their town. Roccantica is a village of 500 residents that annually celebrates a critical event in the history and culture of that village. It was in the year 1060AD that the city provided refuge for Pope Nicolas II as nearby Rome was under siege from invaders from the north. The pope and his entourage fled from the Eternal City and took refuge in this little village positioned high in the mountains and protected by an ancient castle tower. As the story goes, the villagers, reduced by the battle to a handful of men and boys, defended this fortress-like city from the attackers and won the gratitude and respect of the Pope and the Holy See. To this day, there is a document, a Papal Bull, in the city hall that relieves the residents from paying certain taxes due to their loyalty and defense of the pope during the battle. Due to the remote nature of the town, it remains much as it was 1,000 years ago. The narrow streets, built long before the introduction of vehicles, create what is referred to as a pedestrian village. The streets are just wide enough for walkers or the occasional mule bringing firewood to the residents, who for the most part do not have central heating in their homes. The Roccolani, as they are called, are very proud of the special place they hold in the history of Italy during the late Middle Ages.

Due to the vision and organizational capabilities of one man, Andrea Bernabei, and a host of townspeople and supporters, the town celebrates *Medieovo in Festa,* the historical celebration that takes place each August during the festival period known throughout Italy as Feragosto.

Many villages hold some type of Feragosto celebration during the month of August, when most Italians take three to six weeks of vacation. Roccantica provides a very different experience for its residents and the thousands of visitors who come to this tiny village from the 12th to the 15th of August each year. Following months of preparation, the town transforms itself into what it once was, a medieval village. All the residents and many visitors take on the role of medieval residents, wearing authentic clothing whose color and material identify them as members of the local ruling families or peasant workers. The town is lit only by torchlight and a feast of wild boar, pasta, local wine, and sweets is offered late into the night. The main piazza, or town square, which includes the church tower built in the 9th century is the setting for four nights of reenactments of medieval plays, presentations by the tambourini, the medieval drummers; sbandieratori, the flag throwers; dancers, and a display of authentic medieval fireworks. Each year the festival highlight is an elaborate presentation of the events of that famous battle of 1060 AD.

The organizers of the event are aware of the many beneficial results of this annual celebration. The planning and staging of the event bring many one-time residents back to Roccantica, particularly young people who have left the village life for school and work opportunities in Rome and other metropolitan areas. This return is viewed as a very important element of sustainability for the village. While not yet discovered by non-Italian tourists, the village has witnessed the sale of several family homes to residents of Rome who use these second homes as weekend and summer retreats. The longtime residents fear that the village may become full of strangers and lose its character as a mountain village that has retained its character for centuries. By encouraging their children and relatives to return each year for the festival, there is a sense of continuity that will hopefully survive the inevitable discovery of this magical place by an increasing number of outsiders. The event organizers also see the festival as an opportunity to teach and fully involve younger residents in the living history of their village. The town truly becomes a medieval village for those few days in August. The festival, due to the historical accuracy of its plays and reenactments, also attracts many regional and international tourists. There is an observable sense of pride that is shown by the villagers as the piazza fills to capacity each night in order to experience a unique and inspiring celebration and lesson in local history. This remote village benefits financially from the visitors who join in the outdoor feasts or visit the famous glass school or the shops of other artisans and craft makers during these summer evenings. The festival has become the modern identity of the village and continues to be the focal point of social, historical and economic vitality for the village. The website www.roccantica.org provides the virtual visitor a glimpse of the history, art, and festival culture of this unique village.

Given the present financial situation of many local and regional governmental agencies, the most discussed benefit of special events currently is the economic impact that an event may have on a particular community or region. This is, for the most part, a positive development for those who have a passion for special events. Special events can, if properly researched and designed, contribute to the economic success of a region. Acknowledging the importance of the economic impact of special events on communities and regions, chapter four is dedicated to this critical issue.

The Tamburini of Roccantica perform at their medieval festival.
Photo Credit: deLisle

Community Benefits: Well-Being

Generally residents express their approval of special events if they understand the event to have some benefit to themselves or their community. Conversely, if the event is viewed as being problematic to a resident or sector of the community, it may not receive continued support. Research into the role of events as a contributing factor to the overall well-being of a locale is well founded. Derrett (2003) identifies how community-based events reflect the "values, interests, and aspirations of its residents."[2] Events can increase the livability of a place by encouraging local enterprise, serving the needs of the residents, and promoting various elements of sustainability including jobs, environmental protection, and the conservation of community heritage and traditions.

Events draw together real and imaginary elements of the local community so that they can be recalled by residents and observed and experienced by visitors. Derrett (p. 25), explains that a sense of community is influenced by the "biophysical environment," the space and place in which one lives.[3] Where you live influences how you celebrate within your community. A clambake on the beach may be a regular occurrence in New England but is probably not a common community celebration in Kansas. This ability to celebrate one's sense of place contributes to the community's well-being that in turn helps to define the environment in which individuals and groups develop their values and beliefs. What this means is that celebrations reinforce the individual and community perceptions of contentment, satisfaction, and well-being regarding where one chooses to live. This positive reinforcement of choice is frequently the motivation to share the geo-cultural characteristics of a community with visitors, resulting in an event with the potential to reach far beyond the local community.

A festival can define a community's sense of itself as realized through the level of personal and communal involvement that is fostered by participating in the planning and presentation of a festival or special event. See Figure 2.1. Bush (2000) defines a sense of community as the community's image, spirit, character, pride, relationships, and networking.[4]

Festivals can become the soul of the community, that is, the source of meaning and relationship among residents, and the primary means of communicating to others the special values, customs, and images that make a community unique.

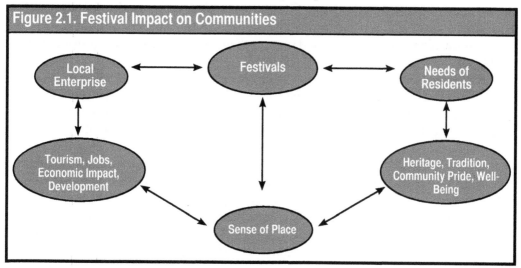

Figure 2.1. Festival Impact on Communities

Communities choose to celebrate those things that they hold dear; commemorating past events that define the community, preserving cultural ideals that may be otherwise lost over time, supporting a sense of community pride, honoring commercial enterprises that have shaped the community, promoting economic development, and addressing the innate desire to break from the ordinary rhythm of life by providing a unique and enjoyable experience for residents and guests. Communities celebrate garlic, mint, blueberries, and all types of fruits and vegetables, livestock, mosquitoes, and other insects and animals that are honored or derided based on their impact on the local community. Famous and infamous residents, diverse cultures, sport competition, music, dance, theatre, and whatever else can be dreamed up in an attempt to create a sense of celebration and connection amongst residents, have become the themes of festivals and special events. This sense of celebration is often extended to visitors in order to share a community's unique perspectives with others.

Richard Florida, in his breakthrough work, *The Rise of the Creative Class and How it is Transforming Work, Leisure, Community and Everyday Life*, identifies the growing dichotomy between authenticity and what he refers to as *generica*. Florida, in promoting the role of the *creative class* in the evolution of American culture, decries the homogenized or "disneyfication" of experiences and products available to the American consumer. One need only travel to the retail area of most American towns and cities to see a duplication of services through chain restaurants, big box stores, and other mass-

Large chain stores contribute to the sense of generica in the United States.

produced experiences. Florida identifies the need to move beyond this malaise to a point of re-establishing a sense of authenticity in our communities.[5] The concept of authenticity mirrors the idea of sense of place defined earlier as the community's image, spirit, character, pride, relationships, and networking. Florida's motivation comes from his understanding of the needs of a new class of worker that he describes as the creative class. Creative people seek leisure activities that reinforce and support their creative energies and provide genuine and life-affirming experiences.

Festivals and events that focus on the unique character or history of an area, its authentic self, have the potential to reshape both resident and visitor perceptions of the location. These activities are sometimes referred to as *heritage tourism*. Heritage tourism, as a return to authenticity, is an appropriate response to the commodification of products and experiences that are forced upon us by corporate interests, because it helps us to return to what is valuable in a community. In this way, events help to create communal self-worth, distinguishing one community from the next, and thereby providing a sense of attachment for residents. Events also provide an opportunity for visitors to enter into a genuine experience of the values and characteristics of a host community. This promotes higher levels of understanding of diverse value systems and provides opportunities to reflect on one's own values and sense of celebration. Social capital and creative capital, both related to the value of the human elements that form a community, are now recognized as critical to personal and communal well-being.

Events, as an opportunity for communication, planning, and celebration, help to bring communities together through a shared vision and purpose. These attributes have been recognized and quantified by researchers and community leaders. Derrett (2003), citing the work of Wills (2001), offers a framework for identifying and measuring community well-being through elements such as democratic governance, active citizenship, social justice, and social capital. Events are identified as an effective means of supporting these values and encouraging involvement on the part of the residents.

Communities that provide festivals and special events oftentimes do not look beyond the immediate benefits that are realized during the actual staging of the event. The immediate effects often include the following:

- an increase in visitors
- the potential for economic gain
- an increased level of civic involvement on the part of residents
- a sense of pride in the promotion and delivery of the event

Organizers must certainly focus on the immediate benefits but must balance this with a consideration of long-term effects of the event process on both the residents and visitors to the area. One must ask whether the character of the event provides for sustainability by meeting local needs and desires as well as providing attractions of sufficient interest to draw visitors on a returning basis.

Understanding the motivations, potential benefits, and the necessary resources associated with the creation of special events within a community provides the framework for the consideration of festival and event management. Underlying this process is the assumption that holding the event will create some level of benefit for the community. These benefits may be very subjective, based on the perceived changes in a community, or may be quite quantifiable in terms of numbers of visitors to a community or the net financial impact of the event.

Case Study: Edinburgh–City of Festivals

Cities and some towns have dedicated a substantial proportion of their resources toward the marketing of their municipality as a prime location for tourism activities. Tourism in some locations is closely linked to event and festival development. The City of Edinburgh, Scotland, hosts fifteen diverse national and international festivals annually as well as several community and participative events. The Edinburgh City Council claims to be making approximately 150 million pounds (approximately $300 million) from festivals each year.

The Edinburgh Fringe Festival encourages all manner of street performers.
Photo Credit: deLisle

Since the late 1940s, Edinburgh has become a hotspot for artistic talent, beginning with the *International Festival* and the *Fringe*. The summer programme has grown to include the *Edinburgh Book* Festival, the largest book festival in the world, the *Edinburgh Film Festival*, a world-renowned showcase of cinematic talent and the *Military Tattoo* in the magnificent backdrop of Edinburgh Castle. The *Jazz Festival* starting in late July and the *Edinburgh Mela* in the last days of August bookend a phenomenal six weeks of arts and culture in the city. The Peace Festival is a new arrival that tackles some of the heavyweight issues facing our world. *Hogmanay* is the world's most famous celebration of New Year, the *Edinburgh Science Festival* is a springtime journey of discovery in its own right, and the *Children's Festival* starts the summer with playful exuberance.[6]

The success of these festivals is due to the efforts of city leaders in developing a *festivals strategy* that encompasses the goals and objectives of the many diverse activities offered in the city. The general goals of this strategy, as outlined by Yeoman et al. (2004), are presented as an example of what a focused strategic plan can mean to the success of festival organizers and to the city in general. They are included in their entirety as they represent a best practices model of strategic goal setting in a multi-event environment.

The city of Edinburgh has created a unified sense of purpose for the many events offered in the city. The sheer breadth of activities suggests a decentralized approach to event planning but is congealed through the overriding master plan presented by the Edinburgh Tourism Action Plan (2000) that states the mission of making Edinburgh "one of Europe's premier capital city destinations with an outstanding built heritage and quality of visitor experience that is second to none."[7] For more on the Edinburgh experience see www.VisitScotland.com and www.edinburgh.gov.uk.

Edinburgh Festivals Strategy

To Provide
- A year-round program of cultural festivals
- A range of independent festivals, satisfactorily balancing the demands of creative ambition, social objectives, and commercial viability
- Maintenance of a summer program that continues to be recognized as the pre-eminent international festival in the world, complemented by a programme of festivals and events at other times of the year which achieves an equally high level of quality and diversity
- The involvement of a broad range of Edinburgh's citizens and encouragement of festival initiatives that address social-inclusion goals
- A learning culture around festivals
- Interconnectedness between the festivals, enabling cooperation, joint initiatives and the sharing of resources, stimulating a positive sense of creative competition
- A healthy relationship with the City of Edinburgh Council
- An explicit recognition of the festivals' worth, which is reflected in appropriate funding
- An effective advocacy and marketing campaign based on the above principles intended to develop Edinburgh's reputation as the festival city and as a city of culture, both nationally and internationally.

www.edinburgh.gov.uk (2001)

For a local parks and recreation department, the identity and positive impression of the department is greatly served through special events. No one may particularly notice the quality and quantity of programs offered by a typical department throughout the year, as residents have come to expect excellent services. But a festival is a unique experience and an opportunity to create lasting memories that can help to establish a very positive position for the department within the community. A special event is a unique and powerful mechanism to create an awareness of the role of a recreation department in a community and develop a sense of loyalty and appreciation of the efforts to provide unique celebratory experiences. Many people say the only time they see old friends is when they attend a special event in their town or city. This type of positive association with the event and the organizing agency can be a critical factor in the long-term viability and sense of importance of the services provided by your department. Festivals and events build communities and are an effective means of negotiating change within a community.

Event as Project Management

Events are, in many respects, a form of project management with many interdependent elements that contribute to the overall product. Project planning theories, models, and practices are very useful tools that can help to move an event from the conceptual stage through the many levels of preparation that are needed to ensure success. There are numerous project management models available in books, through seminars, and online support services. A project is defined as a series of related tasks accomplished in an identified time period in order to achieve a predetermined goal.

PMBOK

The Project Management Institute offers information on the Project Management Body of Knowledge (PMBOK) as an international standard of knowledge, skills, tools, and techniques for project management. A PMBOK guide book, now in its fifth edition, has been developed by the Project Management Institute to provide project managers in many fields with a detailed structure for project management. The guide describes project management as a series of processes including *Inputs* (documents, plans, designs, etc.); *Tools and Techniques* (mechanisms applied to inputs); and *Outputs* (documents, products, events). The guide recognizes forty-four processes that fall into five basic process groups and nine knowledge areas that are typical of almost all projects. The five process groups are: Initiating, Planning, Executing, Controlling and Monitoring, and Closing.

The nine knowledge areas are:
- Project Integration Management
- Project Scope Management
- Project Time Management
- Project Cost Management
- Project Quality Management
- Project Human Resource Management
- Project Communications Management
- Project Risk Management
- Project Procurement Management[8]

The PMBOK model represents a well designed and tested means of accomplishing project goals. If you are anticipating that projects will be occupying a great deal of your time, it is recommended that you spend additional time learning about this project management application. As is the case with many successful systems of this nature, there are now YouTube videos explaining the guide book and some tips if one is choosing to qualify as a project management professional by completing a very rigorous 400-question timed exam.

Each event, due to its content, level of local support, timing, location, and desired outcomes presents unique challenges for organizers and promoters. Despite the distinctive characteristics of each event, there are some general principles that provide a framework for event management. Successful event management is determined by the accomplishment of goals and objectives set by the organizers. *The challenge is to ensure that the goals and objectives of the organizers also meet the perceived needs of the consumers.* An event can be run in a flawless manner but can miss the mark in its appeal to the customer. Conversely, an event can successfully meet the expectations and demands of the consumers but may not meet the organizers goals or can experience a disconnect with the community leaders. Careful planning and a thorough understanding of the needs of all stakeholders help to avoid these less than desirable outcomes. The following is an example of a successful festival that suffered from a few stakeholder issues.

Case Study: World Music Festival—Mission Implausible

As the director of parks and recreation in a fairly diverse shoreline community of approximately 45,000 residents, I embarked on developing a world music festival designed to present a very diverse, high-quality cultural entertainment experience for both residents and visitors in a region that was becoming increasingly dependent upon tourism. Many months were spent planning for this three-day event. The festival was envisioned to feature musical acts, foods, crafts, children's activities, and many other elements from a wide variety of cultures. Celtic music and dance, Andean music, Cajun cooking and Zydeco bands, Blues musicians, Puerto Rican music and dance, Bluegrass performers and workshops, Greek dancers, Senegalese musicians, and other types of entertainment were planned. Several national acts were contracted as headliners for the evening performances. Workshops offered by the performers, further explaining their traditions and techniques of dance, drumming, and singing, were seen as a way of involving the attendees on a more intimate level of interaction. Children's concerts and craft activities, food concessions and souvenirs, safety and sanitation, traffic and crowd control, and the many additional requirements for site management were carefully integrated into the plan.

The event was held at a spacious outdoor venue supported by dozens of volunteers, sizeable crowds, and was blessed with great weather. The combination of sponsorships, entrance fees, and limited municipal support allowed the festival to meet its expenses in its first year. The organizing committee and the recreation department was pleased by the results and committed to carrying the event to the next year. The subsequent year saw an increase in interest from non-resident visitors. During this second year, the event covered all expenses without municipal financial support, although many in-kind services were provided. The event garnered media attention from the New York metropolitan area as well as from arts reporters in the Boston area. As had been the practice during the first year, festival attendees were asked to give their zip code at the entrance gate. This allowed the organizers to determine the point of origin of the attendees and allowed for an evaluation of the effectiveness of the marketing efforts. The data indicated that the majority of attendees were actually from outside a 25-mile radius of the town. The event organizers were very happy with this as it indicated a growing influence of the festival in a much greater geographic area.

To the dismay of the committee and its supporters, the town council, upon learning of the demographics of the event attendees, asked that the festival be discontinued. It was perceived as an event that had no benefit to the local community, as the majority of attendees were not residents. Despite the fact that the festival had a positive economic impact, increased the visibility of the town on a regional basis, provided a very enjoyable and well-received cultural experience, and actually made a profit in its second year, the town manager instructed the recreation department to discontinue the event. The event was cancelled after a two-year run.

The problem was not in the administration of the project, the quality of the event, or satisfaction of those attending the event. The problem rested in the perception of the benefits of the event in relation to the role of the recreation department as imagined by the town council. The world music festival had taken on a high profile in the region and apparently made some elected municipal leaders uncomfortable with the situation. The Council saw the role of the department as primarily serving the residents. However, the overall mission of the department had gradually expanded over the previous years to have a more regional impact. This was common knowledge amongst the departmental employees and those who were actively involved in programs and events. The department offered unique programs and opportunities, including additional cultural events, which attracted non-residents in significant numbers. In fact, most programs offered by the department attracted a significant percentage of participants from outside the boundaries of the town. Oftentimes the inclusion of non-residents, who paid a non-resident surcharge, allowed a new program to be financially successful. The town council, which has up to a 50% turnover in membership every three years, was not educated to the changes that had taken place in the department, and the department had not accurately defined itself through its mission statement. While department officials were comfortable with the regional influence of the music festival and many other events, the policy makers in the town were not aware of the gradual evolution of the recreation department as a regional service provider.

What this case teaches us is that there must be congruity and communication between all stakeholders in the planning and administration of any significant project. Critical to the long-term success of a special event is the link between the event and the mission of the sponsoring or oversight agency. A festival may well meet the objectives of your department or organizing committee, but it is equally important that your efforts also support the goals of the controlling agency whether it is the local municipal government, the board of a nonprofit agency, taxpayers, or stockholders. In addition to the effective communication of intentions of the event, organizations must regularly evaluate their goals and objectives as captured in their mission statement and effectively communicate them to others.

Agency Mission: Process and Product

Typically, a recreational service agency seeks to influence the quality of life in a particular locale through the provision of services and effective management of resources entrusted to them. The details of such a mission are the critical elements in determining the appropriateness of the agency involving itself in the development and administration of a special event or festival. It is advisable that the following steps be undertaken at the onset of the planning stages of an event.

1. Understand Your Mission

Organizational mission statements should be reviewed and potentially revised on an annual basis. This process allows the organization to assess the relevancy of the current document, as well as the efforts made during the past year in the achievement of the related goals and objectives. Having a mission statement that is accepted by the group is vital to the planning process of the organization in general and, in particular, for the introduction or revision of a special event. New ideas for events or programs that are suggested by employees, interest groups, or individuals can be honestly and fairly evaluated by determining if, and to what extent, these ideas support the mission of the organization.

The Annual Checkup

It is recommended that you review the mission statement of your organization annually, particularly regarding its inclusion of special events. If the mission statement is a sufficiently broad statement of purpose, it may be interpreted to include many special events. A more deliberate analysis of your special events should be undertaken to assess the real value of the events offered in terms of the mission of the department.

Many times, a recreational service department is assigned events such as parades and community celebrations because it seems like a logical administrative choice. This situation often creates a situation that puts a great deal of responsibility on staff members, usually during an already busy time of the year, to redirect resources to support the goals of a larger controlling agency such as your municipal government. If your mission does not match the reality of your present involvement in the staging of special events, a decision must be made in consultation with significant stakeholders as to whether the department should and can continue to produce and support festivals and events. If it is in the best interest of your organization, then it is paramount that adequate planning take place in order to meet the demands of regularly scheduled programs while meeting the needs of these special projects. Opportunity costs must be considered when resources are reapportioned to meet the often labor and financially intensive demands of special events.

Examine several mission statements for cities or universities online. Identify some similarities that you find.

2. Establish Goals Relative to the Mission

As the science of management continues to evolve, many different conceptualizations have emerged regarding goals and objectives. Generally speaking, goals reflect the aspirations of an individual or group. *Goals are typically broadly defined, long-term, targeted desires that reflect the mission and outcomes of the organization.* Goals help to translate the mission of the organization or event into characteristics that may be realized over a particular period of time. Goals attempt to set boundaries and provide direction for those involved in the organization's mission. In this sense, goals provide meaning by connecting the daily efforts of the organization to a greater vision and sense of accomplishment. There are many management systems that identify specific types of goals that are relevant to organization and project management.

Internal goals. Well-managed organizations have goals that are designed to meet the desired internal operational outcomes of the organization, as well as goals that are designed to meet desired outcomes for external constituencies. Internal goals may address the need for certain levels of efficiency, proper planning, adequate safety and risk management procedures, and the ability to use time wisely. Internal goals reflect the desire for the organization to plan and present an event making the best use of available resources. Internal operational goals can be classified as *management, adaptation, and positional goals.*

- **Management goals** are designed to support group efforts to use resources wisely and make effective decisions.
- **Adaptation goals** identify the needed efforts to relate to and adapt to change.
- **Positional goals** include efforts to strengthen the relative standing of the organization within the community with the end result being increased support for the organization.

These goals may be directed toward the management of the perceived value of the organization within the community.

External goals. External goals may include the desire to please residents and guests, and the desire of the community to capitalize on the positive benefits of the event for its own self-promotion.

Outcome or external goals can be classified as *official, operative, or operational goals.*
- *Official goals* communicate the purpose of the organization to the public as represented by the mission statement formulated through the process of strategic planning. A properly constructed mission statement serves as the foundation for marketing and public relations efforts.
- *Operative goals* may include market goals, resource goals, innovation goals, productivity goals, profitability goals, and employment development goals, all seeking to increase the viability of the organization or event in the market place.
- *Operational goals* are more specific measures that are managed on a daily basis. These goals direct the efforts of the organization to maintain and potentially expand the impact of the organization. Operational goals lend themselves to the formulation of policies and procedures that guide the tangible activities of the organization on a daily basis. They are related to internal effectiveness and the development policies and procedures that guide the organization.

According to Yeoman (2004), event goals are often a combination of economic, social, cultural, and political motivations.[9] These goals can reflect an overall strategy by a city or region to create tangible benefits from the presence of special events, or can be directed toward the immediate effects or benefits of a particular stand-alone event. Refer back to the Edinburgh case study (p.30) to fully understand this strategy

Economic goals may include the direct economic impact of a particular event on a local or regional economy. Goals may also be considered economic if, by the presence of an event, the locale takes on the role as a destination that will encourage additional spending in the future.

> The potential economic benefits of festivals and events are often emphasized over other impacts, particularly by local authorities and investors. Indeed, the success of a festival or event is commonly measured in terms of its economic contribution to event stakeholders, the community and the region.[10]

Event success is certainly dependent on fiscal viability, but the goals may address issues beyond the financial characteristics of the event.

Social goals may include an increased or renewed feeling of civic pride on the part of local leaders, event organizers, and residents resulting from the sense of accomplishment related to the successful staging of an event. These goals are described in the work of researchers such as Wills (2001), Bush (2000), Derrett, (2003) and others.

The event may be designed to meet *cultural goals* by addressing the specific needs of a particular social, ethnic, or religious group within a community. Special events can also help to strengthen existing bonds and to build new bridges within a community. Cross-cultural experiences are a valuable resource in promoting awareness and understanding of cultural diversity within a community.

Political goals can be realized through the success of a well-received event. If an event is seen as a policy tool used to address social issues within a community or to promote social objectives, there is the potential for political gain. Politically speaking, the effects can be on the macro scale in enhancing the image of an area, or on a micro-level as policy tools used to combat social ills or to promote political objectives.[11]

The tourism industry has identified and appreciated the impact of special events on the goals of location-based tourism. Ali-Knight and Robertson (2004) note,

> In the late 1990s and as now, festival and event-based tourism has become of increasing importance to the public sector, with the notion of place promotion, image regeneration and economic and social multiplier effect ever more central in the strategy and policy pronouncements leading to, or in the retention of, festival and event hosting and management.[12]

Determine Objectives to Meet Goals

As previously stated, goals are broad based and may not be fully attainable—they do, however, lead to more specific statements known as objectives. The use of objectives is optimized if the objectives are considered to be SMART. This acronym tells us that objectives must be Specific, Measurable, Attainable, Realistic, and Time sensitive. The concept was first introduced by Peter Drucker (1954) in his development of the concept of MBO; management by objectives.[13]

Specific—the objectives must be distinct enough to allow for the identification and differentiation between the various tasks selected. Objectives must be clearly written so that they identify what is included and what is not included in each particular objective. Specificity of this type requires more than a superficial consideration of what is to be accomplished and how it will be evaluated; it involves well thought-out details that will guide organizational activities.

Measurable—the outcomes of an objective must result in a quantifiable observation of change identifying what has been accomplished and to what extent. Measurability relates to the control function of management as it allows stakeholders to measure progress and determine levels of success that may lead to the mid-course adjustment of resource allocation and implementation.

Attainable—there must be agreement that the objectives can actually be achieved. This may be supported by examples of objectives being met by others in similar circumstances.

Realistic—attainment of objectives must be possible within the framework of the available resources. Does the organization have the human, financial, and material resources to complete the task?

Timely—Objectives differ from goals in the above ways, but most importantly, objectives must have a predetermined timeline and an agreed upon deadline or completion date. In this way, objectives support the completion of a task so that the efforts have a maximum impact on the product or services being delivered. This is critical to event management, as the event must take place in a particular time frame with the majority of the work completed prior to the event.

This explanation of the SMART guidelines provides a solid foundation for the analysis of objectives that can contribute to the success of an organization or event. Because of the wide use of this acronym, it should be pointed out that the letters have been used to describe other characteristics of effective objectives. You may find the letter A standing for *Appropriate* objectives, meaning that they are properly designed to aid in the achievement of the stated goals. The R is sometimes identified as *Relevant* or *Results-focused*, which also measures the relationship of the objective to the overall mission and goals of the organization or event.

Others (with too much time on their hands), have extended the acronym from SMART to SMARTER to include an E for objectives that are *Exciting* and will help to motivate others. The E has also been associated with *Extending*, suggesting that the objectives should challenge the organization to reach beyond its present capabilities. The additional R has been linked to *Recorded*, emphasizing the need to document and track all progress associated with the objectives. R has also been identified with *Rewarding*, which also addresses the need for continued motivational strategies. Perhaps you can think of a few more words that can support this framework for the formulation of useful objectives?

Objectives are created through the process of determining the needed steps to achieve the desired goals. Goals, being long term, are generally achieved in a progressive fashion. Goals can be complex in nature and may never be fully achievable in some cases, which makes the implementation of SMART or SMARTER objectives all the more important. The allocation of adequate time for the formation of event objectives will have valuable dividends as the project moves forward. Agreements reached in the process of identifying objectives will provide clarity and direction for all stakeholders as the demands of the event require more activity and less time for analysis as the event draws near. Objectives may also be modified if the requirements of the project or the level of available resources change during the planning and implementation stages of the process.

Developing Policies and Procedures

Policies are written and unwritten guidelines that direct and control the activities related to the effective management of the human, fiscal, and physical resources of an agency or event. Policies include regulations or guidelines that are created based on the mission, goals, and objectives established by the organization. Policies reflect major departmental perspectives concerning the provision of services, operation of facilities, management of personnel, and other areas of administrative function. Policies help organizations to comply with standards, organize information and work units, and help to eliminate confusion and ambiguity in the workplace. Policies are critical to the success of a special event as these types of activities typically include many more individuals in the planning and execution of the project than may normally be involved with the agency's daily activities.

Policies are agency-specific, meaning that they are designed to meet the operational needs of a particular project or place of work. Policies help to manage such diverse activities such as hiring and firing of employees, volunteers, and contractual service providers, attendance, dress code, emergency management, and other human resource issues. The collection and disbursement of funds will be guided by financial resource policies. Internet use, permits and applications, risk management, maintenance priorities, and a host of other issues can be addressed through appropriate physical resource management policies.

In addition to creating order and guidance within an agency, policy development contributes to the overall success of an agency or event by shaping values and priorities over time through its influence in the decision-making process. Policies should be clearly specified and included in a manual that is provided to the appropriate stakeholders. It is advisable that all stakeholders be provided with a copy of the policy manual and sign a statement that they have received, read, and understood the contents of the manual. A policy manual and other management documents should also be made available through the internet to the extent that these documents help to inform and guide the behaviors of those who have some interest or level of interaction with your agency or special event.

Communication of policies and the provision of training for employees, volunteers, and contractual service providers is a proactive means to eliminate many problems that can impede progress and may weaken the organizational structures critical to the completion of a project or continuation of the agency agenda. Policies lead logically to procedures that are designed to aid individuals and groups to follow the dictates of the regulations included in a policy manual.

Procedures provide an action orientation to the policies of an organization or planned special event. Procedures relate to policies in a way that is analogous to the relationship between goals and objectives. They are akin to a "how-to" manual or set of instructions that guide specific behaviors and are observable and measurable. One must understand policy in a conceptual way and must then practice or behave in ways that demonstrate adherence to particular procedures. Oftentimes, policies and procedures are included in the same manual, particularly for special event management, which includes a diverse group of stakeholders and service providers for a relatively short period of time.

Procedures identify the daily, task-specific behaviors that are necessary for the completion of objectives within the guidelines provided by the policies. Resource allocation and management, along with the process of evaluation that measures progress for a particular event or project, are greatly enhanced by a clearly written and enforceable set of procedures.

The mission statement, goals, objectives, policies, and procedures are the building blocks of organizations and events. The allocation of valuable human, financial, and physical resources must be carefully determined when considering a new event. Likewise, events that are already included in the annual calendar of a department must be regularly evaluated with regard to the original intent of the event and the possible need for alterations to the existing strategic and operational plans.

A summary of the process can be found in the following statement: *Managers plan, organize, direct, and control, human, fiscal, and material human resources using accepted policies and procedures in order to meet goals and objectives that result in the effective and efficient delivery of services. See Figure 2.2.*

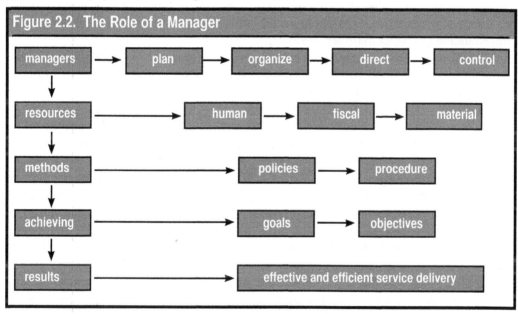

Figure 2.2. The Role of a Manager

Through the implementation of the organizational components described in the preceding paragraphs, an agency can adequately position itself to support a sustainable effort to provide programs and special events that enhance community perception, provide the possibility for economic gain, create a sense of well-being, and promote community involvement. Activities that coincide with the mission of the organization help to strengthen the role of the organization within the community and increase the possibility of success for individual projects.

Defining the Project

A project is defined as a series of related tasks accomplished in an identified time period in order to achieve a predetermined goal.

Most individuals possess an intuitive understanding of what constitutes a project. We all have completed projects and may have even referred to an acquaintance or coworker as a real project! We know that a project requires effort and the expenditure of certain resources including time, money, materials, labor, and sometimes patience. Projects generally have a starting point and a discernible end. If projects are completed on time, using the predetermined level of resources, (on time and within the budget), they are considered, by some, to be successful. Many successful projects are planned for and accomplished in an orderly fashion. Other projects, due to time constraints, a lack of understanding of the principles of project management or the unavailability of adequate resources, are attempted with little or no planning and fail to meet the predetermined goals and objectives. Poorly planned and managed projects frequently result in loss for the organizers. The loss can include financial setbacks, a loss of reputation, a loss of support on the part of stakeholders, or a loss of interest by staff and volunteers. Involvement in poorly planned events is not rewarding and, in fact, is pretty stressful for all involved. Beyond a general sense of what a project is, there is value in defining projects in a more formal way. There are many definitions of projects, each providing useful information and perspectives regarding our understanding of project management.

Keeling (2000) defines a project as "a temporary endeavor undertaken to create a unique product or service" (p.XXI).[14] A project is temporary in that it is not a continuous operational aspect of an organization but has an identifiable completion phase.

Every project has *constraints* or limitations that are defined by the goals of the organization and resource availability. These constraints are traditionally identified by the scope or desired end product of the project, the timing of the project, and the fiscal realities such as the prevailing economic environment, costs, and the perceived value of the project. These three constraints are interrelated and can have both positive and negative impacts on each other. This relationship also introduces the concept of risk or loss if the competing demands of the constraints impede progress toward the completion of the objectives associated with the project.

Masterson (2004) identifies project management as having three additional key factors: external pressures, organizational politics, and personal objectives.[15] These elements, like the previously mentioned constraints, must be identified and incorporated into a planning and management strategy in order to increase the likelihood of success. Identifying these and other elements of a project allows us to understand the role of project management as it relates to event planning and delivery.

Packendorf (1995) defines project management as the "art of directing and coordinating human and material resources throughout the life of a project by using modern management techniques to achieve predetermined objectives of scope, cost, time, quality, and participant satisfaction."[16]

Creating and managing festivals and special events is a particular type of project that requires the implementation of generally accepted management principles as well as event-management processes that are specific to this type of activity. Public agencies must be cognizant both of the needs of their particular constituencies and the need to commit to the use of resources in a responsible manner. This requires one to enter into a process that is referred to as strategic planning, which will be explored in the next chapter.

Planning: Barriers and Benefits

Regardless of the model or method used to pursue any expressed goal or desire, thorough planning is needed. Many barriers have been identified that might inhibit our desire or ability to plan. Planning requires the focused consideration of abstract ideas. One is, after all, trying to bring the future into the present through communication and action. Despite the recognized benefits of planning, many individuals do not adequately plan their professional activities or their personal lives. Planning has costs associated with it. It requires the allocation of resources—oneself, the input of others, the use of time that could be spent doing something else, financial resources, and commitment on both the physical and emotional level to the project at hand. Planning can be hampered by a perceived inability to forecast or imagine the future. Sometimes the fear of the unknown prevents us from looking to the future. Others express a deep-seated discomfort with the planning process. Personality certainly contributes to one's ability, or inability, to embrace the practice of planning, as some individuals lack the experience or task-related maturity to focus on abstract concepts. Risk takers may be more motivated by the somewhat perverse thrill of proceeding without a set plan, preferring a less predictable approach. While this is sometimes acceptable in personal activities, it is not advisable when others are dependent upon your efficient use of their resources.

Benefits of Planning

On the other hand, a realistic assessment of the benefits of planning reveals that it can actually reduce the amount of resources allocated to an event, can positively increase the chances for success, and helps to bring the vision of the future into the present. This allows for greater control of resources and higher levels of effective decision making and self-determination. Planning holds many other advantages. Planning is an integral part of consensus building by fostering and encouraging group input and shared vision. Planning helps individuals and groups adjust to change, allows for the accurate and appropriate allocation of resources and the assignment of responsibility and authority for the use of these resources. Planning contributes to a sense of order; it helps to minimize guesswork thereby reducing time, effort, and money.

Effective planning is a sign of agency and personal maturity. It sends a message that one values and respects the resources and personal commitment of others to the event or project. Planning can always be improved upon through the allocation of additional time to the process combined with increased knowledge and expertise in the planning process. It is also imperative that the event planning process be evaluated with the same energy that the overall event is evaluated following its completion.

Resource Management

Central to the approach of this text is a thorough consideration of resource management as an effective model of event planning and implementation. Resources, as we know, can readily be assigned to one of the following categories.

Fiscal resources. Fiscal resources are the requisite financial means available to fund an activity; for the event planner this would include any internally or externally budgeted funds, grants, sponsorships, the potential for revenue generation, and all expenditures associated with the event.

Physical resources. These include land and other natural resources, facilities, materials, supplies, equipment, and venues; the hardware of the event.

Human resources. Human resources include all stakeholders, staff, contractual employees and service providers, volunteers, and event participants and nonparticipants.

Resource management allows an individual or group to identify the tools available and the expenditures needed to make any project a success. The remainder of this text provides guidelines, examples, and suggestions of strategies and practices that will allow for the most efficient use of the available resources and suggests how the resource base of a special event can be increased. Crucial to the initiation of the planning process is the acknowledgment that there are a multitude of people and organizations that may be affected in positive and negative ways by a planned event.

Stakeholders

Stakeholders are all individuals, informal groups, and organizations that might be impacted by the staging of a special event. There are a few stakeholders that are obvious to all, including the event organizers and all others directly involved in the planning and staging of the event (see Figure 2.3). That is only the starting point for stakeholder management. Stakeholders include supporters, competitors, and detractors. Community consultation is a critical element, as the event will impact the community members whose concerns may include environmental, technological, economic, and quality of life issues that may not initially be viewed as a part of the stakeholder matrix. Crowd control, traffic congestion, access issues, noise and litter are a few of the concerns that might have a negative effect on nonparticipants. It is not enough to please those who are seeking a positive experience by attending an event, as the planning process must be extended to those outside the event, with equal attention to detail.

The event must also consider those who are positioned to realize some benefit from the event. The benefits of an event mentioned earlier in this chapter can provide an ample framework to begin to understand the effect of the special event on various groups within and outside the community. These can include economic benefits; social benefits; cultural benefits, and political benefits. Each of these benefits should be described in detail in order to further identify the positive and negative results experienced by those in contact with the event.

One might ask how does an existing special event presently impact the community, and who are the recipients of these actions. Does the event under consideration fit into the greater scheme of cultural development within your community? Does the event provide something unique and warrant special consideration for funding and support? Or does this event complement a greater strategy on the part of the community or its leaders that identifies attainable goals and a predetermined direction for the community? One must also consider the internal customers: residents, taxpayers, and organizational members, in addition to the external customers, such as tourists, contractual service providers and others, when ultimately judging the value of the event.

Figure 2.3. Stakeholders

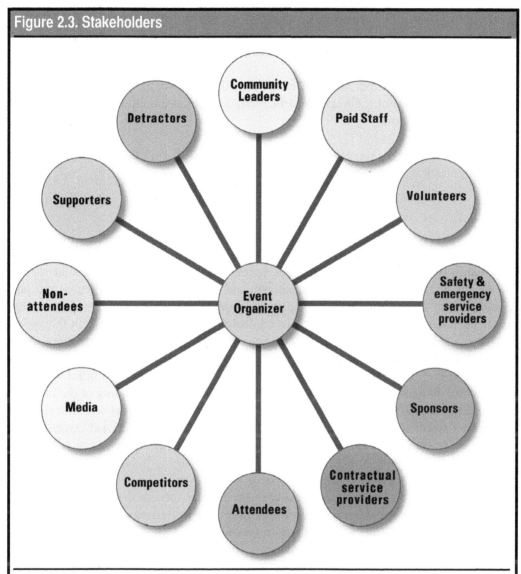

The stakeholder matrix for your event may differ from the example provided. The key point is to properly identify all individuals and groups that may potentially be affected by the planning and staging of a special event.

- **Anticipation**—describes the impressions that someone might have prior to the event. This includes impressions made by planning and marketing the event and the reputation established by the event.
- **Travel/Entry to the Event**—the travel experience can add or detract to the expectations of the individuals as they approach your event.
- **Experience**—all impressions made prior to the event are now reinforced as falling short of, meeting, or exceeding expectations.
- **Closure**—the transition from the event back to ordinary life events also helps to form impressions of the event.
- **Reflections**—memories of the event contribute greatly to the long-term impression of the event. Efforts should be made to reinforce the positive aspects of the event experience.

Understanding these stages of involvement, from anticipation through remembrance, is very important in determining stakeholders' needs.

Feasibility of the Event

There is a certain excitement when a staff member offers a unique idea for a new event or a creative strategy to significantly alter or renew an existing event. The feasibility of this new idea must transcend the initial enthusiasm and find a connection to the real and perceived needs of the community and the resource support needed. Organizers must be very sure of participant or customer needs, not confusing this critical element with the appeal of the product to its creators. The product, or core activities and ancillary attractions of the event, must make sense to those outside of the creative confines of the staff meeting or event administrator's purview. Reality testing must take place before any significant resources are committed to an event. Following efforts to attain a full understanding of the both the internal and external environmental elements that may provide support or constraints for the planned event, a detailed feasibility study of the event should be initiated. Assessing the needs of the community and the capabilities of the organizing group may include both the promotion of positive aspects that constitute identifiable strengths, as well as attempts to minimize or reduce social or economic shortcomings that exist.

With the current climate of decreasing resources and increased expectations for the most judicious use of these limited resources, community leaders must analyze the efficacy of their commitment of time and resources to special events. Oftentimes one is obligated to manage an event that has, for better or worse, become a part of the annual fabric of a community. An event may have served a purpose for the community fifty or more years ago, but could lack significance for today's resident and external market. This scenario can be particularly difficult as there are segments of most communities that favor tradition above all else, due to the perceived sense of security that repetition and ritual bring to their lives. Conversely, it may be the existence of such a long-standing event that is the hallmark of local civic pride and positive community involvement. This potential challenge of determining the present significance of a long-held community event further reinforces the need for adequate and realistic planning and evaluation of these types of projects.

Leadership must also determine whether the activities associated with an existing or proposed event fit into the mission statement of the organization. In order to achieve a point of "buy in" by staff members, as well as external decision makers, the event must further the existing goals and objectives of the organization. A feasibility study uses available environmental information to determine the practicality and economic potential of an event. Figure 2.4 shows a compilation of the components of a feasibility study taken from a number of sources and examples:

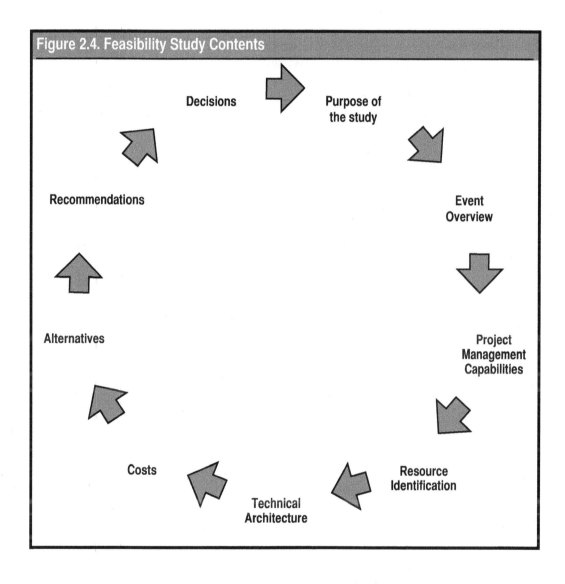

Figure 2.4. Feasibility Study Contents

Purpose and Elements of a Feasibility Study
- Introduction
- Event History

Event Goals
- Identify the Event Objectives
- Determine the Event Scope
- Develop an Organizational Structure
- Identify Relevant Stakeholders

Event Overview
- Justify the event through a business plan
- Demonstrate the viability of event outcomes
- Identify financial, programmatic, and quality controls
- Emphasize the relationship of event goals with organizational mission
- Define performance objectives

Project Management Tools
- Critical Path Analysis
- Schedule
- Risks
- Issues
- Assumptions
- Constraints
- Dependencies
- Decision-making matrix
- Sign-Off Criteria

Resources
- Internal Resource Requirements
- External Resource Requirements
- Contributing Organizations

Technical Architecture
- Site Management
- Service Delivery

Costs
- Budgetary Considerations
- Breakeven Analysis
- Cost-Benefit Analysis
- Opportunity Cost Analysis

Alternatives
- Alternative Event Strategies
- Description of Alternatives
- Benefits and Costs
- Recommendations
- Proceed with Project
- Proceed with Project with Minor Alterations
- Proceed with Project with Major Alterations
- Adopt Alternative Plan – Conduct Feasibility Analysis
- Cancel Event Process [17]

The Planning Process: A Summary

To summarize the planning process in its simplest form, event management seeks to identify the feasibility of holding an event, defines the purpose of the event, establishes goals through communication with stakeholders, and further refines the goals through the delineation of objectives that will serve to achieve the stated goals. SMART objectives are realized through the determination and assignment of manageable work units that allow for the sequential completion of tasks. These activities are managed through the establishment of policies and procedures that provide guidance and control over the creative process. The effectiveness of these efforts is determined for both the planning process and the product through ongoing evaluative analysis.

Discussion Questions

1. Identify five means by which festivals can contribute to community well-being.
2. Name three occasions or themes for community celebrations.
3. Explain why a festival should be coordinated with an agency mission.
4. What led to the cancellation of the World Music festival in the case study? What could have prevented this from happening?
5. What are SMART objectives?
6. Differentiate between policies and procedures.
7. What are some common barriers to planning?
8. Identify some typical stakeholders in a community festival.
9. How would you define a project?
10. What is the purpose of a feasibility study?

1. Retrieved from www.ifea.com.
2. Rappaport, R. (1999). *Ritual and religion in the making of humanity.* Cambridge, UK: Cambridge University Press, p. 5
3. Pieper, J. (1952). *Leisure: The basis of culture.* New York: Pantheon Books.
4. Pieper, J. (1999). *In tune with the world: A theory of festivity.* South Bend, Indiana: St. Augustine Press, p. 7
5. IBID, p. 15
6. IBID, p. 19
7. Rappaport. Op cit. p. 31.
8. Rappaport. IBID, p. 45.
9. Retrieved from www.touregypt.net/featurestories/festival.htm.
10. Miller, S. (2004). *Ancient Greek athletics.* New Haven, CT: Yale University Press, p. 118.
11. IBID, p. 119.
12. IBID, p. 120.
13. Humphrey, C. (2001). *The politics of carnival; festive misrule in Medieval England.* Manchester, UK: Manchester University Press, p. 23.
14. Cosman, M. (1981). *Medieval holidays and festivals: A calendar of celebrations.* New York: Scribner, p. 11.
15. Shivers, J., & deLisle, L. (1997). *The story of leisure.* Champaign, IL: Human Kinetics. p. 59.
16. IBID. p.77
17. deLisle, L. (2002). *Leisure and theology: An analysis of the impact of the Protestant Reformation on the perception and use of leisure.* Storrs, CT :University of Connecticut: Unpublished doctoral dissertation.

3

Strategic Planning

 Events are not naturally occurring phenomena.

Stephen Doyle

Chapter Objectives

- Identify event categories and characteristics
- Understand and implement strategic-planning methods
- Understand the process of decision making
- Identify several event management models
- Identify planning tools and technology
- Understand several research concepts

There is a palpable sense of anticipation when first considering the possibility of staging a festival or special event. The general tendency is to visualize the event in the most positive light. One might imagine throngs of eager individuals lining up to enter an event specifically designed to offer a rewarding set of experiences that may have a life-changing effect on the participants. There is a sense of pride and a real sense of accomplishment associated with creating such an atmosphere. These visualizations are a necessary starting point in developing the enthusiasm and motivation needed to enlist others in the pursuit of such a goal. These positive images, however, are precarious if they are not supported by the intensive, detail-oriented planning needed to address all the issues that may not necessarily reveal themselves in one's initial imaging exercise. Typically, events emerge from the passion of an individual or group in their desire to share a particular type of experience. Events may also support existing agency goals that can be better realized through the types of experiences that are common to events. The preceding chapter listed many examples of the benefits of events for communities, which can be strategically incorporated into the event-planning process. This chapter will guide you through several management models that help in creating a strategic management plan.

Event Categories and Characteristics

Every event is unique due to its setting, theme, attractions, its resource demands, and impact on the local community. It is important to create a model that identifies your event based on its characteristics and anticipated outcomes. Table 3.1 is an example of event categorization used by the National Highway Administration to analyze the impact of events on traffic management concerns.

There is much more on the topic of traffic management in Chapter 15 of this text. This schematic provides organizers with some basic guidelines in the initial design phase of event planning. A strategic approach to define the scope and activities associated with your event is crucial to its success.

Table 3.1. Characteristics of Different Planned Special Event Categories

Discrete/Recurring Event at a Permanent Venue

Event Location	• Fixed venue
Event Time of Occurrence	• Single day, Night/day, Weekday/weekend
Event Time and Duration	• Specific start time, Predictable ending time
Area Type	• Metro, Urban
Event Market Area	• Local, Regional, Statewide, National
Expected Audience	• Known venue capacity
Audience Accommodation	• Cost, Ticket, Reserved seating, General admission
Event Type	• Sporting and concert events at stadiums, arenas, and amphitheaters.

Continuous Event

Event Location	• Temporary venue, Park, Fixed venue
Event Time of Occurrence	• Single/multiple days, Weekends, Multiple weeks
Event Time and Duration	• Continuous operation
Area Type	• Metro, Urban
Event Market Area	• Local, Regional
Expected Audience	• Capacity of venue not always known
Audience Accommodation	• Free/cost, Ticket/ticketless, General admission
Event Type	• Fairs, Festivals, Conventions/expos, Air/automobile shows

Street Use Event

Event Location	• Streets
Event Time of Occurrence	• Single day, Weekends
Event Time and Duration	• Specific start time, Predicable ending time
Area Type	• Metro, Urban, Rural
Event Market Area	• Local, Regional
Expected Audience	• Capacity generally not known
Audience Accommodation	• Free, Ticketless
Event Type	• Parades, Marathons, Bicycle races, Motorcycle rallies, Grand Prix auto races, Dignitary motorcade

Table 3.1. Cont.

Regional/Multi-Venue Event

Event Location	• (Multiple) Fixed venue, Temporary venue, Streets
Event Time of Occurrence	• Single/multiple days, Weekends
Event Time and Duration	• Specific start time, Predictable ending time, Continuous operation
Area Type	• Metro (typically), Urban, Rural
Event Market Area	• Local, Regional, Statewide, National
Expected Audience	• Overall capacity generally not known if continuous events or street use events involved
Audience Accommodation	• Free/cost, Ticket/ticketless
Event Type	• Sporting games, Fireworks displays, Multiple planned special events within a region that occur at or near the same time

Rural Event

Event Location	• Fixed venue, Temporary venue, Park
Event Time of Occurrence	• Single/multiple days, Weekends, Tourist season
Event Time and Duration	• Specific start time, Predictable ending time, Continuous operation
Area Type	• Rural
Event Market Area	• Local, Regional
Expected Audience	• Capacity of venue not always known
Audience Accommodation	• Free/cost, Ticket/ticketless
Event Type	• Discrete/recurring event, Continuous event

Used with permission of NHA

Design an Event with Strategic Planning

Strategic planning is a deliberate and disciplined effort to define and determine the role of an organization. It not only determines what an organization is, but of equal importance, it determines what an organization is not. Strategic planning helps to identify what is most important to the organization and promotes the appropriate allocation of resources. It is about deliberately setting goals that support the agency mission. A strategic plan also allows and prepares an organization to be responsive to changes in their environment.

Street events create a high-impact temporary capacity challenge for a community.

It includes reflecting on the past, the methodical collection of data and experience from the present situation and, to some degree, the ability to anticipate the future. It requires openness to change and the ability to readjust the goals of an organization to meet the realities of the marketplace.

Benefits of Strategic Planning

The benefits of strategic planning include the following:

- Clearly defining the purpose of the organization and establishing realistic goals and objectives consistent with the mission, in a defined time frame within the organization's present capacity
- Communication of these goals to the organization's stakeholders
- Developing a sense of ownership of the plan amongst your group
- Ensuring the most effective use of the organization's resources by focusing the resources on key priorities
- Providing a base for progress and establishing a mechanism for informed change
- Unifying the reasoned efforts of the organization and building consensus
- Providing a clear focus for the organization
- Bridging the gaps between administration and staff workers
- Building strong teams
- Producing satisfaction and productivity through increased effectiveness and efficiency
- Solving major problems[3]

Strategic plans must be guided by past experience but are designed to be implemented in the present in order to effectively shape the future. Strategic plans must be flexible and responsive to change and they must represent the best methods and practices in achieving a specific set of goals under particular circumstances.

Realizing that there is no such thing as a perfect plan, and that the major benefit of the plan is the communicative process that is at the heart of the plan, it is readily noted that strategic planning is very beneficial to all organizations. This process fosters a sense of ownership on the part of the group members. Resource management is also greatly enhanced through detailed planning. Productivity and the effective and efficient use of resources are more probable with strategic planning. The recorded plan offers a baseline for evaluative purposes, which helps to perpetuate effective management for future events.[4]

Contemporary theories emphasize the need for strategic planning that considers the impact of the event on all possible aspects of a community or organization. Strategic planning leads to solutions that address the challenges of event planning while considering the impact on both the present and future well-being of the organization and the many stakeholders with an investment in the activities at hand. Strategic planning, in order to be effective, must be purposeful, focused, and productive. This type of planning can be based on the general mission of the organization, or on specific goals, relevant organizational issues, or requirements of a particular project. Many times the strategic plan incorporates aspects of each of these approaches.

"The process raises a sequence of questions that helps planners examine experience, test assumptions, gather and incorporate information about the present, and anticipate the environment in which the organization will be working in the future."[5]

Strategic plans allow an organization to answer the question as to whether the focus and intentions of the project warrant the efforts put forth. The answer is determined by the role of the project in the greater vision or mission of the organization and whether the project is a viable best use of available resources. This is particularly important for an organization that finds itself concerned with multiple roles and responsibilities within a community. Strategic planning strives to maintain a strict, yet malleable, relationship between the mission of the organization and the projects it chooses to undertake. Strategic planning differs from general planning in that it requires a more deliberate identification of the critical elements necessary for sustained positive results.

Strategic Vacations

All of us, at one time or another, have gone on a trip or vacation. You can plan a trip simply by identifying the destination and determining the means to get there. The experience may be positive or negative depending upon what is encountered along the way and what happens upon your arrival. There is a certain appeal to the adventure associated with a loosely planned excursion.

On the other hand, a trip may be planned in greater detail based on certain things that you want to happen along the way, as well as when you reach your destination. Understanding your motivations for traveling to a certain location will help in the planning of particular activities and choosing specific routes. Also, being aware of the resources available like transportation options, individuals who can facilitate the trip, available funds, time constraints, and the like, will also help you in getting the most out of a trip. You may also be aware of certain outcomes that you would like to accomplish by the end of the trip. These and other considerations suggest a more strategic and deliberate approach to taking a trip. Strategic planning doesn't guarantee success but it increases the possibility of having a positive, fulfilling experience.

Can you think of an example of a strategically planned trip that you have taken during your life? What were some of the factors that went into planning the trip? How were decisions made, by consensus or by a lead individual? How did your planning affect the outcome of the trip?

In creating a special event, much like planning a vacation, strategic planning allows you to be clear about the objectives of your efforts, aware of the resources available, and be able to effectively use these resources to meet goals and objectives. It aids both decision makers and service providers in becoming aware of the present situation and in making decisions in order to effectively shape the future.

Proper strategic planning should lead to decisions that efficiently and effectively make use of present and anticipated resources to the benefit of the organization. Strategic planning involves identifying a definitive purpose for the organization, an understanding of the present environment of the organization, and the ability to respond to this environment through a series of goals and objectives that adequately meet these conditions.

Strategic planning requires strategic vision, the ability to consider the organization in a grand scheme rather than defining it by what it presently succeeds or fails to accomplish. It requires stepping back from the day-to-day exigencies of management to provide the environment and resources for creative thinking and consensus building.

Strategic planning should be entered into at the onset of the organization lifecycle, created in conjunction with a business plan, marketing plan, and financial plan. Both the goals and actions of an organization must adapt to change on an annual basis, if not more frequently. This is particularly true when organizational goals and program delivery are based on the approval or adjustment of an annual operating budget. While the accepted timetable of reviewing a strategic plan annually is commendable, the real value of the plan is its role as a litmus test for all existing and proposed activities.

Reviewing the components of the plan is not the same as reviewing the effectiveness of the plan, which should be accomplished on a quarterly basis or more frequently if the rate of change or challenge calls for greater scrutiny. Effectiveness suggests productivity, which must be monitored on a daily/weekly/monthly basis. Changing the plans for an event must occur when the current results reveal a lack of efficient resource implementation. If your planning process indicates a potential loss of time or money, you cannot wait until the project is over or a new budget is approved to make changes.

Strategic Planning Strategies

There are many models of strategic planning available to an organization, including goals-based, issues-based, and organic approaches.

> **Goals-based planning** is the most common approach, focusing on the organization's mission or values, and the goals and objectives that have been established to accomplish the mission.
>
> **Issues-based strategies** identify the issues that are impinging upon the organization with the intent of developing strategies to address these issues. Prior to the initiation of the planning process, it is important to identify and understand the resources and efficacy of the organization and the relationship of these to the identified critical issues.
>
> The **organic approach** looks at realities of the present situation of an event or organization and projects a desired image for the future.[2]

The choice of one strategy or a combination of these strategies should be based on the perception of your organization and event by significant stakeholders and decision makers.

An *environmental scan* is a tool used to help a group arrive at a common or shared perception of the organization. Prior to an analysis of the project environment, it is helpful to clearly identify the stakeholders and the necessary skill sets needed to complete the project. In addition to the existence of organizational charts for agencies, more detailed representations reflecting the organization structure and span of control, lines of communication and reporting are critical for effective event management. The makeup of an organizing committee should reflect the needs of the event. This means that committee members should have specific skills or characteristics that will benefit the event. Buy-in by the committee needs to happen early and must be nurtured and supported throughout the process.

SWOT Analysis

A widely used technique that aids in identifying the critical issues of an organization or a specific event, prior to the initiation of labor intensive activity, is the *SWOT Analysis* (see Table 3.2). This procedure can be used on the macro-level to ascertain the potential for success for an entire organization or special event and can also be used on a micro level to analyze the subsets of resource allocation needed to achieve the project objectives. *SWOT* refers to an analysis of the *strengths, weaknesses, opportunities,* and *threats* that characterize a particular individual, group or situation.

Strengths. *Strengths* are considered in this model to be positive internal characteristics within the organization. This internal potential is based on the skills, experience, and other intrinsic components that are relative to and support the mission of the organization. Strengths contribute to success if properly identified and utilized by your organization.

Weaknesses. *Weaknesses* are internal negative characteristics or liabilities that may be real or perceived barriers to success that exist within the organization. Weaknesses also must be identified and reduced or eliminated in order to minimize their effect on the success of the project. Weaknesses may include insufficient staff numbers or a lack of experience in staging the type of event envisioned by your organization.

Opportunities. *Opportunities* are externally positioned positive aspects that can provide synergy and increase both motivation and the possibility of success. Opportunities provide situations that allow for greater inclusion of additional stakeholders and the expansion of the sphere of influence of the organization. Opportunities are related to future growth. Potential sponsorships and other types of partnerships can be seen as opportunities that can benefit the efforts to stage a successful event.

Threats. *Threats* are externally located negative characteristics that can prevent success. These must be identified, considered, and adequately managed if goals are to be achieved. For outdoor events, the weather is always a threat. Competition from other events that are in close proximity to your event can also be classified as a threat.

Table 3.2. SWOT Analysis	
Strengths – positive internal factors	Opportunities – positive external factors
Weaknesses – internal liabilities	Threats – negative external factors

Once the strengths, weaknesses, opportunities, and threats have been identified, the organization's capacity for planning and holding an event may be better assessed. This information contributes to the efforts to determine the feasibility of staging a special event.

Prioritizing Tasks

The SWOT factors can then be prioritized as to their impact on, and relative importance to, the potential success of the event, allowing for a more accurate prediction of success (see Table 3.3). Most tasks that confront us in project management fit into one of the four following categories. It is beneficial to train employees to consider tasks from this perspective so that resources are used in the most effective manner.

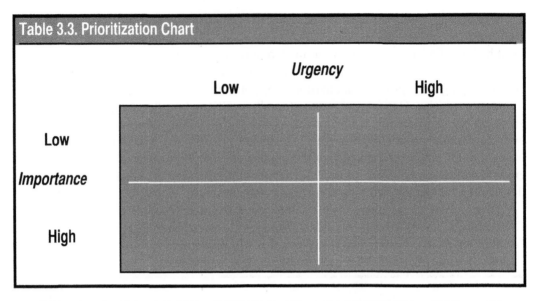

Table 3.3. Prioritization Chart

Following the determination of SWOT factors and a prioritization of issues, the organizers can identify strengths that can be enhanced, weaknesses that must be reduced or eliminated, opportunities to be capitalized upon, and threats that must be overcome or avoided. It is important to address the critical issues that can be effectively addressed given the resources available and the time constraints at hand. This approach allows for a front-loaded, proactive approach to problem solving that will foster greater cohesiveness within the group and will, in the long run, allow for more effective and efficient problem solving. Identifying the issues leads to effective goal statements that will enhance the specific purpose of the event.

Planning Backward

A work breakdown structure (WBS) exercise provides the project planners with the opportunity to identify all the critical elements of the event (see Figure 3.1). A recommended method is to plan backward using the following steps:

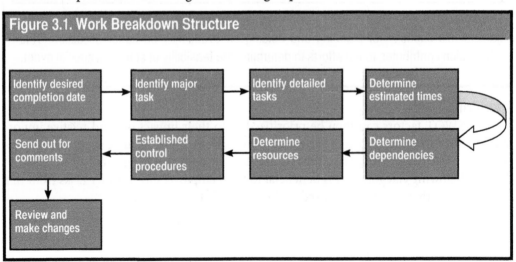

Figure 3.1. Work Breakdown Structure

1. **Identify desired completion date**—In the case of a festival or special event, this is a critical element due to outside forces that may require staging the event during a particular time of the year. Projects frequently suffer from delays that can cost an organization money and opportunity. This is most evident in event management due to the fact that the final product, the festival or event, is planned for a very definite time frame. Hence, the deadline sets the criteria for the sequence of tasks that must precede the actual event. In any multi-task project, there are certain activities that must take place prior to secondary activities. The time frame for planning and staging an event must be positioned to reduce threats to success from competing interests or events.

    By starting with the delivery date, the planned date for the staging of the event, the group can then proceed in an organized and more predictable manner.

2. **Identify major tasks**—The major tasks are essentially the framework of your event. Depending upon the size and scope of the event and the type of activities to be offered, the major tasks will effectively direct the formation of committees or subgroups to analyze and plan all of the significant efforts needed for success.

3. **Identify detailed tasks**—The details flow from a more exact breakdown of the major tasks. The details allow for the assignment of particular jobs and aid in the determination of the flow of the planning process. Simple tasks may only require an action plan, run sheet, or other task-oriented method of completing the elements of the project.

4. **Determine estimated times**—Each task requires a certain amount of time in order to meet the ultimate deadline of the staging of the event. Gantt charts and other technical aids can help in time management will be described later in the chapter.

5. **Determine dependencies**—A critical element in budgeting time and sequencing actions is the need to identify which tasks are sequentially related to or dependent upon other tasks.

6. **Determine resources**—Understanding the tasks to be accomplished and the time needed to complete tasks has a direct impact on resource determination and allocation. A general principle to remember is that in order to accelerate the completion of any task, it is usually necessary to allocate additional resources to that task. More money or more personnel can help to speed up the completion of most tasks. Conversely, if additional time is available, through accurate planning, tasks may be accomplished with fewer resources.

7. **Establish control procedures**—Event management is an exercise in multitasking by many individuals with distinct yet interrelated responsibilities. It is absolutely necessary that a system of controls be established to direct the reporting of progress in each task domain and to ensure that tasks are completed in a timely fashion. Controls greatly aid the decision-making process particularly during the time period immediately preceding the event when resources may be stretched and time is limited.

8. **Send out for comments**—prior to the implementation of a work breakdown plan, it is advisable to have the entire plan reviewed by all stakeholders and perhaps an outside agency familiar with the goals of the project. Time and money can be saved by reducing errors that can be identified at this time. It is better, from every perspective, to identify problems as early as possible in the planning process.

9. **Review and make changes**—any insight gained from the internal and external review process should be incorporated into a revised set of plans for the event. This process should occur prior to initiating the completion of event tasks, during the process to make mid-course adjustments, and following the completion of the event in order incorporate all that is learned through the staging of the event.

Planning backward, using these nine steps or a similar framework, will help to ensure that actions, communications, and controls are properly utilized to ensure progress and the timely completion of important tasks.

Both the SWOT analysis and the work breakdown structure are initial steps in accurate time and resource estimation and allocation. Time must also be allowed for actual project management, meetings, working with internal and external stakeholders, documentation of progress, interruptions by other high-priority tasks, emergencies, and the need for process changes.

In all cases, planning should have both linear and cyclical characteristics. *Linear*, suggesting that the process moves forward (think left to right, or top to bottom on a page) allowing you to visually track progress. Planning is also *cyclical* in that decisions regarding progress might include returning to prior stages of the process to change elements, reevaluate procedures, re-assign resources and the like. Failure to assimilate the cyclical or feedback requirements of a well-planned event may result in one completing the task but not achieving the goals of the event. There are disappointing occasions when the whole is less than the sum of the parts. Feedback should be based on the establishment of performance indicators that provide organizers with predetermined standards that will allow them to sign off on particular tasks when they are satisfactorily completed.

The process of strategic planning is often as valuable as the product that results from the planning of these efforts. The inclusion of stakeholders in the identification and determination of priorities for the organization is in itself an effective means of clarifying the identity and purpose of the group.

Strategic Stakeholders

In strategic planning, a core group of influential stakeholders should be identified and invited to participate in the planning process. The event committee should have a mix of staff and volunteers, each bringing a definable strength to the committee. This includes those who represent community interests that may either benefit or be harmed by the proposed activity. Individuals who can provide key information or have needed expertise should be considered. Those with access to external funding, sponsorships, and other revenue streams are also valuable team members. Individuals with the authority to implement the plan, to choose goals, and to allocate resources to meet the goals are obviously critical to the success of the effort. Following an analysis of the strengths and weaknesses of the group, consideration may be given to contracting with a planning professional to administrate the planning process should the budget allow for this type of service.

The strategic plan should be reformulated into an action plan that will provide direction to the group in determining the objectives of the project under consideration.

All plans are only as valuable as the efforts made to actually implement the details of the plan.

Many departments and organizations have paid enormous amounts of money for plans that serve only to fill bookshelves or gather dust in office closets. Therefore, a timeline for implementation of the plan is critical to effective implementation and the ultimate success of the event.

Check Your Mission Statement

The addition of an event to your agency's repertoire requires the allocation of finite resources that suggests that efforts in one area of programming may necessarily limit activities in other areas. It is critical that any proposed activity or event coincides with the established mission of the organization. Your organization may have an overall mission statement that drives the decision-making process in the determination of resource allocation. The mission statement must be positioned as the guidepost and reference point for subsequent creative efforts. The mission of your particular event must coincide and support the mission of the organization. Failure to do so puts at risk the full support of controlling agencies, staff, and other significant stakeholders. A mission statement should define who you are, whom you serve, and how you serve them. It should be clear enough to act as a test for every action taken by your organization. Time and effort is needed to build consensus prior to the planning of the event. A well-designed mission statement can be used to evaluate the ideas put forward in the early stages of formulating a vision for your event. It is in this sense that all planning must be strategic. Strategic planning also requires taking an encompassing view of a desired activity through the marginal analysis of benefits and costs.

Strategic Management Models

Effective strategic planning should lead to strategic management, a process by which decisions are made in concert with the established mission and priorities of the organization. In its simplest form, strategic management should incorporate a plan that ensures the value of the event, the presence of resource support for the event, and the operational feasibility of the event. Establishing a planning format for events is challenging due to the myriad of details and contingencies that make up the reality of conceiving and producing a complex multi-dimensional activity such as a festival or special event. The amount and quality of time allotted the process of strategic planning will facilitate the clear and effective management of the organization in the present and provide a roadmap for future success. Many authors in the event planning profession offer their vision of strategic management. A few examples are provided in the following pages and summarized in Table 3.4.

Table 3.4. Event Management Models

Salem, Jones Morgan Model	Decision	Detailed Planning	Implementation	Evaluation						
Goldblatt Model	Research	Design	Planning	Coordination	Evaluation					
Masterman Model	Determine objectives	Identify stakeholders	Concept development	Feasibility analysis	Decision to proceed	Implementation planning	Event implementation	Handover	Evaluation	Feedback
Crompton Model	Identify hygiene elements	Identify satisfier elements	Create minimum standards	Communicate desired effects	Implement	Evaluate				

The ensuing models reflect the latest theories and practices in the field of event management. You are encouraged to make use of elements of each model that together will best serve the needs of your particular group and project. Should one particular model seem appropriate for your management style you are encouraged to refer to the bibliography at the end of the book and read about the method in greater detail.

Salem, Jones, and Morgan Model

This model in Yeoman et al. (2004) provides a four-stage process for event management: *decision, detailed planning, implementation,* and *evaluation.* The importance of each stage is relative to the type and purpose of each event, as different types of events will emphasize one aspect of the process over the remaining elements.

Decision. The decision to move forward with plans for a new event must be firmly rooted in core values of the organization and the identification of intended results or project goals. The event must support the mission in such a way that the resources expended on the event make a positive net contribution to the mission of the organization.

Detailed planning. The event should appeal to the largest number of potential customers without diluting the goals of the event. Core activities are determined by the goals of the organization, which must include the perceived needs of the potential participants. In addition to adherence to specific goals and objectives, there must be performance indicators that allow for objective evaluation of the process and results. In many cases success is only measured by increases in attendance and revenue, overlooking the other benefits of event participation. The authors identify several key components that may act as reference points in the planning process. These characteristics include developing a theme, that will determine the activities, services, and experiences that take place at the event. All elements should be directed toward reinforcement of the chosen theme.

The location is also critically important to the overall success of the event. Variables to be considered include the size and capacity of the location; the facilities that will support the staging of the event; the visibility, centrality, and location of the event relative to other services (clustering). The authors suggest designing a list of necessary criteria that can then be used to weigh the advantages and disadvantages of any site under consideration.

Additional elements critical to the planning stage include ticket pricing, financial considerations, marketing strategies, and human resource and operational management.[5]

Implementation. Implementation describes the actual staging of the event. Success at this point is wholly dependent upon the extent of the pre–event planning stage. During the implementation phase, organizers must monitor the event and be ready to make informed decisions in all areas of operation in order to address unexpected issues that may arise. Effective planning includes the development of contingency plans that will allow for the changes to take place in an orderly manner. The authors also address the closing down of the event and the myriad of activities and responsibilities that come with this phase of implementation.

Evaluation. Evaluation, according to the authors, must be relative to the outcomes of the event and the process through which the event was planned and staged. Those involved with the delivery of the event should be enlisted to provide *process evaluation* while the external customers, participants, sponsors, and those who chose not to attend may provide valuable insights into the *outcome* of the event.

Goldblatt Model

Goldblatt (2002) identifies five steps in process of event planning: *research, design, planning, coordination, and evaluation.* The author asserts that there is a positive relationship between the amount of research that takes place prior to event implementation and the reduction of exposure to risk and loss in the process. "The better research you conduct prior to the event, the more likely you are to produce an event that matches the planned outcomes of the organizers or stakeholders."[6]

Research. The *research phase* must be driven by clearly defined objectives so that valuable resources are not wasted on research that serves no purpose to the event planners. Research includes the collection and analysis of data that serves to better define the intended audience of the event. Demographics provide a means of matching the needs, desires, and interests of a particular segment of the population with activities or events that can be designed to meet these intentions. By matching an event with a section of the population, the event may be better marketed to potential audience members, as well as potential sponsors who perceive this audience to be of value to their own marketing efforts. Further research should include a study of similar types of events held in other locations in order to determine best practices, navigate through potential problems, and to generally benefit from the experience of others. It is recommended to seek out the advice of event managers who may be open to sharing information in a cooperative and mutually beneficial environment. By building these types of professional relationships both the organizers and the participants at special events can potentially gain from the synergy of this shared knowledge.

Design. The *design phase*, according to Goldblatt, is the time for creative activity, for brainstorming a wide possibility of ideas that might enhance the event. This author employs a why, who, when, where, what, and how approach to the creative process. He refers to it as *mind mapping,* which is used in order to tease out a basic philosophy that will act as the starting point of the planning process. Of note is the recommendation to event organizers to steadily nurture their own creativity through visits to other arts event, reading great literature, enrolling in creative activity classes, and applying this newly acquired knowledge to one's efforts at creative event management.[7]

Planning. The *planning phase* results from the careful consideration of the feasibility of the project through an objective assessment of the resources needed and available for the successful implementation of the project. Goldblatt recommends an approach to resource management that includes a consideration of time, space, and tempo laws. *Time laws* refer to the actual amount of time available for the planning and production of the event. Time constraints affect all phases of event management and must be realistically considered by the decision makers in the planning process. *Space* defines the actual venue and associated physical resources that either enhance or restrict the creative process. *Tempo* refers to the prioritization of tasks and the allotment of time to accomplish these tasks that impact the quality of the final product.

Coordinating. *Coordinating* the event requires the ability to synthesize all prior knowledge and experience gained from the research and planning phases in order to successfully make decisions that provide direction and feedback to those carrying out the project objectives. Coordinating is the ability to direct the project by breaking down the work into manageable units and delegating the responsibility and authority to complete the tasks to the appropriate staff member or volunteer worker.

Evaluation. *Evaluation* should be an ongoing process that should not be delayed until the completion of the event. Constant evaluation and feedback increase the chance for effective mid-course alterations in the plan, which might contribute to the overall positive outcome of the event. Surveys, interviews, and stakeholder comments all contribute to the accurate analysis of the effectiveness of the efforts made during the event management process.

Masterman Model

Masterman (2004)expands the list to ten key elements including *determining objectives, identifying stakeholders, concept development, feasibility analysis, decision to proceed, implementation planning, event implementation, handover, evaluation, and feedback.*

What is noteworthy in Masterman's approach is the number of steps prior to the decision to move forward with the project. Also, a greater importance is assigned to the strategies for the long-term benefits that can be strategically planned for in the initial consideration of the event.

Masterman's text addresses the particular characteristics and demands of sport event management on the international level. Frequently these types of events require the construction of new, or the renovation of existing facilities. This suggests the need for additional planning both on the pre-construction phase and, perhaps more importantly, the establishment of directives that will guide actions taken following the event. Masterman addresses issues such as handover strategies and the impacts and legacies of major events and venues. Masterman therefore impresses upon the reader the absolute necessity of pre-decision planning in order to determine the long-term well-being of a host city or region.

The author suggests that any desired long-term benefits must be addressed in a strategy that ensures continued success. A cost-benefit analysis is necessary at the feasibility stage. This ensures proper budgeting from the onset and also allows for early support based on projected benefits over a predetermined length of time. Beyond the short and medium term benefits, a 10-year projection must be developed to ascertain the sustainability and legacy of staging an event. The process should also allow for systematic and continuous alignment of these goals of varying length.

Determining objectives. According to Masterman, this initial step answers the question as to the perceived purpose of the event. Identifying the potential for benefit will include a consideration of economic, social, political, and other enhancements resultant from the staging of a particular event. By considering the short, medium, and long term nature of these intended benefits, the needs of the stakeholders may be properly addressed. The scale and timing of the event can have very positive lasting effects:

> In the case of major international sporting events, host cities may well have regeneration objectives such as redevelopment of derelict lands for new facilities, housing and business opportunities. The event in effect becomes the catalyst for the achievement of such objectives.[8]

While most organizations have some event objectives and related benefits, the author notes that they generally lack sufficient detail to be managed properly. There is some debate as to whether the objectives should proceed or follow the concept design. The author suggests (p. 52) that the concept is the vehicle to achieve the objectives and therefore should follow the objectives.

Identifying stakeholders. Stakeholders may include, but are not limited to, ticket buyers, participants, advertisers, sponsors, merchandise buyers, suppliers of goods and services, contractual employees, partners, investors, staff, volunteers, and those who exert influence from outside the realm of the event planners and organizers. In the case of a major event requiring the construction of facilities that will be around long after the event, it is critical to identify and coordinate all plans with the local or regional government authorities. For example, the London Olympic strategic plan included use of the newly constructed facilities in East London as a source of economic regeneration for the area and the starting point for new programs emphasizing school sports and recreational activities for all citizens. The enormous outlay of funds for Olympic construction was, in part, justified by the identification of the opportunities to provide all stakeholders with improved levels of quality of life as a result of the games. See:(https://www.gov.uk/government/uploads/system/uploads/attachment_data/file/78105/201210_Legacy_Publication.pdf) for a full explanation of the UK plan.

All stakeholders must be considered regarding their input, their event experience, and their subsequent reactions to and evaluation of those experiences and the legacy impact of the event.

Concept design. This stage of development, as presented by Masterman, directly serves the objectives of the organization. In this model, the emphasis is on the operational details of the project with minimal attention paid to the creative process. The identification of key decision makers, strategic partners, and stakeholders is combined with a determination of event scale, facility requirements, and other physical resources. A businesslike approach is necessary to adequately address the needs and challenges presented in the design of the event. The conceptual stage directs its energies to answering the questions of what is the event, and what does it look like.[9] All design decisions, according to Masterman, must be aligned with the predetermined objectives of the event. This is truly the key to strategic planning.

Feasibility. With clearly enumerated objectives, and a design that serves these objectives, the decision makers can now determine the ability of the group to allocate the necessary resources to accomplish the objectives. In other words, the event must be tested to see if it will achieve the intended results. In large-scale, venue-driven sports events, this process can take years of effort. Lead-up events that may be staged on a smaller scale can be used to learn the necessary efficiencies to deliver the main event. In addition to any planning issues identified at this stage, it is also extremely important to assess the benefit potential of the event based on the existing objectives and design features. A detailed critical path analysis is necessary due to the multiple layers of dependencies that must be identified and analyzed. A preliminary budget must be developed and a thorough cost benefit analysis must inform the decision to proceed or to abort the project.

The 2014 FIFA World Cup in Brazil is a classic example of the attractiveness of hosting an event clouding the ability to realistically assess its feasibility. By late 2013, it was acknowledged that Brazil was not adequately prepared to complete the construction of the necessary facilities for the event. Brazil has identified systemic risks such as urban chaos, crime, infrastructure challenges, and other important weaknesses inherent in their governmental/social structure. The feasibility of the event was questionable long before the Cup was awarded to Brazil and will provide researchers and students ample opportunity for post-event evaluation.

Decision to proceed. Quite simply, an organization must answer the question as to whether the event will successfully meet the desired objectives and whether the commitment of the necessary resources is worth the effort and will provide satisfactory returns on investment. All identified decision makers must be involved in the process. If the event is not perceived to have the ability to meet the objectives there must be a reevaluation of the concept and the process. If the event is perceived to have the ability to meet the objectives, an implementation plan should be developed.

Implementation planning. This is completed through the development of an operational strategy that includes the accomplishment of required short-term tasks, the determination of performance indicators, and the attention needed to the details of the event. This is the *delivery stage* of the event and includes identifying, organizing, and activating all the physical and human resource elements that are needed to bring the event to fruition.

Implement the plan. This is commonly referred to as the *execution stage*. All previously determined objectives and plans are put into action. The short-term objectives are translated into work units that enable the accomplishment of tasks that allow for the implementation of the plan and realization of the benefits of the event for all stakeholders. Organizers must be able to react to any and all challenges, changes, and emergencies that may appear during the actual staging of the event in order to keep the event on track for success.

Handover. This is an essential element in this particular strategy. Following the completion of the event, the facilities are delivered to other users and the responsibilities associated with the long-term successful use of these assets are realized at this time. The ability to delineate the responsibilities of use by other groups and organizations is critical in determining the level of success relative to the long-term strategy for facility use. This process links the original goals of creating and using facilities that were designed for a specific event but are then to be used again for other suitable events.

Evaluation. The benefits of the event, relative to the costs incurred for short, medium, and long term objectives, are analyzed at this time and will continue to determine the overall success of the event. The event-planning process must be evaluated along with the actual planned objectives of the event. Performance indicators, previously identified in the planning stages, are now used to compare the intended with the actual benefits of the event. For Masterman, who is concerned with extended use issues of major facilities, the evaluation process is not only enacted at the end of the event but also at the end of the process of turning over the facility to other organizations who may realize additional legacy benefits. Not only is the event evaluated but the extended results must also be considered in this process.

Feedback. By developing a process of continuous performance appraisal, feedback is also provided as a part of the cycle of event planning. Recommendations should feed into the event decision-making process for subsequent years. An evaluation report should result from the analysis of the entire 10-step process suggested in this model.

Masterman's overriding premise is that event planning must be a progressive series of actions and evaluations, an iterative process, allowing for adjustments to and realignment of the operational activities to the original objectives of the event. This process must accommodate not only the event goals but also facility objectives which may have a 10- to 20-year life expectancy.

Crompton Model

Crompton (2003) introduces the ideas of Herzberg from the article entitled *The Effects of Hygiene On Worker Motivation*, to explain some underlying principles of effective event design.[10] According to the Herzberg model, the hygiene aspects of a job are those elements that are seen as being necessarily present before a worker could begin to feel motivated about their job. These represent the *minimal conditions* or normal expectations of the job site. This includes things such as company policies, salary, job security, and safe work conditions. These are baseline necessities that if lacking would negate the possibility for satisfactory job motivation. They are referred to as job context *hygienes* or *dissatisfiers*. These are differentiated from job content-related elements that were seen as *satisfiers* or *motivators*. These elements create enthusiasm and commitment and can lead to psychological benefits such as achievement.

Crompton first applied this concept to leisure services in 1980 in an analysis of visitor satisfaction with experiences in recreational facilities. He noted that the physical characteristics of a recreational facility or special event site were analogous to the extrinsic maintenance (hygiene) elements of a workplace in that there are minimum standards or thresholds that, if not met, will surely result in dissatisfaction on the part of a visitor. And like the Herzberg model, if these hygiene elements are satisfactorily met, this in itself does not mean that satisfaction will occur. It only reduces the possibility for dissatisfaction. Crompton suggests that these maintenance or hygiene elements of an event should not be the focus of the manager but rather, due to their routine nature, should be delegated to individuals with the appropriate resources and specific skills to meet the standards set for these elements. His reasoning is that these maintenance elements cannot produce a positive recreational experience, they only reduce the possibility of a negative experience.

The primary task of skilled managers is to focus on the satisfier attributes and use them to create environments that are most conducive to delivering sought social-psychological benefits so visitors have an emotionally satisfying experience. Many managers, according to Crompton, never get beyond direct oversight of the tangible, hygiene elements of the event. This reduces the opportunity to capitalize on the benefits of a well designed rather than just a well organized event.[11]

Maintenance elements, uninteresting and non-unique, include such things as parking, restrooms, availability of basic information, and customer service—these must be perceived to be at least at a minimum level of acceptability. If these meet a minimum level of acceptability, then the satisfiers have the opportunity to influence the intended social-psychological benefits of the event. These benefits include cultural exploration, novelty, regression, socialization with known groups, external socialization, prestige/status, intellectual enrichment.[12] Crompton further explains that the model proposed is non-compensatory, meaning that failure to meet the threshold in a single or small number of elements can result in a negative overall perception of the experience. Compensatory models include trade-offs; that is, poor performance in one area can be offset by good performances in other areas. Because the event experience is itself the product, every experience of the visitor is, on some level, critical to the overall impression of the event.

Applications of Crompton. Crompton's contributions to event-management theory are of critical value for event organizers. With the hundreds of details involved in even the simplest event, it is important to meet the needs of the visitor for basic expected services, as well as moving the event into the realm of higher levels of response and benefit. Organizers should identify both maintenance and motivator elements of an event. Creativity exists in the realm of the satisfiers. By delegating many of the operational elements to the appropriate level within an organization, more time and effort can be allotted to the creative aspects of the event. Research indicates that unique, creative elements elicit higher levels of interest and a greater chance of positive comments and return visits.

Additional Theories

Other theories of event planning have been offered by Catherwood and Van Kirk (1992), Graham (1995), Getz (1997), Watt (1998) Torkildson (1999), Shone and Parry (2001), Bowdin (2001), and Allen (2002). It is advisable to review as many theoretical approaches as possible prior to launching a new project, as each approach offers a slightly different perspective that cumulatively can add a great deal to the knowledge base of your planning group.

What these and other models suggest is that it is not enough to simply complete all of the tasks associated with an event and push forward. Increased levels of accountability are sought to justify the allocation of resources for non-essential activities (a debatable description) such as festivals and celebrations. Impact analysis and benefits determination are critical components to the sustained health of a special event. This suggests the need to incorporate a consideration of these factors early in the planning stage of the event.

Tools of Strategic Planning

Planning technology. Tools and technology have aided the development and advancement of cultural activities for millennia. Due to the critical nature of planning in the overall success of special events, many tools and methodologies have evolved in the past few decades. Prior to the development of planning software packages and websites, there existed a few very useful tools in project management that remain effective and have been strengthened by the software applications associated with these tools.

Organizational charts. Organizational charts are physical representations of the structure of an organization. They generally include an identification of each position in the organization with its position relative to other members of the group. The chart can identify the hierarchical structure of the organization, the layers of authority and responsibility, as well as the chain of command for receiving and delivering information. When assembling a large group of staff, volunteers, and other event stakeholders, it is advised that each team member be provided with the opportunity to examine the organizational chart and be permitted to ask any pertinent questions regarding the work flow as represented by the chart. See Figure 3.2.

Critical Path Analysis and PERT Charts

These tools were developed in the 1950s to manage large-scale governmental projects. The design and development of the national highway system and large public works projects such as dams required multiple layers of planning and coordination. Both tools aid in

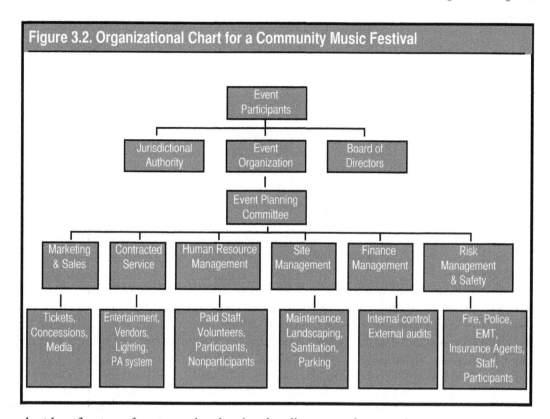

Figure 3.2. Organizational Chart for a Community Music Festival

the identification of project-related tasks, the allocation of required resources, time management, and project progression and evaluation. By controlling for these factors, decisions can be made regarding necessary adjustments to project schedules and resource allocation in a predictable and effective manner.[13]

Critical Path Analysis, also referred to as the Critical Path Method, allows the planner to identify the minimum length of time needed to complete a project by identifying the dependencies and sequential relationship and time requirements of individual tasks. These individual tasks, particularly those that are critical to the completion of a portion of the overall project, provide a graphic illustration of the flow of work. The underlying principle of CPA is that some tasks cannot begin until other tasks are completed. By identifying these necessary critical elements, one can identify the critical path from initiation to completion of the project. Tasks that are not on the critical path may experience some fluctuations in start and finish times without altering the overall time estimate. Changes to the flow of critical elements, however, will assuredly impact the project completion date. Critical elements, once identified, must be given the full attention and priority of the event planners. Non-critical elements may have to sacrifice resources that are then transferred to critical elements in order to keep the project on schedule.

A simple example. I have occasionally asked an audience to determine a critical path analysis for getting dressed in the morning. This exercise is used because there are times when people, particularly at early morning gatherings, seem to skip certain critical steps in the process, this particularly evident with my students who have either slept in their clothes or wore their pajamas to class!. The critical path to getting up in the morning could look like this…

Wake up → get out of bed → remove sleeping apparel → possible showering or other hygiene activities → put on underwear→ find clothes for the day → put on pants→ shirt→ socks→ belt→ shoes→ coat…

Variations include: those who do not wear underwear (hopefully a minority); putting on your shirt before your pants; socks could go on earlier especially if the floor is cold; some people are alert enough to put the belt on their pants before their putting pants on which eliminates missing that one loop in the back; and so on. Prior identification of the necessary steps and the ordering of resources like laying out your clothes the night before, may increase efficiency and may reduce levels of stress and add to the positive characteristics of the experience.

Most students do grasp the idea of a "getting dressed critical path" in that there is a need to put underwear on before your outer clothes (unless you are Madonna). If you want to tuck your shirt in, you need to wait to finish putting your pants on; putting on socks is always better before your shoes. Failure to establish a critical path could result in the situation of trying to get that last few inches of a pant leg to stretch over the shoe that for some reason you were wearing despite a lack of trousers. It seems like a time saver but usually results in pulling the pant leg off and removing the shoes and basically starting over the right way! Critical Path Analysis allows for the sequencing of tasks in the most effective pattern in order to achieve the overall objective in the most efficient way (see Table 3.5).

From this simple example, one can begin to grasp the necessity of sufficient thoughtful, anticipatory planning that is at the heart of the process of critical path analysis. Should a project need to be accelerated in order to meet a deadline, all non-dependent or parallel tasks can be initiated sooner without adversely affecting other sequential activities.

Table 3.5. Key Elements of Critical Path Analysis
• Determining what tasks must be carried out
• Prioritizing tasks
• Sequencing the activities
• Identifying resources needed
• Identifying parallel tasks
• Determining the shortest time to complete the project
• Shortening times whenever possible[14]

A suggested method for using the Critical Path Method follows below:
1. List all the activities in the plan including the earliest start date, the estimated length of time needed to complete the task, the status of each tasks as a sequential

dependent task or parallel or independent task. Identify which task(s) must precede subsequent tasks.

2. Draw the activities as circles with numbers corresponding to the placed task inside the circle. From the initial task circle, draw an arrow to the next task that is seen to sequentially follow the previous task. This graphic illustrates the dependency of one task to the other. The lines should the same length but should indicate the length of time needed to get from one task to the next by writing the time over the arrow. The name of the task being performed during that time is written under the arrow.

3. The linear relationship of the tasks illustrates the need for one task to be completed before the next starts.

4. By adding up the estimated times of each segment one can determine the length of time needed for stages of the project as well as the total time needed as identified by the critical path.

5. Parallel tasks do not initiate from the same point but may become part of the critical path further along in the life of the project.

6. The critical path must receive the greatest amount of attention from the project manager. Any slippage in the completion of sequential events will negatively affect the deadline.[15]

7. See if you can draw a simple CPA Chart.

If projects need to be speeded up due to unforeseen delays or a directive to finish earlier than originally planned, one must allocate additional resources to accomplish the task in a shorter time. This will inevitably affect the project budget as more resources are called into play. Any decision to accelerate the project must consider budgetary and resource constraints and the potential outcomes related to the changes sought.

Gantt Chart

This graphic tool provides the same type of time/task management as the CPA tool. This display includes a task list, identification of resources needed, and a very detailed timeline for the initiation and completion of the task. Similar to CPA, each task is visually represented, in this case by a horizontal bar that extends from starting to finish point of each task. These are calibrated by the timeline provided at the top of the chart. By filling in the bar to the extent that the task is complete, the picture allows for the identification of milestones or checkpoints along the way as well as providing a proportional depiction of the extent of completed work. Based on the starting point of one task relative to the completion of another, Gantt charts can be expanded to track expenditures related to each task allowing for a current accounting of the status of the project budget (see Figure 3.3).

Figure 3.3. Gantt Chart—Event Management

Project Manager: General Manager
Today's Date: 4/5/08

WBS	TASKS	START	END	Duration	%Complete	Days Complete	Day Remaining	1/1/09	2/1/09	3/1/09	4/1/09	5/1/09	6/1/09
											TODAY		
1	Research	1/1/15	3/1/15	90	100	90	0						
2	Feasibility Study	2/1/15	4/1/15	60	100	60	0						
3	Design	4/1/15	5/1/15	30	0	0	30						
4	Planning	2/1/15	6/1/15	120	50	60	60						
5	Coordination	4/1/15	6/1/15	60	0	0	60						
6	Evaluation	1/1/15	6/1/15	180	50	90	90						

Completed

Incomplete

The Role of Communication

In all cases of using planning tools and models such as those described above, the human actions and decisions regarding time estimation, prioritization of tasks, resource allocation, and process evaluation are the determinant factors in the ultimate success of the project. The entire process moves forward based on the best assumptions made by the group involved in the project as well as the external stakeholders who have some significant input in the process. The planning tools, simply put, must use the best available information provided by the event organizers. It is obvious therefore, that individuals with experience in project planning, decision making, resource management, and the ability to communicate this knowledge to others are highly valued. Plans and technological aids are merely tools to help in the process of communication.

Reaching Beyond the Plan

Design suggests more than merely assembling the components of your event. Design calls for a certain level of immersion in the creative process. Creativity has become a some-what utilitarian phrase, as much creativity is directed toward problem solving. Creativity in a broader sense is about new and divergent thinking, seeing things in a different light, and arriving at new relationship with elements of your physical, intellectual, or spiritual environment. To create means to bring something new or original into being. It is possible to assemble all the elements needed for a special event and successfully deliver the event without an ounce of creativity. Designing an event acknowledges the raw materials but also seeks to accentuate those elements that will inspire both the event organizers and the event visitor. Creative design requires an open-minded approach to problem solving. It involves taking risks and may include many false starts. The creative process generally will take longer to achieve the desired end results than a more pedantic approach. It is up to the event organizers to promote creative thinking on the part of staff and stakeholders. Creativity must be a core value of the organization so that it is at the center of the design process. Organizers must allocate sufficient time and other resources to allow the creative process to develop within the organization. The benefits of taking a creative approach should be identified and effort at creativity, regardless of its outcome, should be encouraged and rewarded.

Design: Events are Sensual

Many event professionals suggest that events and festivals need to be sensual. Sensuality in a contemporary use usually connotes sexuality, but sensuality is more than that. Experiences can be very sensual without being sexually arousing. While some are more sensual than others, the point is that the event is a physical experience and we experience things through our senses that then feed our imagination. Our ability to see, hear, touch, taste, and smell allows us to form multi-sensory impressions. An event should be appealing to all five senses.

During the design phase, your planning group needs to ask what your event is to look, smell, feel, taste, and sound like. Research tells us that our olfactory sense, smell, is the most powerful in terms of long-lasting impressions. Smell can also elicit very strong responses from feeling sick, to the pleasant effects of aromatherapy. The folks at Disney understand this quite well. During a tour of the underground world of Disney, I was quite surprised to learn that beneath the pavement of the amusement park are canisters containing scented aerosol concoctions that are sprayed up through the pavement into the path of visitors (and their kids). In particular, I remember the distinct smell of chocolate chip cookies (my favorites) being sprayed directly outside a shop that sold "homemade" cookies. My first reaction was that it seemed a bit diabolical and manipulative in that it assuredly influenced the volume of cookies sales going on at the store. On the other hand it may, for many visitors, simply provide a wonderful memory of a time in one's life when the kitchen smelled of home-baked cookies.

What are some of your favorite smells? How do they make you feel? What are some smells that contribute to the positive experience of a special event?

A less covert approach is to take a virtual, sensual tour of your event and imagine the impact of all elements of your event on the five senses. You may want to alter the experience to eliminate unpleasant sensory experiences and increase opportunities for positive sensory interaction. And if you end up with any leftover cookies, send them to the address at the back of this book!

Summary

Living in an era with diminishing resources, managers are challenged to maintain, and in fact, increase the quality of services provided to their constituencies. It is no longer sufficient to assemble the components of a special event and hope for the best. Event organizers must have a clear understanding of the relationship of their efforts to the greater mission and goals for their respective organizations. Increased amounts of time must be spent in the strategic planning of events to increase the possibility for success. All aspects of event planning must be approached in a holistic manner, considering both the interrelationship of the many elements of the event and their effect on all who are impacted by the planning and execution of the event.

Discussion Questions

1. Identify five types of planned events.
2. What is meant by strategic planning? What are some benefits of this approach?
3. Identify and explain the components of a SWOT analysis. Give an example of each component.
4. What is a work breakdown structure? What are the nine steps in planning backward?
5. Explain Crompton's ideas concerning the Hertzberg Hygiene Model as it applies to event management.
6. What are some common elements to the event-management models presented in this chapter?
7. How can an organizational chart be of benefit to an event planner?
8. Explain the concept of Critical Path Analysis.
9. Describe the structure and purpose of a Gantt chart.
10. What is meant by the statement that an event should be sensual?

1. Retrieved from idealist.org www.nonprofits.org/npofaq/03/22.html
2. IBID.
3. Retrieved from mapnp.org/library/plan_dec/str_plan.htm
4. IBID.
5. Yeoman, I., Robertson, M., Ali-Knight, J., Drummond, S., & McMahon-Beattie, U. (2004). *Festival and event management.* Amsterdam: Elsevier Butterworth & Heinemann. pp. 14–30.
6. Goldblatt, J. (2002). *Special events* (3rd ed.). New York: Wiley & Sons, p. 36.
7. IBID. p.47.
8. Masterman, G. (2004). *Strategic sports event management: An international approach.* Amsterdam: Elsevier Buterworth Heinemann, p. 51–52.
9. IBID p. 54.
10. Crompton, J. (2003). Adapting Herzberg: A conceptualization of the effects of hygiene and motivator attributes on perceptions of event quality. *Journal of Travel Research,* 41, pp. 305–310.
11. IBID p. 306.
12. Crompton, J., & McKay, S. L. (1997). Motives of visitors attending festival events. *Annals of Tourism Research,* 24(2), pp. 425–439.
13. Retrieved from www.mindtools.com/pages/article/newPPM_4.htm
14. IBID.
15. IBID.

Section Two

Indentifying and Managing Fiscal Resources

This section of the book addresses the need to identify and make efficient and effective use of all financial resources at your disposal. This includes budgeting and accounting procedures, understanding economic impact, the role of sponsorships, the challenges of marketing, and the importance of effective risk-management policies and procedures.

4

Planning for a Positive Economic Impact

Planning is bringing the future into the present so that you can do something about it now.

Alan Lakein

Chapter Objectives

- Identify the economic potential of special events
- Understand economic impact characteristics and measurements
- Identify problems with economic impact studies
- Identify modeling systems
- Understand cost–benefit analysis
- Develop strategies to maximize revenue at an event

Assessing the Market

Creating an impact, whether it is social, cultural, civic, or economic, is at the heart of designing and presenting an event. The effectiveness of the impact is closely tied to the resources available to create the event and how these resources are used to achieve the goals of the event.

Justifying the outlay of financial resources and the commitment of time and effort required for the planning and staging of a special event is a critical process for event organizers. In addition, the *substitution costs* of putting on an event rather than allocating these resources to other beneficial activities, must be carefully considered when planning an event. It has become necessary for event organizers, who rely on public funding and in-kind support from governmental agencies, to accurately identify the positive economic and social benefits of their planned events.

Regardless of the other important benefits of staging an event, responsible fiscal management of the process is crucial. Many organizers report the financial outcome of the event based on the accounting of the expenses and revenue associated with the event. A monetary surplus or profit is to be commended and is generally expected by sponsoring governmental agencies, but it is only one aspect in the greater consideration of positive financial impact. Crompton (2001) points out that it is not sufficient to report income to elected city leaders, but also to demonstrate to the resident tax payers that the event has made a positive economic impact that can be realized by residents. It is the residents, through their tax payments, that are the real sponsors of government-supported special events.[1]

In this chapter, we will look at some basic methodologies related to economic impact analyses including the inherent shortcomings of many of the approaches used to justify the allocation of resources to special events. This will be followed by an examination of best practices designed to ensure, as much as possible, the economic success of the event.

The Success of the Festival Format

Frey (2000), in a working paper presented at the Institute for Empirical Research in Economics, observed that many established classical music venues experience financial difficulties, while the less formal festival format has grown in popularity over the past 20 years. Formal music centers, such as symphony halls, opera houses, and art museums in Europe are in what Frey calls a "financial depression." The author notes that publicly supported institutions are challenged by reduced financial support and rising unionized labor costs that drive up the unit labor costs for productions, while labor productivity in the arts remains unchanged. According to Frey, this scenario, referred to as *cost disease*, threatens the continuance of art-based productions, as productivity is not keeping pace with costs.[2]

Festivals have avoided this malaise, and in fact are flourishing due to their ability to be artistically innovative and programmatically creative. Festivals have the ability to reach wider, more diverse audiences. The production costs of festivals are less due to the seasonal nature of the workforce, often supplemented by scores of volunteers. Festivals present an effective model in the delivery of cultural and artistic experiences to the public. Conversely, festivals may be threatened by the overreaching influence of governmental agencies that provide funding and in-kind services and may have jurisdictional authority over the goals and outcomes of a festival or special event. This is particularly true in Europe where a higher percentage of taxes is dedicated to the subsidization of cultural activities. Bureaucratic interference, particularly in the management of fiscal resources, can result in an ineffective system of revenue production and implementation that can cause atrophy rather than artistic and social growth. In other words, dependence upon tax dollars for the support of cultural events runs the risk of causing these events to lose the very qualities of creativity and innovation that make them special events.

Economic Potential of Festivals and Events

Festivals have great economic potential as they attract growing numbers of visitors that, as we will see, may have a positive economic effect on a local economy. Festivals allow residents and visitors to focus on a particular location for a predetermined amount of time. If properly managed, this represents a unique opportunity for economic gain. Festivals are more newsworthy than many other regularly featured events such as a monthly concert series or the newest film at the local movie theatre. Due to the transient nature of the event, individuals must make a commitment at a particular time to attend, or the event will pass them by. Again this is in contrast to a repetitive event at a local venue where the decision to attend can be put off to a later date. The uniqueness of the event will attract the attention of the media, resulting in a raised level of awareness of the event. This is related to the characteristic referred to as *perishability*, the reality that an event has a short and predetermined life span.

Festivals offer multiple opportunities to generate revenue. Ticket sales, sponsorship opportunities, concession and merchandise sales, and special promotions all provide the event organizers the possibility of increasing revenue while meeting additional needs and demands of their customers. Festivals do possess the potential to create a positive economic impact on a local economy, suggesting that strategic event planning include a consideration of this important factor.

What is Economic Impact?

Economic impact is defined as "the net economic change in a host economy, excluding non-market values, that results from spending attributed to the event."[3] For our purposes, it is the measurement of the impact of additional new dollars that enter a community due to the staging of a special event. As we will see, there are many factors that can cloud this type of analysis, and there are many opportunities for promoters to manipulate figures and public perceptions in order to inaccurately portray the positive impact of an event. Economic impact is based on certain assumptions about the potential value of an event to a local or regional economy. Stynes (2001), in describing the Michigan Tourism Spending and Economic Impact Model, provides a basic equation for measuring impact in Figure 4.1:[4]

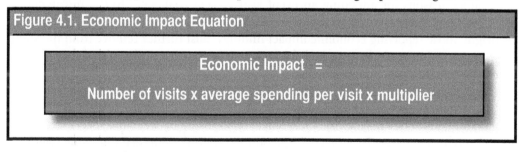

Figure 4.1. Economic Impact Equation

Economic Impact =

Number of visits x average spending per visit x multiplier

The equation is simple enough but the process can be very confusing resulting in large, seemingly unrealistic numbers being provided the experts.

Resident vs. Visitor Expenditures

Some visitors are easier to spot than others!
Photo Credit: deLisle

Non-residents who bring new money to an area are typically referred to as visitors or tourists. Expenditures by visitors within the event host community that are directly related to your event, and would not have occurred if the event was not held, should be the focal point of economic impact analysis. The classification of an individual as a visitor suggests that this person is not a resident of the area and, more than likely, not a taxpayer. The first consideration is to differentiate between residents and non-residents. This is most easily accomplished by identifying the address or at least the zip code of the event participants. This delineation, however, is not enough to begin a study of non-resident economic impact.

When attempting to measure economic impact of an event on the local economy, several categories of individuals must be excluded from the calculations. Residents, while likely to attend an event, and most assuredly spend some money, do not represent new or outside revenue sources for the locale. The money spent by a resident at an event would probably be spent on some other form of entertainment within the same geographic area if not spent on the special event. This is categorized as *switched spending*, and these figures should not be included in measuring economic impact (see Figure 4.2).[5]

Visitor Motivations

Visitors' reasons for attending an event also present challenges to the researcher or event promoter interested in accurately measuring economic impact. To be completely forthright, those reporting economic impact findings must further remove from the study those visitors who would have visited the area at another time of the year if they did not attend the special event.

These are referred to as *time switchers*. Their economic impact is real, but due to the fact that they would have come to the area at another time and most likely have spent a comparable amount of money negates the cause/effect relationship between the special event and the influx of revenue based on the visit. The only exception to not including time switchers would occur if the visitors indicated that they also plan on visiting the area again at another time of the year. In this case, the event-based visit is an additional visit, bringing increased economic activity to the area.

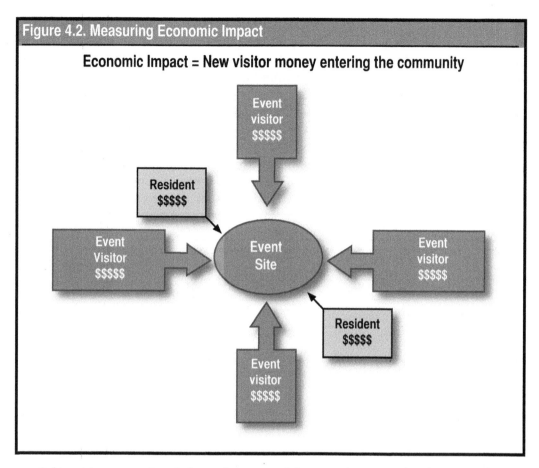

Figure 4.2. Measuring Economic Impact

Economic Impact = New visitor money entering the community

Other visitors may already be in the area and discover the event after their arrival. Once again, the festival is not the direct cause of their presence in the community and thereby cannot be identified as the true source of visitor spending. These individuals are characterized as *casuals* in that their motivation for participation in the event was not intentional, as it was not planned prior to their arrival in the community.

Local residents, time-switchers, and *casuals* must be culled from the respondents to any survey intent on determining economic impact directly related to the special event. Once a proper identification and accurate estimation of significant visitors has been determined, the amount and impact of their spending can be calculated.[6]

The Multiplier Effect

Economic impact determination is closely associated with the concept of the *multiplier effect*, sometimes referred to as the *ripple effect* (see Figure 4.3). Imagine dropping a stone into a pool of water; the effect of the stone is to cause waves or ripples in the water. As the ripples move away from the original point of entry, the ripples become less prominent and eventually fade away. This analogy also describes the effect of new money spent in a community. The money may have an effect, a multiplier effect, in the community. The multiplier effect describes the economic activity that takes place within a community or region based on the re-spending of new dollars that enter the community. The effect is generally greater than the original sum spent by the visitor. The original expenditure has the potential to create additional spending in the community by those who are initially impacted by the visitor's purchase of goods or services. The original visitor expenditure may go toward the income of a part-time or full-time worker, who then spends his/her money at a local grocery store or on some other activity within the impact area. Likewise, the dollars may be respent by a business in the community to restock items that were sold as a result of the special event. In this sense, the dollar creates additional economic activity, which then causes further ripples of activity within the community. At some point, the dollar is spent on goods or services outside the host community. At this time, it is said that the money has *leaked out* of the local economy. The multiplier effect is curtailed if the additional income is spent on goods or services that originate outside of the host community. It is then that the economic impact of the original expenditure ceases to have an effect on the local economy.

Figure 4.3. Ripple Effect of Visitor Spending

The Misuse of Economic Impact Studies

Many event organizers, supporters, and politicians will promote an event based on the projected positive economic impact on their community. Unfortunately there is a tendency for event organizers and supporters to overstate the economic impact of an event on the local economy. According to Howard and Crompton (1995), this is done either deliberately to position the event as a critical element in the local economy and provide for continuing financial support for the event, or due to a lack of knowledge regarding accurate and fair impact analysis methods.[7]

Quite often we hear that an event, like the Super Bowl, will result in the infusion of millions of dollars into the community as a result of money spent by attendees during this now week-long celebration. These figures are relative to the scope and duration of the event and may include factual data from past years' events. There is an initial excitement caused by the figures provided, creating the desired positive image of the event and a justification for further financial support of the project. There is some basic logic in considering that if an individual or group visits a city and attends an event, they will most likely spend some money during their visit. One need only consider the money spent on food, lodging, entertainment, and transportation as an indication that visitors do have measurable financial impact during their stay. However, many event promoters and government leaders use only the most basic analyses, *sales impact*, disregarding the need for a more precise examination of the actual effects of a visitor's expenditures on the community. For those who wish to provide accurate, and possibly more modest, estimates of economic impact, it is important to understand and follow accepted principles and practices regarding these types of studies.

Crompton (1999) presents basic principles for an accurate and honest development of economic impact measures for local community events. The Springfest example provides a framework for identifying variables and conditions that contribute to economic impact resultant from a special event. Accurate economic studies require an understanding of the event visitor's effect on the local economy.

Multiplier Coefficient

Short of coloring or marking the dollars spent at an event (defacing U.S. money is still a punishable offense) the only way to ascertain this multiplier effect is through the use of modeling systems based on mathematical formulae and certain general assumptions about economic activity. These modeling systems determine *multiplier coefficients*, which are used to estimate the additional impact of new money in a local economy. The multiplier coefficient is expressed as a number that reflects the relative probability of a host community consumer purchasing goods or services within the confines of his/her community. This re-circulation of revenue within the community is represented by the size of the multiplier.

The size of the multiplier, according to Stynes (2001), is determined by several factors. The overall size and diversity of the local economy in that region will affect the size of the multiplier. Areas with diverse economic systems may well produce many of the goods or services purchased by local consumers, thereby retaining visitor dollars for a longer period of time. The size of the geographic area considered as the host community also affects the size of the multiplier as a larger geographic area may retain spending for a longer period before it is lost to outside expenditures. The type of business or event under consideration will affect multiplier size as certain sectors, such as tourism and special events, impact different elements of the local economy (labor-intensive vs. product-intensive operations). Finally, the multiplier coefficient is time sensitive.[8] Multipliers change as variable conditions such as price, wages, and inflation define a local economy.

Generally speaking, regions with limited economic development will have smaller tourism-related multipliers. Fortunately, there are individuals who devise software packages and modeling systems that make economic impact analysis a manageable activity for mere humans!

Impact Measurement–Types of Multipliers

Three measures derived from these economic impact models are sales multipliers, income multipliers, and employment multipliers.

Sales Multiplier

The sales multiplier is an indication of additional sales activity based on dollars spent in the community. These are generally the largest numbers available through impact analysis and are quite frequently used to impress the business community. This method is the one most frequently used in "mischievous ways" to inflate the importance of the event to the local community. The sales multiplier measures the total economic activity occurring during the event period. It does not distinguish between resident and non-resident spending and does not account for leakage of money outside the community.

Employment Multiplier

The employment multiplier estimates the number of jobs created by the introduction of the event into the local economy. The data therefore is reported as a specific number of additional jobs. These numbers again allow for the reporting of less than accurate results. The jobs increase reported usually does not specify full-time or part-time employment nor does it determine the length of time that these new jobs will last. This is particularly evident in the types of jobs associated with special events, which tend to be service and contractual jobs of a very short duration. While everyone welcomes job creation in their region, it is important to look beyond the numbers to gain a full understanding of the type, quality, and duration of these new employment opportunities.

Income Multiplier

The income multiplier examines how the spending of one visitor affects the household income of residents and how this additional resident income is spent in the local economy. This indicator is deemed to be the most accurate, and frequently is a much smaller figure than the sales multiplier, but it is a more realistic analysis of real economic impact on a community. Additional income experienced by individuals within the area under consideration has the potential to be re-spent in that area. In this way, it can be seen as having the most meaningful economic impact. The classical definition of income multipliers goes back to the work of Miernyk (1965), who first categorized impacts as direct, indirect, and induced.[9]

The shortcomings of the sales and income multipliers include assumptions that the additional income realized in the community is going to be reinvested in the community. They do not consider the purchase of goods at an event that are not produced in the local area. They also do not account for workers who live outside the region who may earn income in the target area but spend it elsewhere, as well as those who choose to save rather than spend this additional income, and the fact that this additional income may in fact be spent outside the area by residents.

Modeling Systems

Modeling systems such as the Impact Analysis for Planning (IMPLAN) input/output system have been devised to calculate the multiplier effect. It is the most commonly used tool for determining economic impact and deserves further explanation. The IMPLAN model grew out of the need for the U.S. Forest Service to determine the impact of forest-related activities on regional economies. The first publication describing the model was by the Fort Collins, Colorado Land Management Planning Unit of the U.S. Forest Service.[10] Concurrent with the Forest Service efforts was a need on the part of recreational service providers and the tourism industry to measure the economic impact of visitors and special events in their local regions. During the following twenty years, the IMPLAN model was refined and the process was made accessible on the Internet with the first Windows version arriving in 1996.[11] The most recent edition, IMPLAN Version 3.1 is available online and accompanied by a generous amount of free downloads and trial packages and training to assess the value of the software for targeted usage. Additional work has increased the ability of tourism and event organizers to measure economic impact while accounting for an increasing number of variables.

A variation of the IMPLAN model was developed by researchers at Michigan State University, resulting in regional economic models and multipliers that can be accessed by analysts and applied to Michigan-based activities. The Michigan Tourism Spending and Economic Impact Model (MITEIM) is a very useful example of a state-specific tool that provides recreation, travel, and tourism officials with predetermined multipliers and ratios for Michigan's rural, small metro, and statewide areas. This model is easily implemented by analysts and event organizers with little training and limited knowledge of regional economic-impact methods. To download the most recent version or to access additional information regarding the basic concepts involved in economic impact analysis, various methodologies, and some very useful Internet links go to https://www.msu.edu/course/prr/840/econimpact/michigan/MITEIM.htm

Economic Impact: Data Collection

By this time, you might feel that an economic impact analysis would be very beneficial, but it seems to be a little complicated, and who really has the time to figure out the procedures? Critical to developing an accurate economic impact study is to have accurate data on visitor expenditures. Fortunately, a great deal of research has been completed in the last fifteen years that provides event organizers with very practical and relatively easy methodologies for determining accurate and useful economic impact data on the local level. It is recommended that event organizers begin by conferring with local chambers of commerce, tourism boards, and economic development agencies to make use of information that may have been previously collected on local economic impact variables. One must approach this data with knowledge and caution, as less than representative results may emerge from goal-driven assumptions and research.

Creating Useful Data

The basic steps in creating useful, meaningful information include the following:

1. Identify the geographic area to assess the economic change—this may be the boundaries of a town or city, a particular zip code, the county lines, or any other demarcations that allow for accurate assessment and useful application of results. Typically, the impact zone should have some significant interest to the results of

the study. Residents, whose taxes may be providing seed money for the event, may express an interest in the benefits of their investment in the event.

2. Determine a method of measuring attendance at the event. Ticket-controlled entry points are the most accurate. Also, having a turnstile in place creates a very reliable means of collecting attendance data. It is more challenging to count attendees at free events that have open or multiple access points to the event site. In this case, a sampling method must be developed. For example, you might count the number of entrants to the site for a predetermined amount of time at regular intervals throughout the festival. The numbers recorded for a portion of an hour can then be extrapolated to the entire 60-minute period. This might not be totally accurate, as it involves estimation and might not account for multiple entries by the same individual and the expected inaccuracies in the counting procedures, particularly at very busy periods. Hopefully, over the life of the event, organizers can determine accurate and manageable methods of counting attendees.

3. Time must be dedicated to the training of individuals who will interact with attendees in order to present the survey, clarify the purpose, and aid participants in the interpretation and completion of the survey questions.

4. Devise a questionnaire that will identify the place of origin of the attendee and provide additional information about their motivation for visiting.

5. Prior to its implementation, the survey should be tested on individuals who were not involved with the construction of the survey. This *beta test* is helpful in that it might bring to light shortcomings or problems with the survey before it is used at the event. What is of the greatest importance is to differentiate between residents and visitors, as well as visitor time switchers and casuals, so that the visitors who purposefully selected your event will be the only ones to be considered in the economic impact analysis.

6. The information must then be tabulated, subjected to analysis, and be translated into accurate and representative results that can be understood by the general public.

Completing an economic impact analysis of your event is a big commitment of resources that will only benefit the event if there is a predetermined strategy to implement the results. This requires a thoughtful discussion of the goals of the economic impact study. The results may be used to justify the municipal support of the event, indicating that residents' tax dollars are being returned to the community through increased commercial activity. The results may also be used to track the growth of the event over a predetermined number of years. The results may also be used to compare the economic impact of one event with other events within the community. This is only possible if the instrument and methodologies used to study each event are the same. The results may be used to inform both the decision-making process for subsequent events and in order to adjust operational policies that affect the delivery of the event. See Figure 4.4.

Economic impact is only a part of the equation. Economic impact analysis is a very useful and persuasive tool in promoting the benefits of a special event. This impact must be weighed relative to the real and perceived costs of planning and staging the event. A more complete approach to economic impact should include a cost/benefit analysis.

Figure 4.4. Example of a Data-Collection Survey

SPRINGFEST 1999: TOWN OF OCEAN CITY VISITOR SURVEY

DATE:
TIME:

1. What is the zip code at your primary home address?
2. Which of the following days will you be (have you been) at this event? (Please circle all that apply)
Thursday   Friday   Saturday   Sunday
3. How many people (including yourself are in your immediate group? (This is the number of people for whom you typically pay the bills. e.g., your family or close friends)
4. To better understand the economic impact of this festival, we are interested in finding out the approximate amount of money you and other visitors in your immediate group will spend, including travel to and from your home. We understand that this is a difficult question, but please do your best, because your responses are very important to our efforts. DURING THE COURSE OF YOUR VISIT, WHAT IS THE APPROXIMATE AMOUNT YOUR IMMEDIATE GROUP WILL SPEND IN EACH OF THE FOLLOWING CATEGORIES:

TYPE OF EXPENDITURE

Amount spent
in the Ocean City area

Amount spent
outside the Ocean City area

_____ A. Food and beverages (restaurants, concessions, cafeterias, etc.) _____
_____ B. Night clubs, lounges, and bars (cover charges, drinks, etc.) _____
_____ C. Retail shopping (souvenirs, gifts, films, etc.) _____
_____ D. Lodging expenses (hotel, motel, condos, etc.) _____
_____ E. Private auto expenses (gas, oil, repairs, parking fees, etc.) _____
_____ F. Rental car expenses _____
_____ G. Any other expenses. Please identify:

5. Would you have come to the Ocean City area at this time even if this event had not been held?
Yes   No

    5a. If" Yes," will you stay longer in the Ocean City area than you would have if this event had not been held?
    Yes   No
    5b. If "Yes" (in 5a), how much longer?

Days
6. Would you have come to the Ocean City area in the next three months if you had not come at this time for this event?
Yes   No

Used with permission from John Crompton

Other Perspectives on Economic Impact

Jackson et al. (2005) offer a do-it-yourself kit enabling festival organizers to objectively analyze the economic impact of an event and compare results with other events. This methodology is best suited for the economic impact of small regional festivals that are envisioned to be regular events. The information obtained is designed to aid in evaluating past success and informing the decision-making process for future endeavors.[12]

Tyrell and Johnston (2001) provide the framework for a methodology to assess the economic impact of tourist events as opposed to tourism in general. It is referred to as the "net direct expenditures" related to a specific event. Event assessment, according to this method, must consider the source of the expenditure, the geographic starting point of the expenditure, the destination or end point of the expenditure, and the reason for the expenditure. The net economic impact must be differentiated from the gross economic impact, which is the total of all event visitors and participants. This distinction attempts to separate out expenditures that would have occurred whether the particular event was held or not. If a great deal of money was spent by locals on goods at an event, the actual net economic impact to the region would be negligible.[13]

Those spending money at an event will include spectators, participants, volunteers, media, sponsors, exhibitors, and vendors. These expenditures must be tracked from initiation to conclusion to determine whether they have a local economic impact. The reasons for the particular expenditure must also be determined—is it related to the event or to the location regardless of whether the event took place? The economic realities of your local community also play an important role in the planning of a financially successful event. Identifying the goals of the event and the impact of these goals on the local community is critical to the sustainability of your event. If an area has a strong draw for tourism and hosts an event that draws money away from the typical tourist expenditures during that period of time, the event might be seen as having a negative economic impact.

Cost/Benefit Analysis

A cost/benefit analysis is an important component of the initial feasibility study that should be undertaken prior to the commitment of resources to an event. The benefits of the event, as we have said, go beyond economics but must be understood with respect to the various types of costs incurred by planning and producing the event. These costs include the following considerations.

Impact Costs

Impact costs include the costs of additional equipment, supplies, labor, and time invested in the event. An assessment of these items is conducted in order to determine whether the project is worth doing. Costs can be financial or social, and they can be physical or logistical. They include the costs of traffic congestion, vandalism, police and fire protection, environmental degradation, garbage collection, and increased problems for local residents.

Displacement Costs

Displacement costs describe the fact that the staging of an activity by one individual or group may displace activity by other potential visitors. According to information collected by Crompton, the effect of the Atlanta Olympics on the daily average spending of visitors to that area was a net loss for the community. Atlanta Olympic visitors spent an average of $15/day. Normal business travelers spend $350/day. Due to the great influx of Olympic visitors and the pre-event perception of crowding, the availability of visitor services was usurped by low-spending tourists rather than higher spending business people during the weeks of the event.[14]

Opportunity Costs

Opportunity costs addresses the fact that most organizations and municipalities have a limited number of resources available, and the spending of resources on a special event takes away the potential opportunity to do other things in the community. This is a factor that must be seriously considered in the planning phase. Money spent on a festival may take funds and other resources away from new programs or improvements to the infrastructure of the city. Furthermore, setting land aside as a festival site may preclude using the land for other more profitable enterprises. The sale of goods and services within the confines of an event may also limit other business opportunities. If the event provides all the goods and services needed for a visitor, the local economy outside the gates of the event may actually suffer real or perceived loss during the event. All of these examples suggest that due to the reality of resource limitations, particularly the number of potential buyers of goods and services, efforts made in one area, such as the staging of a special event, may result in lost opportunities in other areas.

Event planners should consider the three types of costs mentioned above when considering the net benefit an event may create for a community. It's not all about dollars. The positioning of an event in a community is well served through a thorough analysis of all the costs and benefits associated with the event.

Maximizing Revenue at your Event

Revenue accumulation is not the same thing as economic impact, although both concepts are very important to the success of an event. Event revenue is income that takes place on site including ticket sales, concessions, amusements, souvenirs, and any other revenue that may be realized through related activities before or after the event such as sponsorships, vendor contracts, and fees. One would be hard pressed to continue an event that might have significant local economic impact but does not adequately address the costs of planning and operations. Underlying revenue production is a basic element of economic theory. Revenue is produced through the sale of goods, services, and experiences. Understanding the laws of supply and demand and their relationship to cost are fundamental. These are anchored in our understanding that most people are rational, and make decisions in their own best interest. Accepting this premise, we can readily see that consumers will choose items based on the real or perceived benefit provided to the buyer. This benefit may be one of quality, exclusivity, convenience, conformity, uniqueness, or as a means of gratification or problem solving. The benefit is also controlled through the marketing efforts of the seller, who might consciously manipulate consumers' perceptions relative to the benefit of the product or service.

It is readily accepted that individuals will pay a certain amount of money for the real or perceived benefits of an item or experience. The relative value is influenced by the supply of the product that relates to issues such as exclusivity, perishability, and uniqueness, and the demand for the product, which is generally fueled by advertising and promotional efforts.

Special events have a limited lifespan. This suggests a limited supply of the experiences and goods and services available to the consumer. This is considered a strength for the event planners, if it is properly managed to create both the perception and reality of a high-quality product in limited supply. This perceived scarcity may be enhanced by providing unique experiences at the event—ones that would be difficult to replicate through other life experiences. This can then be combined with the other positive elements of the event to produce the perception of a product of high value. High value frequently translates into increased revenue due to the willingness of participants to pay higher ticket prices and the tendency to purchase more goods and services at a high-quality event. Perceived values can also increase the demand for the event, which might also lend itself to higher revenue realization and the possibility to increase fees.

Event Pricing

Event activity pricing is a challenging task, as one must consider the

- perceived value of the event,
- real costs associated with the event,
- projected attendance numbers,
- competition of other events,
- competing leisure opportunities taking place in the region,
- capacity of the local consumers to pay the price of admission, and
- costs associated with attendance.

The intended market for the event will play a key role in determining pricing strategies. Determining the price of admission to an event is different than considering the cost of the event to the consumer. The ticket price is just one element of spending that must be considered. Other expenses include transportation, lodging, money spent on concessions, souvenirs, and other miscellaneous items that result from the decision to attend the event.

Research tells us that expenditures at a festival are positively related to such factors as length of stay[15]; distance traveled to the event[16]; household income[17]; and family or group size, which has both positive and negative effects.[18,19]

In a study of the spending patterns of jazz festival visitors, Thrane (2002) concludes that the motives of an individual to attend a particular event will impact spending at the event. Specifically, those with an expressed interest in the theme of the event, in this case jazz music, spent more money at the event than those who may have attended the event for reasons such as curiosity, or non-musical motivations. The author also notes that affluent households spent more than non-affluent households at the festival. As the household size increased by one member, the expenditures decreased by 13%, suggesting a need to be cognizant of financial constraints on large families. In addition, the author reports that males spent 25% more than females, older visitors spent more than younger ones, fully employed visitors spent more than those who reported to be part-time employed, and those who planned to attend the festival well in advance of the event spent more money than those who decided to attend relatively close to the time of the event. It is also interesting to note, and is well documented in other research, that non-residents spent considerably more than residents at the event.[20] This would suggest that some types of visitors might be of more importance to the event organizers and might warrant the allocation of additional resources to attract them to the event. Limited marketing dollars are best spent in identifying and reaching out to the types of attendees who have a demonstrated interest in the type of experience being offered at the event.

Ticket Pricing Strategies

Acknowledging that event costs for the visitor extend beyond the price of admission, it is advisable to spend some time and energy in determining ticketing strategies that will result in the maximum return to the event and the greatest satisfaction for the visitor. Research and practical experience suggests that ticketing strategies might include offering reduced rates to those who purchase their tickets well ahead of the date of the event. Those making an early commitment to attend the event might feel rewarded by a reduced admission fee. It is advisable for event organizers to sell as many advance tickets as possible as there are many compet-

Ticket sales are a critical element in realizing financial goals for an event.

ing factors that might cause potential attendees to make other leisure choices as the day of the event draws near. Pre-sold tickets might also help to address cash-flow issues that typically challenge event organizers in the weeks just before an event.

Discounts for families might entice more people to the event, who might then succumb to the attraction of souvenirs, concessions, and other high-profit margin commodities offered at the event. Family events provide additional challenges and opportunities to event organizers. It is important to consider the typical or average levels of pricing for recreational activities available in your area. For example, minor league baseball teams, when entering a new market, carefully study the pricing of family-oriented experiences in the local market when setting the price for game tickets. The area price for cinema tickets is often a good indicator of the capacity of the local economy to pay for recreational experiences. Ticket pricing for general admission to the minor league ballpark often falls slightly below the cost of local movie tickets. Once inside the park, an effort is made to facilitate the separation of additional cash from the attendees through concessions, souvenirs, and the like, all of which are perceived by the consumer to add value to the experience and are welcome sources of revenue for the team owners. Most minor league franchises augment the entertainment experience with additional events such as fireworks, music concerts, and themed days with merchandise giveaways. All of these added features create value in the minds of the potential attendees.

Because a special event is a consumer-based activity, the duration and intensity of the experience may also facilitate organizers in determining the value of the event experience. These are valuable lessons for event promoters in that the entire experience is for sale and a perceived lower entry price, or the impression that the ticket entitles one to more than the base experience, may stimulate additional revenue throughout the event.

There are many other factors that contribute to revenue management and the potential for positive economic impact generated by festivals and special events. Much of the work of designing an event for maximum economic impact has fortunately been researched and formulated in the past decades. Many of these topics are addressed in subsequent chapters explaining the role of marketing, sponsorships, risk management, and other fiscal realities of event management.

Summary

Understanding the basics of economic theory is just the starting point for the responsible fiscal management of an event. Event managers are challenged to make ethical use of economic impact information despite the common practices of hired consultants and politicians. A strategically planned event will assuredly maximize revenue for the event being offered. Superior economic planning will also identify and capitalize on the potential for economic impact that extends beyond the geographic and temporal borders of the event.

Discussion Questions

1. Why do festivals continue to be financially viable while other forms of entertainment are attracting smaller audiences?
2. What is economic impact?
3. What is the multiplier effect? How does it relate to economic impact studies?
4. Why are some economic impact studies unreliable?
5. Why are visitor expenditure and resident expenditures treated differently in an economic impact study?
6. What is a time switcher, and why is this concept important to economic impact studies?
7. Why is the income multiplier the most accurate measure of economic impact on a community?
8. Why is the identification of the geographical impact area important to an economic impact study?
9. Explain three types of costs associated that impact a cost-benefits analysis?
10. What are some ways that a festival can maximize revenue?

1. Crompton, J., Lee, S., & Shuser, T. (2001) A guide for undertaking economic impact studies: The Springfest example. *Journal of Travel Research, 40*(1), pp. 79–87.
2. Frey, B. (2000). *The rise and fall of festivals: Reflections on the Salzburg Festival.* University of Zurich: Institute of Empirical Research in Economics, p. 2.
3. Crompton, J. L., & McKay, S. L. (1994). Measuring the economic impact of festivals and events: Some myths, misapplications and ethical dilemmas. *Festival management and event tourism 2*(1) 33–43.
4. Stynes, D. (2001). *Economic impacts of tourism.* Retrieved from http://web4.msue.msu.edu/mgm2/econ/pdf/ecimpvol1.pdf
5. OPCIT. Crompton, Lee & Shuser. p. 81.
6. IBID. pp. 81–82.
7. Howard, D., & Crompton, J. (1995). *Financing sport.* Morgantown, VA: Fitness Information Technology. p. 55f.
8. PCIT. Stynes.
9. Miernyk, W. H. (1965). *The elements of input-output analysis.* New York: Random House.
10. Siverts, E., Palmer, C., Walters, K., & Alward, G. (1983). *Implan users guide.* U.S.
11. Probst, D. (2000). *Use of IMPLAN to assess economic impacts of recreation and tourism: Chronology and trends.* Retrieved from http://www.prr.msu.edu/trends2000/papers_pdf/propst_implan.pdf
12. Jackson, J., Houghton, M., Russell, R., Triandos, P. (May 2005). Innovations in measuring economic impacts of regional festivals: A do-it-yourself kit. *Journal of Travel Research,* Vol. 43 pp. 360–367.
13. Tyrell, T., & Johnston, R. (Aug. 2001). A framework for assessing direct economic impacts of tourist events: Distinguishing origins, destinations and causes of expenditures. *Journal of Travel Research,* Vol. 40. pp. 94–100.
14. OPCIT. Howard, D., & Crompton, J. (1995). p. 82.
15. Spotts, D., & Mahoney, E. (1991). Segmenting visitors to a destination region based on the volume of their expenditures. *Journal of Travel Research,* Vol. 29, No. 4, pp. 24–31.
16. Leones, J., Colby, B., & Crandall, K. (1998). Tracking expenditures of the elusive nature tourists of southeastern Arizona. *Journal of Travel Research,* Vol. 36, No. 3, pp. 56–64.
17. Asgary, N., De Los Santos, G., Vincent, V., & Davila, V. (1997). The determinants of expenditures by Mexican visitors to the border of Texas. *Tourism Economics* (4), pp. 319–328.
18. Fish, M., Waggle, D. Current. (1996). Income versus total expenditure measures in regression models of vacation and pleasure travel. *Journal of Travel Research,* Vol. 35, No. 2, pp. 70–74.
19. Taylor, D., Fletcher, R., & Clabaugh, T. (1993). A comparison of characteristics, regional expenditures, and economic impact of visitors to historical sites with other recreational visitors. *Journal of Travel Research,* Vol. 32, No.1, pp. 30–35.
20. Thrane, C. (2002.). Jazz festival visitors and their expenditures: Linking spending patterns to musical interest. *Journal of Travel Research,* Vol. 40, p. 281–286.

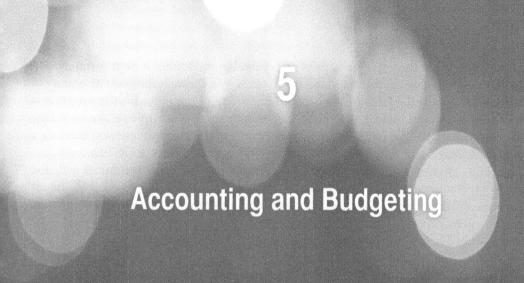

5

Accounting and Budgeting

 The very best ideas simply cannot survive without the money to bring
it to the market and sustain it until it achieves profitability.

Joe Goldblatt

Chapter Objectives

- Understand accounting principles
- Discuss the relationship of budgeting to planning
- Understand how a budget acts as a tool for planning, daily management, communication, and evaluation
- Differentiate between fixed costs and variable costs
- Understand feasibility and break-even analysis
- Understand the process of establishing a fiscal calendar
- Understand the process for identifying revenue sources
- Understand the purchasing process

Successful event management requires the capacity to manage the fiscal resources needed to adequately address the goals of the project. Fiscal management is the most critical element of event management. This is due in part to the nature of special events. An event presents a relatively short period of time to capture revenue. While expenses frequently occur throughout the fiscal year, the majority of the income generated is realized during the event period. Planning for the maximization of revenue collection during this brief period is both challenging and absolutely critical to success. Additional funds can and should be gathered throughout the year via sponsorship relationships, pre-event ticket sales, and a long-term fundraising strategy.

It is possible, and frequently is the case, that one might initially stage an event without a full understanding of the fiscal demands. Many agencies approach the event-planning process with a great deal of enthusiasm, creativity, and vision, which might carry the momentum through one cycle of the event, but it does not lead to sustainability. Responsible individuals, agencies, sponsors, and taxpayers, through the evaluative process, must realistically face the issue of the economic viability of the event for the future. It is frequently not sufficient these days to just break even or arrive at a surplus at the end of the event. The goals of many events are tied to greater efforts to increase tourism, enhance a community's image, and achieve other monetary and non-monetary goals. Investing time in a feasibility study as an initial stage of strategic planning is highly recommended. The extent of preplanning analysis is proportional to the complexity and resource demands of the project. The financial risks and opportunities presented by the event must be fully discussed and incorporated into the strategic plan.

As described in the previous chapters on planning and economic impact, we know that all stakeholders must understand the mission and goals of the organization. This might also require the completion of key financial partnerships prior to moving forward. The objectives of the particular event being proposed must be in concert, or at least not in competition, with the objectives of any outside organizations that invest in the event. These event objectives then guide the decisions regarding the scope of the event under consideration. This synchronicity must accompany all decisions made at each phase of project development. It is possible for an individual event to be considered successful by the event committee while the larger organization might view the event as a failure based on goals that were not correlative. For example, a local craft festival might attract many vendors and a satisfactory crowd but might not contribute in a substantial way to the goals of the local tourism board that seeks to increase overnight visitors to the area. If the tourism board provided initial funding for the event, they might not be inclined to provide future funding due to the lack of success from their perspective. The fiscal realities of the event can become very challenging as the event grows, but the basics of sound fiscal management remain constant.

Fiscal Management

Many times, well-intentioned enthusiasm gets the best of planning, and money is spent that might not directly or significantly impact the event in a positive way. "You spent HOW MUCH on flowers for the guest speakers?!" It is wise, from the onset, to have a committee or staff member whose primary task it is to exert fiscal control over the decision-making process by repeatedly examining each financial decision in light of organizational and event objectives and the available resources. Fiscal management is about the recognition of the scarcity of resources and the enactment of strategies to prioritize needs and make best use of the resources available. Hopefully someone who is forceful and vigilant without being too annoying can be enlisted for this job!

Preliminary budget formulations are an important part of the feasibility analysis that should take place before significant resources are committed to the event. The budget must address the operational objectives of the project. This will be based to a great degree on the pricing and level of services to be offered at the event. An important consideration at this point is whether the event is being designed to meet specific pre-existing fiscal goals or whether the event, on its own merit, deserves fiscal support. If an event is proposed for the specific purpose of increasing revenue at a particular venue or to increase overall revenue for a department, then the substance and theme of the event can be determined based on maximizing income. Conversely, if the goal is to increase civic involvement and pride, the project might take on a completely different character with a lesser emphasis on profit making. This process of fiscal planning must recognize these realities *and* be rooted in acceptable accounting and budgeting principles and practices.

Accounting Principles

Underlying the budgetary process is the science and art of accounting. Accounting practices are based on policies and procedures that support the mission, goals, and objectives of an organization. Accounting, despite its inherent lack of appeal to most of us, is a very powerful tool. Major corporations, both in the United States and abroad, have used accounting as a means to prop up failing companies, misinform stockholders, and avoid paying obligatory taxes. They have also paved the way for many business executives to spend a considerable amount of time in prison. Other organizations have dutifully managed accurate and transparent accounting records, building a high level of trust with all stakeholders.

Financial practices based on accurate accounting are necessary for the daily control of expenditures and revenue. Generally accepted accounting principles (GAAP), as developed by the Financial Accounting Standards Board, provide organizations with a set of guidelines and conditions that will help to ensure that the methods used to record transactions and prepare reports support the credibility of your organization. A certified public accountant (CPA) can help your organization establish sound accounting principles that will provide you and your stakeholders with clear, understandable practices for cash-flow management and reporting.

If your event is one program of many offered by an organization, or if the event is affiliated with a governmental agency, it is wise to meet with the appropriate finance officer to review and assimilate the necessary procedures to ensure smooth, crisis-free fiscal operations. Expense and revenue accounting procedures will be in place that should address most of the needs of the event. Governmental agencies are legally required to follow more stringent procedures in accounting for revenue and expenditures.

Depending on the particulars of the governing agency, the opportunity may exist for setting up a special revenue account so that the fiscal management of the event may address the event needs more effectively. Special revenue accounts and enterprise accounts, depending on the language of the particular agency, might allow for an operational approach that does not have to strictly follow the guidelines established for other governmental spending. Special revenue accounts within a governmental structure can avoid the return of revenue to the general fund and can then be designated for the continued financial support of the event. Purchasing regulations can also be streamlined if the funds are handled outside of the traditional governmental system. The advantages and disadvantages of these options should be fully discussed with the finance officer of the agency and with the committee members and decision makers working on the event.

Special events are particularly challenging as they often involve a significant number of volunteers and committee members who might not be familiar with the fiscal procedures of the organizing agency. It is of paramount importance that any individual involved with the expenditure of funds or the collection of revenue be made fully aware of the importance of following the procedures necessary for the successful financial management of the event. A lack of attention to these details can erode the best intentions of an event committee if it is perceived to be operating in violation of the accepted fiscal principles of the governing agency. The principle of *public trust* requires that public agencies act in such a way that the funds entrusted to them by residents, sponsors, and others be managed in an honest, transparent, and professional manner. Once approval has been given to expend funds, decisions must be made in the best interest of all stakeholders. Levels of responsibility and authority must be clearly delineated so that each committee member understands the boundaries of his/her individual role regarding fiscal resources.

Accounting Defined

Accounting is defined as the process of recording, classifying, and summarizing financial transactions. See Figure 5.1. The receipt and disbursement of funds are recorded and reported. Records are created to document the financial activities of the organization. These activities take place in what is called an *accounting cycle*. The specifics of this cycle depend on existing policies and procedures and the particular characteristics of your event or organization. The accounting system used by event organizers will be dependent upon the existing expertise of the organizing committee, the time available to devote to bookkeeping, and the complexity of the event business.

Figure 5.1. What is Accounting?

Accounting includes the following functions:
   1.   Tracking daily sales transactions
   2.   Purchasing of goods and services
   3.   Periodic posting and reporting of debits and credits
   4.   Issuing and administration of debt
   5.   Fiscal evaluation of the risk management program
   6.   Budget preparation and administration
   7.   Preparation of an annual financial report

For the small, independent organization whose sole purpose is to plan and deliver a special event, it is critical that an effective accounting system be introduced prior to the initiation of any financial activities. Software programs provide many alternatives for record keeping and should be compared to find one that best suits your needs. A new organization would benefit from having a CPA provide guidance and perhaps oversee the financial management of the event. The committee must decide whether it is cost effective to manage the accounting for the event in-house or to contract with a professional to manage the accounts. In either case, it is also advisable to consult with tax professionals to ensure that the methods chosen meet the requirements for local, state, and federal tax reporting. Sales tax and payroll taxes such as federal and state income tax, FICA, unemployment insurance, and others can make for a labor-intensive and somewhat technical challenge for event organizers with limited accounting expertise. Understanding your needs and allocating resources to contract for support services contributes to a realistic and potentially successful strategy for fiscal management. If outside assistance is needed, it is best, at a minimum, to understand the accounting process to determine the extent of professional services needed. Oftentimes, a consultant can help an organization to set up an accounting system that allows for the daily recording of transactions and summaries without the use of a CPA. Professional accounting services can then be used for the more complex annual reports and tax-related activities associated with the event or organization.

The Accounting Process

The accounting process includes the following procedures:

1. **Identify the basic transactions of the business.** Identify how and why money is spent and the source of any revenue realized.

2. **Set up accounts.** The business transactions are separated into categories referred to as accounts. Setting up accounts is best achieved after the group identifies the major and minor tasks associated with the event. The major tasks may well become the cost centers used to manage the various operations of the event. The chart, or list of accounts, becomes the framework for recording transactions. Many easy-to-use software products are available to help in the set up and control of the accounts.

3. **Record transactions.** There are several ways to record business transactions. Generally, transactions are recorded as debits or credits in a double ledger system. A balance sheet and other journal entries may be used to further detail and track all transactions. Learn what options are available through software packages and select a suitable tool for your operations.

4. **Summarize transactions.** All business activity should be tabulated and summarized according to a schedule that contributes to a manageable system for the organizers. Off-season transactions may be minimal and require weekly or monthly summaries, while the transactions that take place during a special event might require hourly tabulations in order to maintain control over a manageable workload.

5. **Prepare reports.** Depending upon who is going to use the accounting information and when this use is to take place, reports must be planned for and prepared to meet the needs of the organizers, sponsors, tax authorities, and decision makers.

6. **Analyze the reports.** To determine the financial condition of the event, the results of a carefully designed and executed accounting system can be very valuable in the decision-making process regarding the allocation of future resources for the special event. The accounting reports provide a fiscal history of the event that can help to identify strengths and weaknesses in the operations, marketing, and resource management of the event. Effective evaluation of the fiscal history of the event along with other evaluative measures, should guide future strategic decisions.

Accounting procedures accompany the decision-making process throughout the life-cycle of the project. Future event planning may be limited by the available fiscal resources and the financial history of the event. Accurate financial information allows for the analysis of the current situation and the opportunity to forecast potential future success. The ability to utilize this type of financial information effectively often separates a highly successful organization or event from the rest. Financial reports also support the development of performance evaluation criteria for the event as well as for the professionals who manage the event. Organizers might include financial goals in the contract of a professional event organizer or financial manager of an event.

Procedures for the handling of all financial transactions must accompany the accounting system. Basic controls regarding the handling of funds include requiring that no one person is responsible for the entire accounting procedure. This is commonly referred to as *separation of duties* and should be accompanied by a system that requires more than one individual recording and signing off on all transactions. This suggests that at least two people should count all deposits, sign balance sheets, and review payroll reports. This will reduce human error and possibly reduce the temptation to steal funds and defraud the agency.

Case Study: Lack of Controls Can Lead to Theft

Some years ago, a college athlete, whom I coached in soccer, confided in me about a scheme that he was involved in during his summer employment. He was assigned to collect money at a public parking garage attached to a major sports stadium in an east coast city during summer rock concerts. He was to collect five dollars per car and give each driver a ticket like the ones used in raffles—numbered and duplicated for record-keeping purposes. After several concerts, he learned that many of his co-workers were collecting the money but not handing out the tickets. The concertgoers, mostly not familiar with the venue procedures, did not ask for a ticket and went on their way. The money collected was to match the number of tickets handed out. By retaining the tickets, it was possible for the employees to pocket large sums of money each night. My player and his coworkers were never caught and stole thousands of dollars that summer. Except for guilty consciences and the possibility of eternal damnation, they suffered no averse consequences.

This example illustrates the fact that effective accounting systems and procedures must be designed to reduce loss, to minimize fraud, and provide for the best interests of the organization. Corporate accounting scandals remind us that, no matter what the safeguards, individuals who are strongly motivated can find a way around the most sophisticated systems. The other lesson is that, in the long run, most people will get caught!

How could the concert promoters have designed a system to reduce this type of theft by their employees?

Fraud can take place in high-end investment firms and the local Little League board of directors. It can occur in both public and private sector organizations. Fraud can result from trusting employees too much, lack of proper accounting procedures, or failure to enforce procedures that are in place. A lack of attention to details or failure to have multiple levels of reconciling transactions and reports caused by poor communication or unclear lines of authority all can create a scenario in which fraud can occur.

It is recommended that all event organizations make use of finance professionals in establishing accounting practices and procedures for the organization and train all those who will have some role in the handling of funds. Training should include appropriate procedural requirements and should strongly emphasize the need for honest and ethical behavior.

Budgeting

Accounting provides a framework for managing funds. A budget is then designed to plan for, allocate, and spend these funds. A budget is a multiuse document in that it helps the organization to establish and adhere to spending limits that reflect the mission, goals, and objectives of the event. A budget is a *planning tool*, as the financial resources must be allocated and used to the maximum benefit of the event. The budget reflects the intentions of the organization and identifies the specific resources needed to accomplish the project goals. A budget is a *daily management tool* used to control fiscal activity and to make decisions that affect the outcome of the efforts of all stakeholders in the event process.

Decisions made regarding the purchase of materials or services should be guided by the funds allocated during the budget process. The budget acts as a *communication tool* by the priorities it sets for spending. One can learn quite a bit about an organization by studying its budget. The areas designated for funding communicate the values and priorities of that organization. For example, a large-scale event budget that does not allocate funds for safety and risk management communicates a less than acceptable level of concern for its visitors and stakeholders. The budget is a *control tool* supporting the enforcement of organizational policies and aiding in the evaluation of the management of not only the financial resources, but the entire event process.

The budget process must begin long before the first purchase order is written and, like all other facets of event planning, must consider the needs of all identified stakeholders. A *fiscal year* must be identified that either matches that of the larger controlling organization or is chosen to reflect the needs and fiscal activities of the event. A fiscal year is an identified 12- month period used to manage the financial resources of an organization. The fiscal calendar need not follow the traditional calendar in that it can start on the month that is most convenient for the organization or that conforms to the fiscal year of the larger organizational structure. For example, many municipal budgets start on July 1, while the federal budget begins October 1. When formulating a budget, it is also advisable to solicit input from any individuals who have a vested interest in the event. Relying upon the expertise and experience of stakeholders, and a fair amount of research, should help in accurately addressing the funding needed for the various aspects of the event. The most efficient budgetary system is one that clearly identifies both the amount of funding requested and appropriated, and the intended use of these funds. An *appropriation* is the amount of money approved for spending and may be less than or exceed the amount of the original request.

Line Item Budgeting

A *line item budget* is generally considered to be the most accurate means of managing appropriated funds. Line items specifically identify personnel needs, materials, and services that will be purchased to support the event. A line item budget identifies areas of expenditure that are coordinated with the purchasing policies and procedures of the organization so that both the budget document and the means of accessing the funds for expenditures are conceptually and practically linked. Line items can also be used to identify different types of revenue that will be realized through the event. These line items are organized into cost centers, which typically represent major areas of activity/expenditure for the event.

Creating a budget document should begin with the identification of major and minor tasks and time constraints associated with the event. This will foster the development of a cost center system that will mirror the major tasks and the necessary resources. The line item method assigns a number or code to each cost center and line within the budget. This creates an accounting system that utilizes these numbers in the budget planning, accounting, purchasing, inventory control, and reporting systems for your event. It is important to design a budgetary system that best reflects the needs and activities of your event, and adheres to any requirements of the general accounting procedures of the organization. Major tasks associated with many festivals and special events that may be designated as cost centers include the following categories listed in Tables 5.1 and 5.2.

The retention of accurate budgetary information over the life of the event is critical to effective and successful management. Past expenditures and revenue levels contribute to the planning as well as the evaluation of the event. While budget management is often the weak point in organizational operations, it is by far the most critical element in the continuing success of the event. In Chapter 16 we will take a look at the many reasons why events fail; high on the list is the mismanagement or lack of sufficient funds.

Table 5.1. Expenditures
Administration
Financial management
Overhead costs
On-site office expenses
Legal expenses
Office expenses
Consultants
Taxes
Interest or finance charges
Planning
Research
Committee recruitment
Planning meetings and materials
Insurance/risk management
Insurance coverage
Permits—state and local
Site inspections
Security
Event Documentation/Evaluation
Video records
Sound recording
Evaluation materials
Photography
General materials and supplies
Office supplies
Miscellaneous items
Site Management
Site planning
Groundskeeping

Table 5.1. (Cont.)

Decoration
Seating
Other furniture
Staging
Lighting
Traffic and pedestrian controls
Parking
    Signs
    Fences, cones, and barricades
Booth set up
Site breakdown and cleanup
Law enforcement

Utilities
Telecommunications
Electric
Water

Transportation
Mileage reimbursement
Guest transportation
On-site vehicles

Marketing/Advertising
Advertising design and printing
Postage
Web design and maintenance
Shipping
Public relations
Print costs
Radio advertising
Television advertising

Sponsorship
Solicitation and recruitment
Sponsor packages
    Advertising and promotion
    Hospitality
    Gifts
    Recognition
    Post-event communications

Concessions
Solicitation
Registration

Table 5.1. (Cont.)

Food
Beverages
Payment to vendors
Dining area
Admissions
Tickets
Guest identification
Comps
Registration and record-keeping materials
Merchandise
Items for sale
Administrative costs
Entertainment
Sound reinforcement
Sound engineers
Lighting engineers
Stage crew
Stage lighting
Entertainer contracts
Transportation
Food
Lodging
Royalty payments
Rentals
Sanitation
Trash receptacles
Environmental controls
Hauling fees
Staff/Volunteers
Full- and part-time salary allocations
Food
Recognition and incentives
Meeting expenses
Contractual Services
Any additional services not provided by agency/sponsors

Table 5.2. Income/Revenue
Ticket sales
Pre-sales
Premium sales
Group sales
Additional ticketing strategies (seniors, students)
Vendor fees
Booth or space rentals
Percentage of food sale revenue
Gross returns self-managed food concessions
Merchandise sales
Gross returns from souvenirs and other items
Percentage of contractual vendor receipts
Sponsorships
Cash payments
Service values
Trades
Advertising
Brochure sales
Fundraising
Solicitations
Donations
Parking
Grants
Loans

Understanding Fixed and Variable Costs

In order to avoid the perils of fiscal mismanagement, you must develop an in-depth understanding of the impact of the financial operations of your event. This means that expenses must be further categorized and analyzed. Costs are generally categorized as fixed or variable, also referred to as *indirect* or *direct costs*. *Fixed costs* are those expenses that will be incurred regardless of the impact (attendance numbers) of your event. *Variable costs* will fluctuate depending on the volume of business experienced.

For example, the cost of the rental of the stage and sound system may be $5,000 for a weekend event. This is a fixed cost. It won't matter if one hundred or one thousand people attend, the cost will be the same. Administrative expenses like insurance, site management, and preparation expenses and many other items are set simply due to the fact that the decision was made to hold the event. Fixed costs vary in the sense that they can be negotiated through a bid process or by price comparisons, but the agreed-upon cost will not be influenced by attendance or other variables. No matter how many goods or services are sold, fixed costs must be paid. Likewise, the contract price for entertainment is agreed upon before the event begins and is a fixed cost. Fixed costs are also referred to as *sunk costs* as they are committed to the operation of the event. Some fixed costs can be converted to variable costs. If the entertainers were guaranteed only a share of the gate receipts based on attendance revenue, then this would be considered a variable rather than a fixed cost.

Variable costs are those expenses that fluctuate with the number of goods sold or services provided. Any expenses that rise or fall with the number of visitors or attendees can be considered variable costs. For example, the costs related to merchandise inventory or food will vary with the number of people served, and are therefore a variable cost.

It should be a financial objective to try to reduce fixed costs, as these can have a very negative effect on an event if anticipated revenues are not met. A percentage of each ticket sold goes toward the fixed costs. By reducing fixed costs or by increasing ticket sales, the percentage of each ticket dedicated to fixed costs can be reduced. Variable costs, having a direct relationship to sales, can increase with additional economic activity and have a more predictable relationship to profit margins. Each item, whether it is a ticket to the event, food, or merchandise, has a predetermined profit margin incorporated into its pricing. The markup value of sales ensures that increased purchasing will be accompanied by increased revenue and profit. The only restriction on this lies in the fact that events are perishable, they are of a relatively short duration, which may preclude the selling of all merchandise allotted during the time of the event. There is little sales value to last year's t-shirt once the event is over, unless of course the shirt becomes a "collectible" and is once again in demand.

The value of this type of characterization of expenses is realized in determining the *break-even point* for the event. The break-even point is defined as the number of sales needed to produce sufficient revenue to cover all fixed costs and the variable costs of the event. This is the point when the production of the event is covered by revenue and you can begin to realize a profit from any additional sales. This method can be used to analyze an entire event or to project necessary sales for a particular item at the event.

Example: Another Look at T-shirt Sales

Many organizations sell t-shirts that commemorate their event. Assuming that the fixed costs for shirt sales includes items such as booth space, transportation, a vendor fee, and advertising costs, the total for our example is $2,500. The production costs for one t-shirt (a variable cost) are $3. We project a *total sales* of 300 shirts at $15 each during the event. The long-hand calculations are provided in order to understand the process. However, there are many web-based tools that allow for the calculations to be completed using free software programs Take a few minutes to understand the data in Table 5.3.

If there is a sincere desire to responsibly estimate the fiscal feasibility of the event, this type of break-even analysis should be undertaken for all sales items including tickets, food and beverage, merchandise, and any other revenue-producing items. Sales projections are difficult in the first year of an event but will provide the necessary data for future-year projections. Accurate financial projections greatly aid the decision-making process for the allocation of funds to such items as marketing and sponsorship packages and will help in the prioritization and possible reduction of fixed costs in the future. If a significant outlay of funds has little or no return to the event, chances are you are not spending money wisely.

Table 5.3. Break-Even Analysis

Projected Unit Sales	300
Sales Price Per Unit	$15 = this is the selling price of the shirt
Variable Unit Cost	$3.00 = this is what it costs you to produce each shirt
Total Variable Costs	$900 = 300 shirts x $3 per shirt
Fixed Costs	$2,500 = these are the overhead costs of selling the shirts
FC + VC	$900 + $2500 = $3,400
Total Revenue	$4,500 = 300 shirts x $15 per shirt

$4,500 − $3,400 = $1,100

The break-even point occurs when 208 shirts are sold. This is determined by examining the income produced by the shirts in quantities of 10:

Break-even Analysis

Units	Fixed Cost	Total Cost	Total Revenue	Profit
0	$2,500	$2,500	$0	- $2,500
10	$2,500	$2,530	$150	- $2,380
20	$2,500	$2,560	$300	- $2,260
30	$2,500	$2,590	$450	- $2,140
40	$2,500	$2,620	$600	- $2,020
50	$2,500	$2,650	$750	- $1,900
60	$2,500	$2,680	$900	- $1,780
70	$2,500	$2,710	$1,050	- $1,660
80	$2,500	$2,740	$1,200	- $1,540
90	$2,500	$2,770	$1,350	- $1,420
100	$2,500	$2,800	$1,500	- $1,300
110	$2,500	$2,830	$1,650	- $1,180
120	$2,500	$2,860	$1,800	- $1,060
130	$2,500	$2,890	$1,950	- $940
140	$2,500	$2,920	$2,100	- $820
150	$2,500	$2,950	$2,250	- $700
160	$2,500	$2,980	$2,400	- $580
170	$2,500	$3,010	$2,550	- $460
180	$2,500	$3,040	$2,700	- $340
190	$2,500	$3,070	$2,850	- $220
200	$2,500	$3,100	$3,000	- $100
208	**Break-even Point** --			
210	$2,500	$3,130	$3,150	+ $20
220	$2,500	$3,160	$3,300	$140
230	$2,500	$3,190	$3,450	$260
240	$2,500	$3,220	$3,600	$380
250	$2,500	$3,250	$3,750	$500
260	$2,500	$3,280	$3,900	$620
270	$2,500	$3,310	$4,050	$740
280	$2,500	$3,340	$4,200	$860
290	$2,500	$3,370	$4,350	$980
300	$2,500	$3,400	$4,500	$1,100

Along with the importance of understanding the break-even scenario, it is also important to plan for the cash-flow requirements of your event. This factor is greatly influenced by funding sources in that most organizations have a predetermined fiscal year that determines the timing of annual appropriations. If the fiscal year does not match the spending needs of your event, you must creatively manage funds so that they are available when needed. This is common challenge if you are involved in a public-funding relationship with a municipal agency, or if your funds are provided by renewable grants.

One method to keep funds beyond the limits of a fiscal year is to *encumber* them. This process allows you to designate and retain funds for specified purposes despite the closing of the fiscal year. The encumbrance of funds is but one strategy that can be used in the management of the fiscal resources that are associated with purchasing.

Purchasing

Purchasing is the process of procuring materials, supplies, and services that have been included in the detailed budgeting plan and are necessary for the planning and staging of your event. Purchasing involves detailed record keeping and tracking procedures and is an important function of the overall accounting system for an event. Large organizations have a trained professional, the *purchasing agent*, who is responsible for the administration of all policies and procedures that control the expenditure of allocated funds.

Purchasing policies may include regulations controlling the timing of purchases, ethical guidelines for making purchases, vendor rules, the need for comparative pricing or a bidding procedure, requests for qualifications (RFQ), requests for proposals (RFP), quality-control specifications, bulk or cooperative purchases, emergency purchasing procedures, inventory controls, property disposal, petty cash use, and any other rules that might be necessary for the administration of funds. Purchasing agents can get pretty busy!

Most organizations have a purchasing manual that provides details on these and other elements of the financial management of the organization. If you are a startup organization, it is imperative that you develop purchasing policies and procedures that coincide with the mission of the organization and meet accepted standards for purchasing that comply with federal, state, and local laws.

Purchasing systems generally make use of a form called a *purchase order* that is used to initiate the process and to track, verify, and close out the purchase after the items or services have been delivered. A purchase order is a written contract and is subject to federal and state contract law. Records of purchase orders should be stored, either in hard copies or electronically, for seven years. Purchase orders include all the pertinent information about the purchasing organization including shipping and billing addresses, as well as the identification of the vendor, and descriptions and quantities of the items to be purchased. The PO also identifies the cost center and line item of the budget to be charged for the purchase and is identified by a unique number (the PO number) that is used when referring to the transaction. The purchase order, once signed, encumbers or holds the funds, set by the predetermined purchase price, so that the vendor is ensured of payment upon delivery of the items. In our earlier discussion of cash-flow management, the idea of *encumbrance* was mentioned. A signed purchase order may hold funds beyond the end of a fiscal year as an encumbrance, so that items may be purchased at a later date. This strategy helps to address the, sometimes inconvenient, cyclical nature of funding provided by the municipal agencies based on the accepted constraints of the fiscal year.

Blanket purchase orders may be issued to vendors that have repeat business with an organization. A blanket purchase order may remain open for a predetermined amount of time allowing for easier transactions and reduced paperwork. This also allows for a periodic billing and payment schedule.

Years ago, purchase orders were often filled out in quadruplicate (four copies) so that the buyer, vendor, and finance office had plenty of paper to stack on their desks. Today much of this paperwork has been eliminated through computer-based purchase order systems and electronic fund transfers. Many purchasing agents have been challenged by the new technology, in that they were forced to find new materials to pile upon their desks in an effort to look busy.

Purchasing Strategies

Purchasing decisions and strategies can have a noticeable effect on the financial success or failure of an event. Some basic cost-saving purchasing strategies include timing purchases when the demand for an item is at a low point, purchasing in large quantities or in cooperation with other agencies to get bulk pricing, standardization of materials, replacing items before repairs outpace cost efficiency, and requiring increasingly stringent price comparisons for increasingly expensive purchases. Anyone given the authority to make purchases must also understand the regulations regarding taxable items, tax exempt documentation, and laws that may impact the final price paid for materials and supplies.

With the large number of items to be purchased, and the mingling of staff, volunteers and visitors at an event, it is also imperative that tight inventory control procedures be enacted and enforced to eliminate the inevitable and costly loss of materials through breakage, mishandling and theft. Up-to-date lists of all durable goods and a sign-out system for the use of tools, supplies, and equipment will help to control loss.

Capital Budgets

Capital budgeting provides a parallel budget system for purchasing items or making improvements to facilities that involve expenditures that fall outside the normal budgeting guidelines. This occurs when the item to be purchased has a multiyear life expectancy, exceeds a predetermined threshold for spending, or is a non-recurring expense over a certain dollar amount. Capital budgets are another tool that aids in creating an understandable, manageable, and transparent means of administrating budgetary funds. Capital expenditures, often in the tens or hundreds of thousands of dollars, are separated from the operating expenses of the organization as they require a different level of scrutiny in the budget planning and approval process and should be managed with a longer planning and execution strategy. A capital budget item may extend beyond the annual fiscal year allowing for activities that fit better into a three, five, or ten year plan. If your event has the luxury of permanent home, as do many fairs and festivals, a plan may be developed to finance improvements to existing structures or to build and maintain new facilities. Capital budgeting documents and procedures are the appropriate means of realizing these types of activities.

Capital budgeting for equipment has changed over the last 15 years to include a greater amount of leasing. Leasing spreads the costs out over a longer period with a lesser impact on the budget. Leasing allows for a more frequent turnover of equipment, which may aid in keeping up with changes in technology.

Summary

For the experienced manager, financial management is a positive aspect of event management that provides an important tool in achieving success. Fiscal responsibility, as mentioned earlier, is a critical aspect of event management. Those entrusted with the financial resources of an organization or event have responsibilities that extend far beyond budgeting and paying the bills. There are many legal requirements that must be adhered to in order to ensure success and to stay within the boundaries of local, state, and federal law. It is always advisable to solicit the advice of finance and tax consultants when planning and delivering any special event.

Discussion Questions

1. What is the relationship between accounting and budgeting?
2. How is accounting defined in the text?
3. What are the six steps in the accounting process?
4. Why are controls a necessary aspect of accounting?
5. How is a budget used as a tool?
6. What is a line item budget?
7. Differentiate between fixed and variable costs.
8. What are some typical sources of revenue at an event?
9. What is the purpose of a purchase order?
10. Why do some organizations establish a capital budget?

6

The Nature of Sponsorship

 Our ambitions must be broad enough to include the aspirations and needs of others, for their sakes and our own.

Cesar Chavez

Chapter Objective

- Understand the role of sponsorships in event management
- Explain why sponsorships are so popular
- Identify sponsorship benefits for the event organizers
- Identify sponsorship benefits for the sponsoring agency
- Understand the relationship between consumer decision making and sponsorships
- Discuss the risks associated with sponsorship contracts
- Identify the steps in the soliciting a sponsor

Why Sponsorships?

The evolution and growth of event sponsorship in the past three decades has been exponential. Despite the threat of over commercialization and loss of event identity, involving commercial businesses as an element in the strategic planning of events has been a very successful and beneficial development. Sponsorship is far more sophisticated than fundraising and other philanthropic approaches in securing resource support from the business sector. *Sponsorship is a negotiated exchange of mutual benefits between two or more parties.* Each party has in mind a specific set of benefits to be gained through the association with their contractual partner. It is imperative that event organizers have a clear understanding of their needs and must determine who can best meet these needs and what the currency of exchange will be. It is also very important that event organizers understand the needs of the potential sponsor, both in terms of standard sponsorship expectations and the specific marketing objectives that the business seeks to achieve through association with your event. Potential sponsors must be researched and selected in such a way that the transaction is mutually beneficial. The possibilities for benefit exchange are diverse, constrained only by the creative interpretation of the needs of both organizations.

Sponsorships present a unique opportunity for two disparate organizations to benefit from their respective and combined strengths. Event organizations can always benefit from an influx of cash, in-kind services, additional marketing exposure, and a host of other more specific advantages provided by the business community.

For many businesses, sponsorship is a preferred means of commercial advertising and promotion due to the evolution, or some might say devolution, of traditional promotional outlets. Television expanded from three or four national stations (depending how good your antenna was) to hundreds of specialized stations that arrive at our homes by cable, satellite, Internet, and mobile device. With this product expansion comes a multiplication of advertising spots associated with all these new outlets. In addition, modern technology allows viewers to avoid commercials altogether. Television, despite its continued popularity, is now a less effective means of advertising due to the sheer volume of messages presented to the viewer, the increased costs to the advertiser, and less predictable outcomes.[1] Radio is also experiencing enormous change as downloadable music minimizes the need for live radio. Satellite radio has nationalized a service previously offered by local stations, reducing the availability of localized advertising opportunities. Print media continues to expand to very specific audiences through specialty magazines, while newspapers are losing market share to Internet sources that can be conveniently read on a home or office computer, tablet or mobile device. Television, radio, and print advertising have become prohibitively expensive for many businesses, rely on a somewhat arbitrary distribution, and might not reflect the most effective means of promotion for the future. To further complicate matters, the expanding influence of Internet marketing has not only created a new and sometimes overwhelming set of marketing opportunities but has also caused traditional marketing outlets to adjust their strategies.

The growth of product lines has also created a more defined need for differentiation as competition between products increases. There are many more choices for items that were previously represented by a few easily recognizable national or international brands. One need only think of the number and type of sport shoes available to the public. Not only are there many more brands, but each brand now specializes in various types of shoes that are designed to meet specific activity requirements. The tennis/basketball shoe of forty years ago has evolved into running, walking, biking (road and mountain), cross training, hiking, indoor soccer, aerobics, sock shoes and many other types of activity-specific shoes. The reality facing shoemakers and event promoters is one of differentiation and capturing an appropriate segment of a potential market.

While each of these issues presents challenges for commercial businesses, they represent a real opportunity for event managers to market the value of their event to a sponsor as a unique way to connect with potential customers in a defined market. As products become more specific, so do the needs and tastes of consumers and audiences. This can strengthen the promoter's efforts to attract specific sponsoring agencies. Events allow the consumer to be introduced to, and interact with, a product in a recreational setting. Most event attendees are there voluntarily and have the anticipation of a positive, enriching experience. It is the perfect setting to initiate or further develop a relationship between a product and a potential customer.

What Does Your Organization Need from a Sponsor?

The answer to this question can only be fully answered by your staff and event committee. The specific characteristics of your event are what make your event attractive to a potential sponsor. Conversely, these same characteristics and the costs associated with making the event a success make the resources provided by a sponsor necessary for continued growth and success. Prior to determining your event needs, it is important that event managers have *quantitative demographic information* regarding those who attend their event. The right mix of age, income, spending patterns, family size, and other characteristics represented by a sufficiently large number of attendees is the type of information that is of the greatest importance to the potential sponsor. The information obtained during the strategic planning of the event, particularly an assessment of existing and needed resources, will help organizers to identify those needs that cannot be adequately met by the organization. It is helpful to organize these internal weaknesses, along with strengths in such a way that they might be connected with the opportunities presented by potential sponsors in the business community (refer to the discussion of SWOT in chapter 3).

Organizational shortcomings and resource limitations help to define the parameters of potential sponsorship opportunities. Organizations can always use extra cash directed toward areas of the budget that would most benefit from additional funding. It is a helpful exercise to ask your organizing committee what it would do with an additional sum of undesignated funds, $10,000 for example. This discussion will help to focus the group on needed improvements or opportunities for the enhancement or expansion of the event. It will also help to define needs that can be met by securing appropriate levels of sponsorship. This can allow for higher quality entertainment, new attractions or concessions, or increased promotional activity, all of which might eventually lead to higher attendance and additional revenue for the event.

In-kind services are those benefits provided by a sponsor that support the event but are not necessarily a financial resource. The sponsor can provide their own personnel whose expertise greatly enhances the event and might include administrative support, technical support, live personalities acting as emcees, and representatives of the business community who support the event. Sponsors might provide *product support*, including food, beverages, and other items that improve the attendees' experience. Depending on the potential sponsor's line of business, the event might benefit from *technical resources* that support communication, safety, logistics, entertainment, or concessions. Most potential sponsors are looking for increased opportunities to expose their product or service to new consumers. From this perspective, it is important to consider the value of obtaining media sponsors for your event. The event might also benefit from the association with certain high-profile businesses that are perceived to be community leaders. The value of association with successful enterprises lends credibility to an event that cannot be manufactured through a public relations campaign. The challenge rests on the event organizers to inventory the opportunities available to local businesses as partners in the promotion and management of your event.

What Is The Sponsor Looking For?

There are generic, textbook answers to this question that can provide a framework for developing specific and effective sponsorship packages for potential sponsors. And since this is a textbook, they will be presented here.

Typically, marketing staff create a sponsorship program using a fundraising model employing various levels of sponsorship identified by color, platinum, gold, silver, or other means of differentiating the individual level of commitment. This can be effective, as each level of involvement includes an incremental increase in benefits. This old-school approach to sponsorship is usually a prepackaged bundle of benefits presented without an opportunity for input by the potential sponsor. Sponsorships of this type require annual arm twisting and rely on the altruistic disposition, or sense of community obligation or guilt of the local businesses. It often becomes a dreaded exercise akin to professional begging that is usually delegated to the least senior member of the staff or to the oblivious optimist who is immune to the stress of asking for money. Depending on the level of sophistication of the event and of the local business community, this method can provide the necessary benefits for each party on an annual basis. At some point, due to financial restraints or boredom with the repetitive nature of this sponsorship dynamic, businesses may choose to withdraw their support.

What Is The Sponsor Really Looking For?

If your intention is to build a strong, positive, mutually beneficial business relationship with sponsors, it is best to take the program to the next level. Sponsorships, if properly designed, create motivation for business involvement. Sponsorship must be viewed as a business relationship. The sponsor is looking for a *return on the investment (ROI)* for the resources dedicated to the event opportunities. It is a very deliberate, targeted form of marketing that seeks to promote a business service or product to a specific group at a specific time. The marketing mix, as we know, includes *product, price, position or place, promotion, and public relations.* Sponsorships allow a business to maximize positional and promotional advantages while placing their product in the hands, or at least the minds, of potential customers through their association with your event.

Howard and Crompton (1995) offer a functional analysis of business benefits to be derived from a sponsorship that includes four categories: *increased awareness, image enhancement, product trials or sales opportunities, and hospitality opportuntities.*[2] A business may be looking for *increased awareness* of their product or service through name recognition or association with the event. Visibility is the starting point for increased awareness. Name recognition can be achieved through repetitive exposure of the product to the event visitors and by the strategic placement of advertising at the event. Awareness at some point must move beyond name recognition to provide the opportunity for the potential customer to learn more about the product. This challenge requires a more in-depth strategy that allows the sponsor to build upon name recognition oftentimes by providing an opportunity for product sampling. This type of scenario provides the sponsor with a cost-effective means of putting the product in the hands, or mouth, of the consumer.

A second sought-after business objective is that of *image enhancement*. Image enhancement addresses the need for differentiation between products. The sponsorship provides the opportunity for a business to improve the perception of the product to a select group that attends a particular event. This improved image may result in a change in the relationship between the business, its product, and the consumer. If this change results in a more favorable attitude toward the product, the consumer may move toward a decision to accept the product and make a purchase. Potential sponsors review the personality and amenities of an event to determine if it is the right environment to enhance their product. Sporting events, cultural festivals, parades, and other civic events are situations that evoke many favorable emotions. It is beneficial for the sponsor to have the consumer make contact with their product in such a positive, fun environment. Sponsors are not seeking out natural disasters or tragic events as launching pads for products or services, although given the effectiveness of the sponsorship model, it is not unfathomable in the future.

Events provide the unique setting of contacting hundreds, if not hundreds of thousands of people enjoying themselves in a voluntary, recreational setting. The fact that events by nature are experiences outside the normal realm of daily life is very attractive to a sponsor. Attendees are there because they want to absorb the unique experiences of the event. This may include absorbing more food and drink than is their habit. There is a certain freedom that one experiences when an entire event has been assembled for personal enjoyment. Individuals will try new things, take chances, stay up late, and embrace the spirit of the event. It is an ideal setting for introducing a new product to an audience that is pre-disposed toward experimentation and new experiences. This is a strong selling point for sponsorships that seek to benefit from product trials at the event.

A third benefit for sponsors is a *free trial of a product* that may be accompanied by the sponsor wanting booth space in order for the consumers to have the opportunity to purchase the product in a standard commercial portion. The sponsor has achieved several objectives as awareness of the product has increased through the sample, and sales have increased through the activity at the booth.

Hospitality opportunities allow a sponsor to entertain select customers, vendors, and business associates in a unique way that takes advantage of the strengths of the event. Hospitality benefits may also be used as incentives and rewards for the sponsor's employees as they receive special treatment and privileges. Typically, hospitality opportunities include free tickets, reserved seating, convenient parking, elaborately designed sponsor areas with cocktails and hors d'oeuvres, backstage passes, and interaction with entertainers, and other benefits that may be developed through the input of the sponsor. The strategy is to ascertain the benefits that are meaningful to the sponsor and provide them with as much style and attention to detail as possible. By successfully meeting the expectations of the sponsor, within budget limits, event organizers have effectively created a team approach with the sponsor in allowing them to host an unforgettable experience for their own guests. In the most simplistic analysis of sponsor hospitality, your event is being paid to entertain the guests of the sponsor. The key to this type of sponsor benefit is to provide value and quality to the sponsor without expending all the funds provided by the sponsorship.

These four variables, *increased awareness, image enhancement, product sampling, and hospitality* are recognized as the basis of many sponsorship decisions. The motivation of a particular company to designate a portion of the marketing budget to sponsorship is not done for philanthropic reasons. The decision-making process includes a consideration of the needs of the business and the potential to meet these needs through affiliation and exposure through special events. See Table 6.1.

Table 6.1. Corporate Objectives

Objectives that may influence the decision for a business to enter a sponsorship agreement:
- Increase public awareness of the company or product
- Alter or reinforce the public perception of the company
- Identify the company with a particular market segment
- Involve the company with the community
- Build goodwill amongst decision makers
- Generate media benefits
- Achieve sales objectives
- Create advantage over competitors
- Gain unique opportunities for hospitality or entertainment
- Secure entitlement or naming rights

Mullin, Hardy, & Sutton (2000)[3]

Case Study: Fireworks Show Saved by the Sponsor!

The Town of Groton and City of New London, Connecticut, had for several decades jointly hosted a fireworks show the weekend after the 4th of July. Staging the event the weekend after the 4th allowed for a fireworks show that was second only to New York City in terms of the size and impact of the show. The fireworks were launched from several barges in the Thames River that separates the two municipalities. Due to the length of the accessible shoreline on either side, the event attracted several hundred thousand spectators. The expenses for the event were addressed through the municipal budgets of each city. For many years, the event continued unthreatened by change and went virtually unnoticed by the business communities. When the town leaders were presented with the possibility of closing the town library on Sundays at a savings of approximately $25,000, the fireworks show became a potential and very sensible alternate cut. Recognizing the marketing potential of the event and the goodwill that would be realized through saving the fireworks, the event committee inventoried the potential benefits that the event would provide a sponsor. Within a two-year period, an event sponsor was identified, naming rights, entertainment, and hospitality benefits were presented and accepted by the new sponsor, and the event grew tremendously in the ensuing years. The sponsor also enjoyed media benefits along with the image enhancement as the fireworks show was now broadcast live on statewide television.

Due to the enhanced publicity of the event brought about by this major sponsorship deal, the event committee was approached by a company marketing a new lemonade drink on the east coast. The company recognized the benefits of having thousands of thirsty fireworks attendees gathered to watch the event and maybe needing a cool drink. The company offered the event organizers a refreshing $10,000 to provide free samples of their drink to the crowd. The sponsorship required no expenditures by the event organizers, offered a welcome treat to the attendees, and allowed for increased awareness and product trials for the sponsor. The additional $10,000 was used to improve the entertainment presented prior to the actual fireworks show.

Positional Advantages: Understanding the Consumer Decision-Making Process

There is a third beneficiary in a sponsorship strategy that is integral to the success of the sponsorship agreement. If a sponsoring business really seeks a marketing advantage from their sponsorship, there must be a direct connection between the benefits offered by the sponsorship and some planned effect on consumers. Understanding a consumer's relationship to a product is important information for all parties to consider when formulating a sponsor package.

AIDAR

Consumers go through a somewhat predictable process in making a decision to buy a product. There are several models to describe the process. An appropriate model of consumer behavior for use in sponsorship formulation is the AIDAR (awareness, interest, decision, action, reinforcement) approach. This typology is common knowledge in the marketing world but is particularly well explained in the sport finance text of Howard and Crompton.[4] While originally identified as AIDA, savvy marketers also include the R for reinforcement as a means of retaining and rewarding customers who have made a purchase. This approach reflects a consumer learning process that positions the product relative to the current relationship between the consumer and the product. The sponsor identifies consumers at one of five levels of knowledge regarding the product or service being offered.

The first step is that of *consumer awareness*. The consumer becomes aware of a product but has limited information or knowledge of its attributes. This represents the relationship between the consumer and a new or unknown product in the marketplace. Understanding that the consumer has little or no knowledge of the product, the sponsor wants to develop name recognition and initiate a feeling of familiarity with the product. A sponsorship that includes the naming rights for the event is a very effective way to have a repetitive exposure to a company or its product. Consumers may at a later date be disposed to recognize the name and progress to the second level.

Developing a sense of *interest* on the part of the consumer requires providing more detailed information about the product. The presentation must move beyond name recognition so that the consumer can internalize some favorable facts about the product. If the product, due to its presence at an event, becomes recognizable and has no negative associations, the consumer may move beyond interest to the third level.

If the consumer recognizes the product and can recall favorable information about the product, there may now be a feeling of *desire* on the part of the consumer. The consumer might now want to try the product. This might only involve a mental trial, imagining what it would be like to own and use the product, or it might include sampling the product prior to purchasing. At this time, the consumer might have enough information and a sufficiently developed opinion of the product to be moved to *action*. Depending on the merits of the product, whether it meets the needs of the consumer, the action taken will either be to accept or reject the product. Marketers also seek to create a sense of urgency, though sales and special offers, to coax the consumer from desire to action.

Moving the consumer through these levels of relationship with a product requires the allocation of a significant number of resources on the part of the business. Once a consumer has taken action to purchase a product, it is advisable that efforts be made to solidify the consumer's decision through an appropriate means of *reinforcement*. Ultimately, the goal is *brand loyalty*, so that the efforts made to get to the point of purchase do not have to be repeated for that particular customer. Brand loyalty is supported by many factors, including the quality and durability of the product, the personal sense of reward provided by the purchase, the perceived value of the product, and by subsequent marketing efforts designed to reinforce the customer's purchase.

It has been observed that 80% of all purchases are made by 20% of the consumers in any particular market. This suggests that extra effort must be made to capture and retain the loyal customers that comprise this 20% demographic.

Consumers can be identified as preferred customers based on their frequency of purchase and are often rewarded by receiving information on new products, accessing owners' areas of websites and can receive preferred treatment as special guests at a sponsored event. In the final analysis, consumers evaluate the entire experience, including the activities presented at the special event and the efforts of sponsors to expose them to new products. A favorable evaluation or experience of satisfaction results from the consumer's perception that the benefits of the event and the product exposure are greater than the costs associated with the experience. This holds true for all three parties in the sponsorship relationship:

Benefits – costs = level of satisfaction

Many times, particularly for local events, the potential sponsor becomes involved due to community connections and a desire to help out. The event organizer should certainly take advantage of these favorable attitudes. The sponsor will feel doubly rewarded if the event organizers take the time to explain and help identify the real potential of the sponsorship. The desired sponsor benefits can be directly targeted to the potential customer, based on the present and anticipated level of consumer knowledge that will be affected by the sponsorship activities. This process starts before the consumer contacts the product and continues long after the purchase is made. Each phase of this relationship can be enhanced by a well-designed sponsorship package that focuses on the needs of the customer. Event organizers, understanding the value of each of these stages, can structure the expenses associated with the sponsorship based on the levels of interaction between the product and the customer. Just as the sponsor is looking for certain levels of response and relationship from the customer, the event organizers can develop the partnership between the event and the sponsor so that it grows from year to year. The greatest effort is expended in the initial securing of a sponsor. Therefore, the initial contract should be structured to promote a multiyear enhancement of the sponsor benefits and increasing levels of investment in the relationship by both parties.

Contractual Expectations

Understanding that the sponsorship is a business relationship, it is recommended that all elements of the sponsorship be enumerated in a clearly understandable written contract.

A well-written contract identifies all parties, states the intended goals of the sponsorship, identifies the responsibilities of each party, describes satisfactory levels of performance, and provides for compensation if either party fails to meet the agreed-upon expectations of this relationship.

In this way, the sponsorship becomes an independent entity that can be managed separately from any preexisting relationship that may exist between the sponsor and the event organizers. It places the sponsorship on the level of a manageable business agreement that is not wholly dependent on the personalities of the signers. Inevitably, things might go wrong at your event and someone ends up disappointed or feeling shortchanged. A contract helps to isolate these shortcomings and provides a solution that allows for a continuation of the sponsorship relationship in the future. The contract also helps to eliminate assumptions and presumptive expectations that can lead to dissatisfaction, mistrust, and the eventual termination of the relationship. If a business sponsor has a bad experience with your event, it will undoubtedly become a negative topic of discussion at the next Chamber of Commerce meeting, effectively limiting the opportunity for additional support by the business community.

The contract requires both parties to develop specific, quantifiable outcomes. This not only supports the accountability of both parties, but requires a thoughtful consideration of what is being sought through the sponsorship. The event and its attendees must represent a good fit for the sponsor. This means that the demographics, scope, size, timing, and opportunities provided by the event allow for a successful return on investment for the sponsor. The match between the sponsor and the event must rely on the link between the product and the event, and the product and the audience. Sometimes the linkage is obvious as there is a direct product tie-in, such as sporting goods at sporting events. Other obvious links exist between certain types of events and particular products; golf tournaments partner with luxury cars, while professional team sports seem to appeal to beer drinkers. Other times,

Case Study: A Time When Tennis Was Smoking!

In the 1970s, tennis, as both a recreational activity and a spectator sport, was experiencing unparalleled increases in visibility and growth. At one time, a women's professional tour was established in the United States, featuring the best talent in the game. The sponsor of the league was a cigarette company. The Virginia Slims Tour was a partnership formed between women's professional tennis and a nicotine delivery system, as we like to call it nowadays. Smoking was not publicly identified to be the addictive, carcinogenic product that we know it is today. However, the link between the product and the event was not based on the players' endorsement of the product nor through free samples being provided at the events. Players were not even required to smoke during their matches! The link between cigarettes and a highly aerobic sport worked because a woman's tennis league and a distinctly women's cigarette both appealed to the women's liberation movement that sought freedom from the traditional boundaries of contemporary western society. The hook was not the product, but image enhancement of the product through association with an event that was representative of the cultural advancement of women exemplified through the women's tennis league. Over time, the attendance at these tournaments dwindled, and interest in the league and the potential benefits from sponsorship evaporated. It was a great experiment in tennis and sponsorship strategy that was grounded in a very important time in the women's rights movement.

The lesson evident in this example is to be creative, think outside the carton, find connections that might not seem obvious but might, through their creativity, provide an advantage for the sponsor to differentiate their product from the competition in a unique way.

Both parties can realize the maximum potential of a sponsorship relationship if sufficient thought is given to the desired objectives. The ideal situation is one in which the event staff assigned to manage sponsorships is motivated and excited enough to provide excellent customer service to the sponsor. It is easy to forget about the benefits accrued by the event organizers if the staff is fully focused on providing the best possible results for the sponsor.

the link might be the result of more creative analysis of the relationship that initially may seem misplaced.

Risks of Sponsorship

Sponsorship relationships are not without risks. There is the danger that, once the sponsor is secured, the event organizers might not deliver the anticipated benefits to the sponsor. The level of risk is generally related to the complexity of the event and the amount and quality of attention paid to the sponsorship before, during, and after the event by the partnering agency. Lack of performance can happen for a variety of reasons, some of which can be avoided and others are beyond the control of the event organizers. These generally fall into several categories.

Sponsor mismanagement introduces a potential for loss if the sponsor's needs are underserved or overlooked at some level by the event organizers. The organizers might not deliver the exact amount of promised exposure. For example, banners might be smaller than promised or their placement might not match the expectations of the sponsor. Providing a level of quality in hospitality that is below expectations can also cause a sponsor to lose trust in the sponsorship relationship.

Attention to detail is the only appropriate response to the contractual elements of the sponsorship package.

The overall quality of the event might not match the hype produced in the marketing efforts to attract the sponsor prior to the event. It is better to maintain a conservative and factual presentation of the event while generating a sense of excitement and unique opportunity for the sponsor. This is commonly referred to as underselling and over delivering on the event. Ideally, the written contract will eliminate most miscommunication between sponsor and organizers. To further reduce the possibility of unmet expectations, it is best to put all pertinent information including necessary alterations to the original plan into a written operational plan so that changes are identified and agreed upon prior to the event.

Event mismanagement includes both factors that are within one's control and those that lie outside or beyond the influence of the best efforts of event management. Should a crisis arise that is clearly beyond the control of the organizers, oftentimes a sense of understanding and forgiveness might be displayed by the stakeholders. Having a headline performer become a no-show at an event is a crisis and a great disappointment for all concerned and can create a strain on a sponsorship relationship. While the organizers must have a contingency plan for the event attendees, there must also be a backup plan to meet the requirements of the sponsors. But when problems occur due to oversight, bad planning, inadequate decision making, and other issues that are perceived to be within the control of the organization and could have been avoided, you have problems. A poorly managed event reflects negatively on both the organizers and the sponsors.

The associative relationship of sponsor and promoter, if done correctly, should link the two parties in the eyes of the participants. This can have dramatically negative effects when things go badly. It is necessary to switch to crisis-management mode in order to minimize the impact of the problems for the participants. Many events have been saved due to quick thinking and implementation of corrective measures. Sponsors must be made aware of the problems at an appropriate time. If you can fix the problem first, without causing alarm for your sponsors, you can then calmly and clearly explain the issues and the solution put into place. It is always best to be as open as necessary to maintain the trust and confidence of the sponsor. After all, it is all about relationship—it must be based in honesty, trust, and the ability to meet the sponsor's needs. The key to damage control is to tell the truth, tell it as soon as possible, and take responsibility for solving the problem.

Environmental conditions include weather-related obstacles such as rain or the threat of weather that might be too hot, too cold, too windy, or so perfect that people choose to do something else with their time. Contingency plans can address some threats by having a predetermined rain date or an indoor location. Some marketing impact for the sponsor can be lost due to the necessary changes, but the event might still hold some potential for the sponsor at the later date. Postponement or cancellation involves additional expenses that should be addressed in the sponsorship contract. Failure to do so can result in a sponsorship that, because of necessary adjustments made due to a change in date or venue, might actually cost more to the event than the actual value of the sponsorship. Reprinting of event information, rescheduling entertainment, concessions, and myriad other challenges must be considered when coordinating contingency plans with sponsors.

Low attendance is another environmental condition that despite all the best efforts can contribute to not meeting the expectations of the sponsor. It is imperative that you share data and analyses with the sponsor if attendance did not meet expectations so that event organizers and sponsors can work together to improve results at subsequent events. Despite the lack of satisfaction resultant from low attendance, the problem might provide an opportunity for a closer working relationship and an opportunity for the sponsor to increase their ownership commitments for the future.

The Value of Media Exposure

One very positive component in attracting a sponsor is increased visibility through media outlets. This can be difficult to manage as the contractual goals of providing media exposure for the sponsor is sometimes in conflict with the media outlets that might be seeking to increase revenue through advertising sales related to the event. Many times, media outlets will omit the mention of event sponsors in news reports as they see it as lost advertising revenue. The best way to manage this challenge is to bring a media outlet onto the team as a sponsor. Their sponsorship, usually an exclusive relationship, would consist of the providing the event with a predetermined amount of coverage quantified as column inches in print, or a specified number of minutes of air time on radio or television. It might also include placement of the event on the sponsor website. A clear understanding of the allowable uses of this media space is necessary. The media outlet might allow the event very liberal use of the space that could include mention of other commercial sponsors. However, it is generally the case that restrictions will be placed on allowing the event to use the media space to highlight additional business sponsorships. If the naming rights of the event have been sold to a sponsor, this can and should be considered permissible by the media sponsor. Prior to offering a commercial sponsor any placement in media releases, it is important that a full understanding of the parameters of the relationship with the media outlet be explored and put into writing.

Sponsor Solicitation

The previous pages have explained many of the underlying concepts and practices included in sponsorship development. This final section will aid in the actual process of identifying and approaching potential sponsors.

The first step is to understand your event and its potential to attract sponsorships. What is your basic attraction and who is affected by it? Who attends and why? Assess your resources that can be devoted to sponsor development and support. Does your organization have the personnel and skills to develop and manage sponsorships, or should you stick to less complicated forms of fundraising? The answers to these questions will help you to develop a fact sheet for your event.

Who are Potential Sponsors?

Questions one must consider in identifying sponsors include the following:

- What is the makeup of the local business community and what contacts exist between your organization and potential sponsors?
- Who should be approached and by whom?
- What are the marketing and public relations needs of the potential sponsors?

Sponsorships are successful if they solve an existing problem for a business. You must be aware of the actual fiscal year of the targeted business in order to know the right time of the budget cycle to approach a business. In order to create a sustainable relationship, your event must make its way into the sponsor's marketing budget for the following year.

Research the Company

Chances are, your sponsorship proposal is not the first one to cross the desk of your targeted company. If a business frequently receives sponsorship requests, it will have policies and procedures for reviewing them. Some businesses only consider certain types of proposals from specific types of organizations, such as educational agencies or non-profits and might only accept proposals during a particular time of the year. It is useful during the initial research stages to obtain as much information as possible regarding these issues either through individuals who have specific information and experience with a particular company or by inquiring directly to the marketing, advertising, or public relations department of the business. Time is well spent on this type of research and will better prepare you to make informed decisions and to appear well prepared for the eventual interaction with the company. Office and support staff, if engaged in a friendly and respectful manner, might readily share information about the review process and the idiosyncrasies of a particular manager. It is also wise to learn the types and amounts of sponsorships awarded in the past. Contacting those agencies that have contracted for sponsor support in the past is very helpful in learning the particular needs and expectations of a business.

Pricing the Package

It is important that the benefits of a sponsorship reflect real market value for the opportunities being offered. To arrive at values that will be accepted by the business community, it is necessary to research the local advertising market. While benefits like community goodwill and psychic income cannot necessarily be measured, it is important that all other benefits be accurately quantified. Research is needed to develop pricing for signs, banners, column inches of print, radio and television spots, photos, and logos placed in different locations on all advertising pieces. Booth space, product sampling, hospitality opportunities including free tickets, reserved seating, refreshments, and backstage passes all have a monetary value that must be known and appreciated by the potential sponsors and the event organizers.

A custom-designed package is a very attractive alternative for a potential sponsor. It allows the event organizers the opportunity to meet the needs of the sponsor while controlling the flow and cost of benefits. This is best accomplished by researching the value of all potential benefits before initiating the negotiating process. If benefits are sought by the sponsor that are not identified and priced, be open to the possibility but ask for time to get back to them with answers for those particular items.

Contacting Prospective Sponsors

Ideally, the initial contact should be made by someone familiar with the business and hopefully has a friendship with an executive or decision maker within the organization. If this is not possible it is helpful to take advantage of any contact with the business so that more can be learned about the needs of the organization. A top-down approach will allow the initial contact person to recommend that the firm's marketing individual follow up on the request. Use the interaction with the marketing staff to gather any additional information about the organization and its marketing goals prior to the presentation. The approach to the initial meeting must be a blend of gratitude for the opportunity to present the proposal and a strength that comes from the knowledge that what you have to offer is a legitimate benefit for the potential sponsor. One must remember that this is not a philanthropic setting relying on the goodwill of the sponsor but is a business proposition with the exchange of valuable commodities by both parties.

Presenting the Proposal

An overview of the history of the event and a description of past attendance, demographics, as well as prior media exposure, are important starting points in an effective presentation. A fact sheet describing the past success of the event in terms of attendance, media coverage, and community involvement is a helpful tool. Prior information about the business and its marketing needs allows for the connection to be made between the event and the sponsor. Once these basic parameters have been established, it is time to present a preliminary sponsorship package that will list possible benefits that meet the needs of the potential sponsor. It is advisable to include a cafeteria-style list in addition to a specific benefits package as the potential sponsor may respond more favorably to being able to customize their benefits. You want to make the initial meeting as easy as possible for the sponsor, which might mean getting together at a time and place that suits their needs. Try to arrange meetings in settings that can accentuate the positive elements of your organization and yourself. Distractions from the purpose of your meeting should be kept to a minimum. It is important to keep the meeting focused, so that both parties understand the conditions of the proposal and can accurately assess the benefits. At the same time, you must be conscious that some business people enjoy the ego boost derived from being approached for a sponsorship, and these, like all sponsor needs, should be addressed in an effective manner.

The presentation must accentuate the potential benefits of the sponsorship opportunity relative to the need of the business for benefits that can be realized through event sponsorship. It is also necessary at this point to listen carefully, allowing the sponsor to imagine the results of the sponsorship. Probing questions and note taking will allow you to assimilate the additional information gathered through this process. A contract template with space to add benefits that meet the specific needs of the sponsor provides the rough draft for a final document. If the sponsor has no idea of the needs of the organization that can be met through sponsorship, a standardized contract with opportunities for exposure prior to and during the event should be presented. The goal of this process is to summarize the needs of the sponsor, attach a monetary value to the elements that make up the contract, and to move the sponsor to agreeing in principle to the terms as developed through the meeting.

Opportunities to involve the sponsor in official capacities, such as a grand opening or other interaction with the public that are not specified in the contract, should be considered and implemented as these features often add value to the package and help to develop long-term involvement in the event. Although they might not be a part of the sponsor package, these perks should be carefully planned and positioned in the sponsorship strategy.

Case Study: Avoid the Away Game!

In attempting to attract a very successful local business owner to become the lead sponsor for a local music festival, I agreed to meet for a round of golf at a fairly exclusive private club. The sponsor saw the opportunity to enjoy an afternoon away from the office, entertain a few friends, and consider sponsoring a new local event. Despite managing a municipal course, I was, at best, a bad golfer. With a set of very old clubs and some cheap golf balls, I showed up for the match. I declined the pre-game drinks in the bar and set out to bond with these guys. My playing partners obviously spent a lot of time on the links, sporting equipment that I'm sure cost more than my first car. They displayed all the trappings of the ritual golfer and had a comfortable swagger about themselves. At the first tee, I was up third, following two of those long high drives that seem to disappear in the sky before landing in the center of the fairway. Trying to hide my unease, I approached the tee and took a full, rushed swing that resulted in the ball slicing at 90 degrees through the pines bordering the tee box, ricocheting off a car in the parking lot and returning to the fairway about 60 yards away. I certainly got everyone's attention and luckily managed to get the ball past the women's forward tee, avoiding additional ridicule.

It only got worse from there. By the back nine, I was rattled and trying too hard to play golf. My partner's comments went from playful ridicule to the type of pitiful support that only magnified my incompetence. I never got around to pitching the event to the sponsor and tried to save face by thanking them for the round of golf. It was several weeks before I could make the call to discuss the sponsorship and ended up with less than hoped for from this particular sponsor.

Follow-Up

It is imperative that follow up to the initial meeting be immediate. By the end of the next working day, the sponsor should receive the final contract for approval and signature. Lost time is lost opportunity as the passage of time permits obstacles, second thoughts, and competing interest to cloud the decision. Ideally, sponsorships should represent a long-term commitment of three to five years in order to experience the maximum return on the effort and resources invested. Once the contract is in place, it is important to remain in communication with the representative of the business so that the details of the agreement are fully understood and properly planned. This also fosters buy-in on the part of the sponsor that helps to deepen the relationship between the sponsor and the event. Some sponsors may enjoy further involvement, while others may give the investment little attention. Your relationship with the sponsor must be sufficiently developed for you to understand the feelings of the sponsor in these matters.

A successful sponsorship does not end when the lights are turned out on the last night of the event. Post-event responsibilities include adequate communication with the sponsor to assess the success of your relationship, to identify areas for improvement, to develop new ideas for the coming year, and to thank the sponsor for their support. Keeping major sponsors in the communications loop during the year allows for creative input by both parties and the fostering of an attitude that next year will be better than ever. When appropriate, the sponsor should be included in the mailings for your agency to remind them of your status within the community, and that the special event is not the only positive contribution your agency makes to the community. The annual report for the event should be provided to each sponsor using the report as an additional opportunity to identify and thank the sponsors.

Previous year sponsors should be afforded the first right of refusal for the following year's sponsorship opportunities. Basic pricing levels of sponsorship in subsequent years should be adjusted to reflect any increases in the costs associated with providing the sponsorship benefits. If the sponsor experienced quantifiable gains or advantages from their participation in the previous event, it is the right time to offer a higher level of sponsorship for the next event.

Summary

Sponsorships are complex dynamic relationships that have become indispensable in the management of programs and events. They are also a very positive opportunity to create new working relationships and friendships in the local business community. Economic conditions make this type of support almost mandatory for the continued growth of community and cultural events. Fortunately, sponsorships provide for real returns on investment and are perceived as an effective means of reaching an intended market through a unique and enjoyable medium. As in all endeavors, accurate needs assessments and creative strategies are the key ingredients to successful outcomes.

Discussion Questions

1. Why are sponsorships such a popular way of commercial advertising?
2. What are some potential benefits of sponsorship for the event organizers?
3. What are some potential benefits for the sponsoring organization?
4. What are the four steps of consumer behavior related to the purchase of a product or service?
5. Why is customer retention such an important concept for a business?
6. What is meant by ROI, return on investment?
7. Identify several risks associated with a sponsorship relationship.
8. What are some important points when soliciting sponsorships?
9. What are important things to remember about post-event follow up?
10. What is the difference between sponsorship and fundraising?

1. Howard, D., & Crompton, J. (1995). *Financing sport.* Wheeling, WVA: Fitness Information Technology, p. 235.
2. IBID. p. 225.
3. Mullin, B., Hardy, S., & Sutton, W. (2000). *Sport marketing* (3rd ed.). Champaign, IL: Human Kinetics, p. 265.
4. Op. cit. Howard & Crompton, p. 243.

7

Marketing

 You are in the business of brain surgery... not as a medical doctor but as a modifier of minds.

Leonard Hoyle

Chapter Objectives

- Understanding the product and the audience—basic marketing principles
- Identify the who, what, when, where and why of marketing
- Explain market segmentation
- Understanding the marketing mix—product, price, placement, position, promotion, and public relations
- Differentiate authenticity vs. generica
- Marketing vs. advertising
- Understanding destination marketing
- Identify visitor motivations
- Explore Internet marketing
- Identify marketing evaluation tools

The success of a special event is unquestionably dependent upon the unique characteristics of the event, the theme or purpose of the event, the entertainment or attractions provided, the location, the time of year, and more. All contribute to the potential for meeting the goals of the event. But even with all the elements well planned and executed, it is the ability to market the event that will determine the attention drawn to it and the corresponding level of participation by the public.

Marketing is about informing, attracting, nurturing, and retaining customers and supporters for your event.

Marketing must be intimately linked to the goals of the event. A marketing plan must use the mission and goals of the event as guidelines for the development of a marketing strategy. By having the goals and objectives clearly identified and the operational details of the event aligned to support the marketing plan, a synergistic gain in effectiveness can be realized by event organizers. What does that mean? It means that all the efforts of the many committees and other stakeholders must be joined toward a clear and singular mission. This mission must include the recognition that effectively marketing the event serves a multitude of beneficial purposes. When each facet of the event is consciously linked to the other seemingly unrelated parts of the whole, all aspects of the event benefit from the mutual gains realized by the successful accomplishment of the objectives assigned to each committee. For example, choosing a favorable site for the event will enhance the marketing of the event if it is in a well-known, easily accessible site that lacks any real or perceived barriers associated with getting to the site. If the event is placed in a run-down or unsafe part of town, this will take away from the appeal of the event and will make it more difficult to market. If, on the other hand, the goal of the event is to revitalize a particular neglected part of town by bringing the public to the site, then the choice of the site, despite inherent negative qualities, remains central to the marketing plan.

Marketing is about getting the word out; it involves advertising, public relations, and promotional activities. For an agency managing an entire event from conception to post-event evaluation, marketing is much more than the alphabetic approach of the 5Ws (who, what, when, where, why) and the 5Ps (product, price, promotion, place, and position) that are typically associated with event marketing. For many agencies, a festival or special event is a unique opportunity to reach out to new audiences, to create a greater base of support in a city or region, and to create a source of civic pride and positive social interaction. The event, as has already been explained, should add to and support the general goals of the agency.

Marketing Should Be Fun!

If you believe in your event and are confident of the value of your product, the marketing campaign should be a combination of a well-conceived plan and unbridled optimism. It is the time for staff and supporters to get others excited, involved, and anticipating the great things to come. Equally as significant is the fact that your agency has devoted countless hours and innumerable resources to an activity that may only last a few hours or days. The stakes are even higher in that many events are held only once a year!

The marketing plan cannot be reduced to simply advertising the event. While we have in recent times equated marketing with advertising, it is but one element in a marketing plan. Hoyle (2002) tells us that marketing must be an integrated process that combines the goals and efforts of all stakeholders with the expertise of the marketing staff so that marketing efforts support the predetermined expectations and standards of success for the event.

Marketing must enter the planning process at the onset as the marketing experts will provide input as to how the tools of marketing can be used to support the event goals, or may point out that the desired goals do not provide tangible benefits that can be supported by marketing efforts.

> Print media, electronic media, human dynamics, group dynamics, internal public relations, external public relations, press relations, promotions, advertising, sales and merchandising, sponsorships, and special celebrations as forms of marketing must all be used in concert with organizational goals.[1]

The Right Person for the Job

Few agencies, except perhaps large, well-funded urban departments, have the luxury of a full-time marketing specialist. Nor do many agencies have the budget to hire an outside marketing firm to handle the responsibilities of marketing your event. You may be fortunate to have a volunteer with some expertise, but usually it falls to a staff member to handle this critical area of event planning. How does one determine the best fit between staff abilities and the multidimensional task of marketing? An ideal marketing person possesses unwavering optimism, is enthusiastic, a storyteller by nature, yet understands the quantitative realities of finance and sales. The optimum person is one who is flexible, a true negotiator who can keep others focused on the big picture while attending to very important details. It is someone who can delegate through a clear explanation of tasks, requirements, and expected outcomes. It is an individual with a keen understanding of human nature and what it takes to get others excited about an idea. It is the person who can deftly move from concept, to strategy, to implementation, and follow through while keeping others accurately informed. The fact is, this person probably doesn't work for you right now! It may require that you develop a marketing mentality throughout your agency. Just as some agencies inculcate a sense of risk management in all employees, it is equally beneficial to encourage all staff to think in terms of optimal marketing opportunities. It may mean that additional time and resources must be allotted for the training of a staff member with an expressed interest and personality suitable for this type of work. It may take time and practice gained through smaller, less challenging responsibilities that will build toward the skill level needed for the management of a major marketing plan for an important signature event.

Marketing Success—Two Basic Principles

1. Understand the Product

Understanding what your product is, and how the audience will receive it, is a critical first step in the marketing process. Most events provide an anticipated audience with a unique experience that can be readily quantified. An event or festival can offer a certain number of hours of music, drama, merchandise sales, social interaction, and other activities that must be marketed in the most effective way possible. You must determine how the available resources, including marketing strategies, can be best used to introduce this product to the public. The event must be well conceived if it is to appeal to a sufficient number of potential attendees. There must be an understanding of both the appeal of the event to select market segments and its overall appeal to the general populace. It is also important to understand

Case Study: Marketing Enthusiasm!

A new marketing position was formed at an upscale community center that offered a half a dozen annual events that had become the trademark of the organization in the eyes of the local community. It was agreed upon that the new hire should have quantifiable skills that would support the marketing efforts of these events. The individual chosen for the position had little tangible evidence of related work experience but had great social skills, was charming, seemed well organized and, in many respects, was a good fit for the organization. The reality was that this person had minimal experience in marketing. However, in the three-year period after her hiring, the success of the agency's events increased markedly. This individual worked very hard despite some noticeable shortcomings, and held strong to her mantra—enthusiasm! This word found its way into most conversations at staff meetings and was the key phrase in presentations to the board of directors, to potential sponsors, and to the media. Enthusiasm drove the marketing strategy, attracted talented people to the organization, and effectively sold not only the annual events to the public, but the role of the agency to the local community. Eventually this individual outgrew the opportunities of the agency and opened a public relations and marketing firm that found success in many projects in the region. The particular skills needed for effective marketing were learned and refined along the way, but the commitment to create enthusiasm on the part of her clients was the key element to success. Repetition, reinforcement, and an identifiable product, in this case enthusiasm, created an environment characterized by optimism and a true sense of excitement for the agency and its stakeholders. The lesson here is that knowing one's strengths and weaknesses and turning them all into viable tools for the accomplishment of the challenges presented is a remarkably useful strategy for individual success and can contribute to the long-term success of an agency.

What are some characteristics that you or your agency possess that can help to drive a marketing campaign?

why the event does not appeal to other segments of a community (non-attendees) if the marketing plan is to be effective. The event must be distinct in that it must be perceived to offer a unique experience for the participant. The concept of *differentiation* suggests that the event must be conceptualized and presented in such a way that it gains some market advantage over the competition.

Van Der Wagen (2005) tells us that it is precisely the nature of special events that influences the marketing strategy. Special events, according to Van Der Wagen, are defined by three unique characteristics that have bearing on the formulation of a marketing plan:

Variability—the services or products provided vary greatly from one event to another resulting in no two events being exactly the same. This is an advantage referred to as differentiation. The challenge is to cut through the media clutter and clearly define and communicate the essence of the event to the public.

Inseparability—the actual product or services provided and the experience of the visitor are inseparable. Special events are about the experience, which includes every possible detail of the event that will impact the visitor's perception and memory of the event. Understanding the whole experience from the viewpoint of the visitor will help to shape the marketing efforts.

Perishability—events are usually not long-term activities; they happen during a specific time frame and then are relegated to memories and to the anticipation of next year's edition. Each time the event is offered, it is different due to the conditions of that particular version of the event. Entertainment will vary, weather is rarely the same year to year, trends in society will impact interest levels, and expectations change over time. This suggests that marketing efforts cannot merely rely on last year's strategies, as so many conditions that influence success can change over time.[2]

2. Understand Your Audience

Marketing is like dating; depending on your goals, a certain level of resources and effort must be allocated to the process. A well-conceived first date may lead to a long-term and mutually beneficial relationship. Likewise, marketing requires knowledge of what is being offered and an estimation of the interest level of the potential recipient. Once the product has been identified, it is important, in fact necessary, to learn as much as possible about the "other." This suggests the need for consumer research that should include a demographic analysis of the potential attendees and their spending patterns, a thorough understanding of visitor needs, insight into the decision-making process of potential visitors and their expectations regarding quality. It is through this research process that the initial stages of relationship are initiated. Marketing is a beautiful thing!

Market Segmentation

Events are steadily growing in popularity, creating increased competition for attendees and their discretionary dollars. This, combined with the ever-increasing costs of promoting an event, makes it necessary to develop highly efficient and effective means of marketing. Identifying the behavioral characteristics of the anticipated market segment that will attend your event is critical to achieving the best results from marketing efforts. A clearly defined market for an event allows for specific marketing to targeted groups, improves the ability to project attendance figures that impact resource allocation, makes the event more attractive to sponsors, and contributes to the strategic planning efforts that affect all areas of event management.

Marketing, as mentioned, is about developing relationships. Customers must relate to the organization as well as the event being presented. Based on the content of the event, planners should identify potential customers and seek to gain insight into their decision-making process regarding their choice of recreational activities. Potential customers must be motivated to allocate some of their disposable income in order to attend your event. It is commonly understood that certain events attract particular demographic subgroups based on their interest and knowledge of the product being offered. Prior to the development of an advertising campaign, research into the relationship between the product and the consumer must be explored. A fan base can be established by determining the core group of supporters for a particular event.

This is obvious in the types of advertising that we see during televised golf tournaments. Luxury car companies, cruise lines, investment companies and others understand and use demographic research to place their products in front of the right audience. Golf tournament sponsors also make use of the known demographics of the golf enthusiast in order to effectively disperse their sponsorship dollars in the most effective way.

- *Can you describe the demographics of a typical golf fan?*

- *What products might be marketed to a golf fan that would not be attractive for an NFL fan?*

Expanding the Fan Base

One of the challenges of marketing is to attempt to expand the fan base and attendance without compromising the expectations of the committed supporters of your event. A balanced sensitivity toward the needs of both audiences must be incorporated into the marketing plan. For example, symphony orchestras are challenged by the need to hold on to their base of support—generally an older, wealthier, and more sophisticated audience, with the challenge of developing the next generation of listeners. The more progressive organizations have expanded their programs to include repertoire and special performances by soloists and ensembles that attract a different and generally younger audience. Pops concerts, themed events, and the use of very recognizable mainstream stars have been enlisted to attract younger audiences. When classical music was first presented centuries ago, it was considered popular music played on the instruments of the day. It was innovative, exciting by their standards, and sometimes controversial. Above all, it was beautiful and inspiring. Today's orchestral executives must understand that the existing audience may appreciate, and in fact prefer, the standard classical repertoire but the audience is really there for beautiful music, including music that is new, innovative, and challenging.

It is a very satisfying experience to develop a relationship with those who attend your events and programs. But like any relationship, it cannot be left to chance, it requires constant and appropriate attention, and the right amount of surprise, to keep it vibrant and growing.

Marketing Success—Understanding the Marketing Mix

Marketing has existed for centuries. Evidence exists in both ancient Greece and Rome of handbills enticing the masses to attend sporting events, theatre presentations, and outdoor assemblies and parades. Today's special event organizers must understand the various means of reaching the potential audience and influencing their attitudes so that they choose to spend both time and money on a particular activity. Although not developed in the times of the philosophers and gladiators, there are some classic notions about the possibilities and opportunities for marketing an event. In order to achieve the greatest advantage in the marketplace, organizers must capitalize on five characteristics of the marketing mix. The five Ps mentioned in the opening section of this chapter provide a reliable roadmap for a thorough approach to marketing a product or event.

Product

Your organization must expertly understand the product—your event. Organizations that have experienced decades of success have developed a culture particular to their event. This includes knowledge of the history of the event, the current goals to be achieved, the perception of the event by the community by both attendees and those who choose not to participate, the impact of the event socially and economically on the community, the planned lifespan of the event, and the strength of support for the event. All of these aspects help to define the event for organizers, sponsors, attendees, and the greater community.

Richard Florida (2002) discusses the idea of *generica*. By this, he means the homogenization of American culture represented by big box stores, chain restaurants, and places of amusements that offer generic experiences that can be identically repeated from Kissimmee to Kalamazoo.[3] A special event by its very nature should work to counter the generica phenomena. By offering an experience that is unique, an event can successfully capture the imagination of its audience.

Marketing means understanding what will appeal to your target market!
Photo Credit: deLisle

Price

Pricing an event is an interesting combination of quantitative fiscal information, agency goals, and consumer perceptions. Pricing is not an exact science and can frequently benefit from an intuitive understanding of the relationship between the event and the potential customers. One must, however, start with the facts. The organizing agency may, by choice or dictate, need to realize a certain level of financial return on the event. Some organizations, due to grants or other outside sources of funding, do not focus on bottom-line or break-even strategies. Others are quite satisfied with covering the operational costs while allowing their agency to cover the administrative, personnel, and other overhead costs of a particular event. More progressive agencies and commercial ventures must measure a significant portion of the success in terms of past event surplus funds or profit margin. The longevity of the event is often tied to the achievement of the stated goals of the organizers and their superiors. If profit is not a standard for success it is still advisable, and certainly responsible, to pursue means of becoming a self-supporting entity.

An analysis of the operating and overhead costs must take place as the initial step in determining price. Combined with the event costs is the need to gather information from past events, or from similar events if yours is a first-time venture, in order to project the needed attendance and revenue targets for the event as realistically as possible.

In addition to the mathematical requirements of price determination, there exists the need to determine the real and perceived value of the event. This process involves researching the price of similar events that are attended by similar segments of the local market. Furthermore, the perceived price of the event is related to the real or perceived value of the product. If your event includes multiple activities, has regionally or nationally recognizable entertainment, and provides a high-quality experience, the price of the event should reflect these realities.

Finally, one must consider the difference between the *price of the event* and the *actual cost* of the event for an attendee. For our purposes, the price of the event is the ticket price that allows for admission to the event. The cost of the event includes the ticket price and any other money spent related to attendance. This would include the travel and parking expenses, perhaps the cost of a babysitter, money spent on concessions, souvenirs, programs, and other impulse purchases associated with the event. The costs of the event are often greater than the price of admission. Frequently, event producers will keep the price low, anticipating additional revenue associated with the costs incurred by visitors to the event. While this may seem diabolical, the consumer actually has the opportunity to expand upon their event experience by purchasing additional items, memorabilia, food, refreshments, and other items that can add to the overall enjoyment of the event. If properly managed, this strategy can produce positive results for all parties.

Place

Place defines the method of making your product available to the consumer. It is sometimes referred to as *distribution*, which starts with a D, and wouldn't fit into the mnemonic device of the 5Ps. In event marketing, the place of distribution for your product begins with advance marketing and ticket sales and continues through each activity or experience associated with the event. Deciding where and how to make tickets available to your audience plays an important role in the perception of the event by potential visitors.

Position

It is imperative that organizers understand how a particular event fits into the flow of events in the area. You must determine which needs in the local community are met by holding your event. This is both a process of researching existing events and of educating the public about the particular benefits of your event. Positioning is based on understanding the competition and filling a particular niche in the local market. This position, relative to other events, is determined by the unique elements that your event offers. Admission pricing, related expenses, and the level of quality of both product and service that is experienced by the participant determine the perceived value and position of your event. Positioning requires research in order to collect and coordinate quantitative and qualitative data. Research methods may include the analysis of the competition, using representative focus groups, and conducting surveys in sufficient time so that the results can help in the strategic planning of the event.

Promotion

Promotion is the means by which the message of your event hits the ground and begins to influence people's attitudes and behaviors. Promotion is the marriage between message and medium. Based on a very secure understanding of the benefits and attractions of the event, the proper mix of promotional methods must be determined. Promotions can include advertising, public relation efforts, and other awareness-raising strategies.

Promotions are about communicating the who, what, why, where, and what of your event. Promotional budgeting presents challenges in determining how much and where dollars are spent. Organizers must accurately identify the *primary markets* for their event and allocate sufficient resources using appropriate techniques. Primary markets are those groups of individuals who historically show a predisposition to attend the type of event being presented. It is important to measure the levels of awareness of this group concerning the upcoming event and then increase awareness through promotional efforts. *Secondary markets* are those that might not be the most obvious targets for attendance at the event but might add to the overall attendance and revenue for the event. Efforts here might be a combination of educating the public about the benefits of the event and raising awareness. Goldblatt (2002) offers a checklist for determining promotional strategies in Table 7.1.[4]

Table 7.1. Promotional Strategies
• Identify all elements of the event that require promotion.
• Develop strategies for allocating promotion resources with efficient methods.
• Identify promotion partners to share costs.
• Target promotions to the market segments that will support the event.
• Measure and analyze promotion efforts and make necessary midcourse corrections.

Promotional Strategies

A well-planned promotional campaign will use of mix of media tools to inform the public. These may include paid advertising, flyers, posters, presentations and speeches, mailings, radio, television, Internet presence, signs and banners, brochures, mini-events, sponsorship links, media kits, computer-generated materials such as cds and dvds, newsprint, text messaging, public service announcements, celebrity endorsements, government publications, contests, ticket giveaways, cross promotional opportunities, and more. The selection of a particular method must be based on the anticipated goals of each promotion, the available budgetary resources, and the effectiveness of the promotion as indicated by tracking the results of the response by the public. Promotions seek to engage the consumer by raising awareness and interest, by connecting with the consumer, and moving them toward making a positive decision regarding your event. The process must be properly timed so that the decision-making behaviors peak at the appropriate time. Commitment to attend, either by advance ticket purchase, making plans with others to attend, or scheduling the event into a personal calendar, must be sufficiently close to the event so that the interest level created through the promotions carries through to the day of the event.

Public Relations

Public relations is a particular method of event promotion that deserves to be examined separately from the promotional strategies previously addressed. Public relations is the means of creating a positive image and attaining credibility through the managed perceptions of supporters and potential customers via the media or through direct contact. Public relations involves media relations, community relations, customer relations, employee relations, sponsor relations, and government relations. If properly directed, public relations can be the most cost-effective means of promoting an event.

Public relations is about building a perception of your event for the potential customer, the general public, and all other relevant stakeholders. Public relations uses the event as the launching pad for related stories, human interest pieces, descriptions of unique characteristics or personalities associated with the event, and even the challenges faced by the organizers to make the plan a reality. Through the development of opinions about your product, customers help to inform your marketing efforts through their expressed perceptions of the event.

Public relations differs from *publicity* in several important ways. *Publicity* is any attention given by the media to an event or organization. This attention is controlled by decisions made by the media in support of their goals and can result in both positive and negative reporting about your event. Public relations is directed by the event organizers in order to develop a mutually beneficial relationship with news media that can only help your event but does not eliminate the possibility of bad publicity.

Event organizers can influence media coverage by employing several positive strategies. The organizers must first *identify the publicity messages* that they want delivered to the public through the media. This may develop into a theme or subplot for the event. Secondly, the event marketers must *provide the media with accurate information* that will help to shape the opinions of the event for the public. If organizers can create scenarios that the media characterize as news, the event will receive additional attention from media outlets. Basic information in the form of press kits must precede this effort so that the media has a general idea of the shape of the event. What will catch the attention of the media is an angle that will allow the media to sell their product: newspapers, television reports, website visits, and radio shows, by using the unique characteristics of your event to stimulate readership or viewing. News reporters in all media are challenged to deliver stories that appeal to

Promotional strategies include using traditional advertising media tools.
Photo Credit: deLisle

their audience on a daily or weekly basis. They, like anyone else, appreciate having their job made a little easier. In a survey of 5,500 journalists worldwide, 38% said they got at least 50% of their ideas for stories from publicists who provided materials and story lines regarding events, personalities, or public interest items.[5]

Due to the fact that news media are also involved in public relations for their own benefit, they value stories that allow them to deliver news in a public service format. In this way, the event organizers can achieve media coverage that is mutually beneficial to the event and the media reporters.

The planning given to the treatment of the media representatives who attend your event also has a bearing on the type and extent of coverage provided by media outlets.

Providing the media with visual supports such as photos of the event entertainers, shots of the crowd enjoying the event, video footage and other materials, increases the probability of high-level coverage. Providing journalists perks like free admission and concession tickets helps to ensure their attendance and can help to create a positive impression of the event. For larger events, establishing a pressroom with the necessary technologies such as phone, fax, computer lines, maps, schedules, and other support materials helps the reporters to do a thorough job of reporting the event. By understanding the needs of the media, by providing reliable, timely, and interesting information and stories, and through a continuing relationship with local reporters, your event will realize maximum results from publicity and public relations efforts.

If an event benefits a social cause, oftentimes the recipients of the proceeds from your event make for a compelling story as to how their situation will be improved by the success of the event.

Media coverage can be greatly enhanced by creating a sponsorship relationship with the media outlets. An official radio station or television station for the event allows for a team approach to covering the event. Public service advertising, a predetermined number of ad slots during peak listening periods, media personality endorsements, and appearances all help to promote the event. A live remote broadcast from the event is a very effective way to draw attention to the event while it is being staged. Having a media partner will also enhance the status of the event in the local or regional broadcast area. This relationship may also attract other corporate sponsors.

Advertising

It is a commonly accepted axiom that 50% of all advertising dollars are wasted, the problem is no one can determine which half is being wasted and which is producing results! Advertising, a necessary part of any marketing campaign, is a means of paying for the opportunity to explain the details and benefits of an event from the point of view of the organizers. There are many marketing tools used to get the word out to the public and to create a positive image of your event. Advertising is critical in that it sets the stage, presents the facts, and serves to keep an event in the public eye. An advertising budget is necessary to fill the gaps in the information being provided by the media through public relations efforts and promotional activities. Funding, combined with research and creativity, will help your organization make the best use of limited advertising dollars. An advertising schedule should be developed so that valuable resources are used at the appropriate times to move the public toward making a decision to attend your event.

Web Marketing

Effective marketing in the 21st century must consider the benefits and challenges of web-based marketing. We will address the technology of event management in a later chapter, but special consideration must be afforded the necessity of using the Internet as a marketing tool.

The Internet emerged in the mid-1960s from the need for the Department of Defense to devise a means of having governmental information systems talk to each other so that scientists could readily exchange information. In 1965, The Advanced Research Project Agency (ARPA) was created, without the help of Al Gore, to serve the research and security needs of the federal government, introducing the concept of computer-based information sharing to the world.[6]

Over one billion individuals have email addresses and can connect to over 600 million website addresses. The strength of the system is in its ability to narrowly define searches in order for users to access desired information with a minimum of effort. According to the *Wall Street Journal* (http://blogs.wsj.com/digits/2012/02/27/online-retail-spending-at-200-billion-annually-and-growing/), over $200 billion is spent annually on Internet purchases with growth expected to be over 10% in subsequent years. Despite the availability of this remarkable tool, most advertising dollars continue to be dedicated to traditional means of marketing such as newsprint, radio and television, and printed materials such as flyers and brochures.

The key to efficiency is to understand the role of each tool in the overall marketing plan. It may be necessary to disseminate introductory information through traditional outlets as you seek out the consumer and create awareness. This type of information can then direct those seeking additional information, or desiring to make contact with the event to satisfy their curiosity, to a well-designed website. It is at this point that websites can provide the greatest returns. Properly designed websites are created to address particular issues related to marketing through a deliberate identification of objectives to be achieved by the site. Initially sites were strictly informational and not interactive. Websites are moving from static advertising to becoming their own category of application software wherein a consumer can access and interact with a product or service. Sites that only provide information are being replaced with opportunities to make reservations, check schedules, listen to the performers, ask questions, review last year's event highlights, purchase tickets and merchandise, and get fully involved with the event. This increased level of personal investment and commitment on the part of the consumer prior to attending the event is a strong and effective means of building your event community.

Web access is constant, a 24/7 opportunity that can reach well beyond the traditional geographic and temporal advertising boundaries. The cost of web marketing involves the investment of staff time and a modest fee for development and hosting. It is critical that resources be allocated for the regular and accurate updating of information on the site. Outdated and incorrect information can have a very negative effect on visitor confidence and interest in your product. Having a web page dedicated to your event adds to the perceived importance of the event on the part of the viewer. This positive impression must be supported by adequate site maintenance. Web advertising strategies also allow the event site to capitalize on sponsorship relationships by offering the placement of sponsor information and links on the website as another potential benefit of sponsorship. Providing additional links to other relevant sites featuring entertainers and products available at the event serves to enhance the educational objectives of the site, as well as to deepen the viewer's interest in the event. Depending on the objectives of the site, the visitor may be able to make online purchases, take advantage of premiums offered on the site, secure desired benefits, tickets, merchandise, and have questions answered in a most convenient and efficient setting.

Are there any negative consequences to web marketing?

What Research Tells Us: Motivation in the Marketplace

It is important to understand that visitors to a festival or other special event have varying motivations for attending an event. Formica and Uysal (1996) found a correlation between residency status and motivation for attending an international jazz festival in Perugia, Italy. Those identified as residents of the area identified socialization benefits as the major reason for attendance with entertainment as a strong secondary consideration. Non-residents, including many international visitors, identified the entertainment factor as the strongest factor, with the novelty of the event as the second leading motivation.[7] These results make intuitive sense if one reflects on the perceived benefits of a local event. Residents use the event opportunity to see friends and neighbors in a unique but easily accessible environment. Many residents comment that the only time they see certain friends or acquaintances is at an annual local event. Visitors to the area are obviously not attending to see neighbors but are attracted to the theme and entertainment offered. Oftentimes an event is attractive due to the purpose of the event being out of the ordinary, either beyond the visitor's normal range of experiences, or due to the quaint simplicity of the event. This characteristic attractiveness of an event is referred to as *cultural exploration*.[8] Organizers must understand these factors in appealing to local supporters and in developing strategies to attract visitors from outside the region.

It is also relevant to determine other motivating factors that play a role in the decision to attend an event. Iso Ahola (1982, 1989) presents a dichotomy that identifies motivation as either a *seeking behavior* or an *avoiding behavior* in order to obtain an optimal level of arousal. Event attendees can be analyzed using this strategy.[9] Nicholson and Pearce (2001) describe Crompton's (1979) seven socio-/psychological motivational categories or domains that influence recreational pursuits:

- novelty
- socialization
- prestige/status
- rest and relaxation
- educational value/intellectual enrichment
- enhancing kinship relations/family togetherness
- regression.

Further studies of multiple events in New Zealand support the need to ask open-ended motivational questions that allow for a greater range of answers than a predetermined list of motivational categories and statements in order to understand visitor motivation. This is due to the distinctly diverse character of events and the varying motivations and interests of attendees.[10]

Destination Marketing

Events are an important part of a greater strategy to market a destination to the tourism sector. Events like Mardi Gras, the Newport Folk/Jazz festivals, national and international sporting events and others are used by governments and tourism organizations to draw people to a particular city at a particular time of the year. The Olympic Games provide governments with the opportunity to promote their country as a member of the world community in ways not previously afforded them. This had positive long-term effects on tourism and Chinese cultural identity following the 2008 games. Russia is currently struggling to position the winter Olympic games in Sochi (2014) as an invitation for the world to visit. This is despite the governments restrictive policies regarding human rights for many groups of citizens in their country.

Well-planned strategies are very effective in creating brand-name destinations based on events. From this perspective the marketing of a particular event will also benefit from the larger goals of creating destinations that capitalize on the characteristics of the area and the special attractions that are offered.

Evaluating Marketing Efforts

Due to the many marketing options available and the variability of events, organizers must become adept at determining the most effective means of getting the message out to the public for each particular event. A successful strategy for one event may not be the right choice for other events, including the same event one year later. Marketing dollars are mistakenly the first things cut from many budgets, because other elements of the event, fixed costs, require a large share of the operating budget. This is particularly unwise if the marketing plan is an efficient and effective means of generating public interest and revenue. The negative effects of a reduction or misuse of marketing dollars may not show up in the year the cuts are made, but the long-term results can be a reduction in awareness and participation in the event. Most marketing plans identify these two elements, awareness and participation, as key objectives in the marketing strategy. Marketing must remain fresh and creative and be able to adroitly change in order to meet the interests and trends of the consumer market. Organizers must meet the challenge of reduced financial resources by devising marketing relationships and opportunities that maximize event exposure to the desired market segment. To best equip the organization for the needed flexibility that results in effective marketing, evaluation should take place during the process of marketing the event and as an important element in post-event analysis. A majority of organizations would benefit from additional time and effort spent on post-event evaluation. The challenge generally comes from the fact that agencies complete one event and must move immediately to the next project on the radar screen. Evaluating the marketing effort is doubly challenging, because it is a difficult and complex area to standardize and measure results.

Evaluation of the effectiveness of marketing must be structured to measure quantifiable objectives emanating from the original strategic plan of the event. This link to the project goals and objectives is the key to evaluation, progress, and the future viability of the event. There are no industry standards for event marketing evaluation attributable to the fact that marketing oftentimes affects complex factors such as perceptions, attitudes, and other less than tangible characteristics.[11] Measuring these changes requires the formulation of instruments that consider both the affective domain (attitudes and feelings) and the stated objectives of the event. Tangible results such as increased attendance, sales, and event visibility may be logically credited to the marketing plan but are often done intuitively rather than based on empirical, quantifiable data. Evaluation allows the event team to confirm results and plan future strategies.

In order for evaluation to be fully effective, it is advisable to conduct pre and post event research, particularly in the areas of awareness and relationship, as these two areas may be greatly altered through the marketing process. One of the difficulties of evaluating the event marketing strategy is the occurrence of *cross-marketing influence*. The participant may bring a coupon to the event in order to receive a reduced admission, but the decision to attend the event may be the result of prior knowledge or personal interest in the theme of the event that was then supported rather than determined by the coupon offer. Other detracting factors are elements, such as the weather, that can have a deleterious effect on many of the traditional measures of marketing effectiveness. The marketing might have been first rate and very effective only to be derailed by threatening or inclement weather.

Tangible Results of Marketing

Media coverage/exposure rate and content quality can be assessed through the number of column inches devoted to the event, the minutes of air time on radio or television, new or improved relationships with sponsors, increased number of sponsors, increase in sponsor dollars, returned promotional coupons, Internet site hits, and other quantifiable results of a marketing campaign. Quantifiable information is important in measuring the effectiveness of resource allocation to the marketing effort.

Intangible Results

Intangible results might not be as easily quantified but can be measured based on input from key stakeholders (see Table 7.2). The *identity* of the event can be successfully portrayed as it relates to and supports the organizational intentions for the event. The *image* or how the participants view the event and the organization can be influenced by the marketing campaign. *Awareness* of the event by the general public results from information provided by advertising, promotional, and public relations efforts. Has the *relationship* between the event and the consumer changed—can this be attributed to the marketing campaign?

Table 7.2. Tangible and Intangible Results	
Tangible Results	media exposure; increase in number of sponsors; increase in sponsor dollars; ticket sales; concession sales; coupon returns; Internet site hits
Intangible Results	event identity establishment; image enhancement; increased awareness of event/destination; change in consumer relationship

Evaluation Tools

Marketing evaluation requires internal and external information. *Internal information* refers to the data collected from organizers, workers, volunteers, contracted employees, and sponsors that helps to clarify the achievement of the event marketing objectives. Questionnaires, staff and volunteer wrap-up meetings, written reports by supervisors and line staff all can contribute to the greater picture of the marketing impact.

External information comes from participants and other stakeholders not involved in the planning and implementation of the event, but are crucial in ascertaining the effectiveness of the marketing campaign. According to Yeoman et al. (2004), event sales, staff reports, sponsorship feedback, meeting minutes, customer service feedback, complaints, and compliments all contribute to the feedback matrix for event marketers. Surveys, visual observance, follow-up letters and surveys, emails, focus groups, and other forms of questioning will help to elicit responses from those outside of the organization regarding the effectiveness of marketing efforts.[12] Evaluation can be designed to gather information from the consumer regarding the levels of satisfaction experienced in all aspects of contact between the event marketers and the customer.

Summary

Marketing is the soul of commerce. The development and viability of any product, particularly a special event, is critically linked to the organization's ability to tell its story.

Understanding the tools of marketing and making effective use of all available advantages inherent in a special event will support but not guarantee a successful marketing effort. Trial and error, with accurate documentation of each marketing success and failure will help to focus and refine future marketing efforts.

Discussion Questions

1. Why is the marketing plan inserted very early into the strategic plan for the event?
2. Identify and explain the three unique characteristics of an event according to Van Der Wagen.
3. What are some qualities to look for in a marketing professional?
4. Why is it important to understand the potential audience for your festival?
5. Explain the concept of market segmentation.
6. Explain the five Ps of marketing.
7. How does a public relations strategy contribute to marketing your event?
8. What are some advantages of web-based marketing for events?
9. How can an event contribute to the marketing of a destination?
10. How would you evaluate the marketing efforts for a special event?

1. Hoyle, L. (2002). *Event marketing*. New York: John Wiley & Sons, p. xix.
2 . Van Der Wagen, L., & Carlos Pearson, B.(2005). *Event management for tourism, cultural, business, and sporting events*. New Jersey: Prentice Hall, p. 60.
3. Florida, R. (2002). *The rise of the creative class and how it is transforming work, leisure, community and everyday life*. New York: Basic Books, p. 165.
4. Goldblatt, J. (2002). *Special events* (3rd ed.). New York: Wiley & Sons, p. 254. Department of Agriculture, Forest Service Systems.
5. Braun, M. (2000). Courting the media: How the Spoleto festival USA attracted media coverage. *International Journal of Arts Management, 2*(2), p. 54.
6. Leiner, B., Cerf,V., Clark, D., Kahn, R., Kleinrock, L., Lynch,D., Postel, J., Roberts, L., & Wolff, S. *A brief history of the Internet*. Retrieved from http://www.isoc.org/internet/history/brief.shtml
7. Formica, S., & Uysal, M. (1998). Market segmentation of an international cultural-historical event in Italy. *Journal of Travel Research, 36*(4), 16–24.
8. Crompton, J., & McKay, S. L. (1997). Motives of visitors attending festival events. *Annals of Tourism Research. 24*(2), 425–439.
9. Iso-Ahola, S. E. (1982). Toward a social psychological theory of tourism motivation: A rejoinder. *Annals of Tourism Research, 9*(1), 256–262.
10. Nicholson, R., & Pearce, D. (2001). Why do people attend events: A comparative analysis of visitor motivations at four South Island events. *Journal of Travel Research, 39*, pp. 449–460.
11. Eckerstein, A. (2002). *Evaluation of event marketing: Important indicators to consider when evaluating event marketing*. International Management Master Thesis No 2002:25 Göteborg University ISSN 1403-851X Printed by Elanders Novum.
12. Yeoman, I., Robertson, M., Ali-Knight, J., Drummond, S., & McMahon-Beattie, U. (2004). *Festival and event management*. Amsterdam: Elsevier Butterworth & Heinemann, pp. 246–257.

8

Risk Management

 To be alive at all involves some risk.

Harold Macmillan

Chapter Objectives

- Identify the benefits of risk management
- Understand risk and legal responsibilities
- List the components of a risk management plan
- Organize a risk-analysis project
- Develop risk management policies
- Identify risk management options

Risk management is included in the fiscal resource section of the book for several reasons. First and foremost, risk management is the exercise of common sense and prudent responsibility. Maximizing personal enjoyment and minimizing threats to your event and its participants should drive the process of identifying, assessing, and managing risk.

In a more complete consideration, *risk management* is described as reducing liability and loss through a planned program of education, prevention, control, and evaluation.

Loss can take many forms, most of which result in either the outlay of funds to cover a loss or a reduction in revenue resultant from imprudent behavior or an unforeseen crisis. Because dealing with risk involves costs that have an impact on the financial well-being of an event or an organization, it is considered a financial component of a management plan.

Benefits of Risk Management

According to Tarlow (2002), it is significantly less expensive to manage a risk prior to an occurrence than after a crisis has occurred. Additionally, by creating a risk management plan, expenditures associated with loss can usually be reduced, allowing the event managers to allocate these savings to other areas that may increase the value of event-related experiences.[1] Other benefits of an effective risk management plan are included in Table 8.1.

Table 8.1. Benefits of Risk Management
• Protects the financial well-being of the organization
• Reduces loss of time, materials, personnel, and participants
• Maintains participant safety, satisfaction, and loyalty
• Upholds moral principles of service orientation
• Creates a safer work environment
• Encourages active involvement of all staff members
Tarlow, 2002

Personal injury and loss of life are the worst-case scenarios of a risk-related incident, the consequences of which can effectively and permanently end an event. Event organizers must consider a wider scope of possible losses when planning a risk management strategy. The event itself, with all its interrelated parts, is also subject to risk.

What Can Be Lost?

Loss encompasses more than just the financial implications of the critical and possibly negative occurrences associated with an event. It may also include loss of reputation, loss of public support, loss of confidence by stakeholders, loss of loyalty on the part of customers or volunteers, and loss of market share and competitive advantage which may lead to additional financial losses such as sponsorship, outside funding, ticket sales, and so on.

Incorporating a risk management strategy at the onset of designing and planning an event is strongly recommended. Understanding and identifying the risks associated with each type of resource utilized in an event can provide a systematic and practical means of mitigating the greatest number of possible occasions for loss. Risk management helps organizers to ensure a safe event site for workers, volunteers and the general public. Risk management practices result in fewer accidents, increase productivity, and frequently contribute to higher morale and favorable attitudes among all stakeholders.

What Brings About Liability and Loss?

Events present one of the most challenging scenarios for managers, as there are numerous variables and elements of risk associated with staging an event. Lack of planning, poor communication, lack of technical knowledge or skills, false assumptions, carelessness, and a lack of attention to detail are frequently mentioned as contributing to a loss occurrence.[2] These can be categorized as acts of *omission*—not doing something that should have been done, or *commission*—doing something that should not have been done. This categorization will be explored later in the chapter as these terms have important legal significance.

Prior to the identification of the sources of risk, one must adequately comprehend the underlying principles of risk management. We are confronted with multiple risk-producing situations on a daily basis. Whether it is driving on a busy interstate, playing competitive sports, or forgetting to bring home the groceries at the end of the day, life is full of dangers. We quite naturally identify and avoid or control most risks on a daily basis. For the event planner, the major categories of risk include accidents and injury, fire, theft, breach of contract, and numerous opportunities for lawsuits.

Underlying Mechanisms in Risk Management

While authors offer various theories of risk management, it is fairly straightforward to identify the following important steps in developing a risk management plan.

1. Identify all risks—i.e., weather, accident and injury, technology, mismanagement
2. Assign value to each potential occurrence
3. Develop data systems to record and monitor all risk occurrences
4. Assess risk occurrences
5. Develop education and training program for employees, volunteers, and participants
6. Develop the risk management plan and process, including reports, emergency response procedures, standards for performance and reporting, and process-evaluation materials.[3]

We will now take a closer look at the parameters of *education, prevention, control,* and *evaluation* as the main activities associated with risk management.

Education

At the heart of the education process is a thorough knowledge of the elements of risk inherent in your activity or event. Risk identification and assessment is the starting point of this awareness. Simply put, research reduces risk. Once the pertinent information regarding the risks associated with an event is assembled, it must be shared with those involved in your event in an appropriate and effective manner. Event risks include health, safety, and food-quality issues, unexpected weather occurrences, accidents, and injuries, structural failures, technology failures, contractual difficulties, negative publicity, the impact of competition, theft, vandalism, fraud, sexual harassment, misuse of facilities, civil disturbances, and the potential for violence, and the perception of problems associated with these issues that may lead to a crisis.

In the planning process, it is important that each of these variables and others that may be particular to your situation, be analyzed to determine your ability to gather information regarding the potential for problems in each area. A suitable educational program should be developed by identifying the most typical types of problems that might arise and designing a strategy to address these issues. Determining the relationship between any real or perceived problem and the costs associated with each occurrence will help to prioritize your risk management efforts. The prioritization of event risk elements is further aided by understanding the parameters of your event. Specifically, the projected attendance figures, the demographics of anticipated attendees, the risks inherent in the type of activities being offered at the event, and the probability of occurrence of particular types of incidences all impact the process of identification, prioritization, and education.

Standards and Codes

Following a thorough analysis of event-related risks, it is imperative that all quantifiable data be shared with the relevant and appropriate stakeholders. Along with the sharing of this type of data, it is also necessary to disseminate all information regarding acceptable standards and codes for the provision of the services associated with the event. These standards include food-handling regulations, building and construction codes, electrical codes, traffic codes, and other regulations that have been developed to improve safety. Additionally, appropriate procedures for all identifiable risks including traffic and crowd control, inclement weather threats and others, must be developed and provided to all involved through adequate training. Ironically, the potential risks that receive inadequate attention and insufficient training are frequently the areas that present problems during the event. Identifying and involving all relevant regulatory and enforcement officials very early in the risk management planning process will ensure that continuous and effective communications become the accepted standard for risk management for your event. The cross-pollination of ideas and prior practices can also serve the risk management goals of the event.

Education and Training of Staff and Volunteers

Ensuring event safety is a personal and personnel matter. Those actively involved in the planning and delivery of the event must be trained in personal safety. This may include receiving training to qualify for a particular set of responsibilities such as first aid provider, emergency medical service responder, food handler, traffic control, lifeguard, and other specific, certifiable programs. Others will require in-house training to raise the safety awareness relative to themselves and the event. Ideally, all staff and volunteers should be trained as risk managers in the sense that all are aware of and actively involved in the process of risk management. This general training should, over time, include visitors to your event so that all stakeholders are conscious of the need to be personally responsible for themselves and for the well-being of others involved in the event. Along with this heightened level of awareness, staff and volunteers must be taught to be proactive, that is, to take immediate and appropriate action at the first sign of a potential risk situation. This type of strategy may then become part of the organizational culture of your event.

Given the many responsibilities of event organizers, the possibility of making use of the expertise of local safety officials, including local police and rescue squads, as primary trainers for your event is advised. This will provide staff and volunteers with the most up-to-date information and training, and will also open the lines of communication between the your event workers and public safety professionals. This early contact and familiarity may prove to be instrumental should a crisis arise during an event that requires collaborative efforts between your staff and outside help.

Education and Training of Participants

Invited guests to the event, defined as those that pay an admission price or are actively recruited and welcomed to the property, create the greatest potential for accident, injury, and associated loss. It is usually not possible to provide prior training for event participants. Onsite communication including focused efforts at informing participants of potential risks associated with the event is critical in reducing the occurrence of loss. Once again, the knowledge and expertise of safety professionals, as well as the advice of the event insurance providers, will help to lower the potential for loss. Standardized procedures exist for many situations, including rules and codes that have been developed for public assembly. Effective communication of these guidelines to the public through a planned presentation of safety expectations communicated through visuals, such as signs and flyers, must be accompanied by public address announcements concerning the need to adhere to these pre-established guidelines in order to promote a safe and enjoyable experience for all.

The New York Five Boro Bike Tour successfully guides 32,000 riders through the streets of New York. Educational websites and emails prepare the riders for the challenges of urban trekking months before the event.

Prevention

No one can prevent an accident or loss from occurring at all times and in all situations. One can only hope to reduce the frequency and severity of such events. Preventing loss begins with involving all stakeholders in a dynamic process of developing an agency culture wherein all members take on the responsibility of being a risk manager. This team approach strengthens the possibility of the majority of problems being identified and solved prior to the experience of loss. Loss prevention begins long before an event takes place. Risk assessment and education allow the management team to prescribe preventative actions to lessen and eliminate potential problems. See Table 8.2. Education, as previously noted, is the starting point for this process.

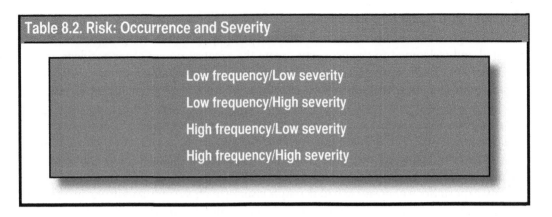

Table 8.2. Risk: Occurrence and Severity

Low frequency/Low severity

Low frequency/High severity

High frequency/Low severity

High frequency/High severity

Prevention also requires *record keeping* so that areas or activities of high risk can be identified based on historical data. Past records are a key to understanding possible future risk. While there are many models available to develop risk strategies, the choices provided below should prove to be very helpful for most situations. When confronted with a potential risk, one must determine certain characteristics of the potential occurrence. The categorization of these occurrences can be determined by the estimated frequency of the occurrence and an estimate of the maximum severity of loss for each occurrence. This means that one must determine how often an accident might occur and the potential seriousness of each occurrence.

It is a valuable use of staff time to identify and classify all potential risk occurrences included in the various elements of the event. A master chart depicting all known risk factors and their occurrence and severity classification is an important step in preventing loss. Depending on the classification of each identified risk, a prevention strategy can be assigned. Again, acknowledging a myriad of possible approaches, four major preventative actions can be taken based on the frequency and severity of a particular risk.

Eliminate the Risk Entirely

This strategy is recommended for risks that cannot be accommodated within the risk management plan. This includes risks of high occurrence and high severity. If a particular activity lends itself to frequent and catastrophic results, there is no justification for the continuance of this activity. While insurers and programmers have incorporated many "high-risk" activities into recreational programming, one must continually ask the question as to whether the probability of risk and injury is worth the costs. Many event organizers have experienced negative legal and social consequences due to the sale of alcohol at events. Alcohol sales generally are large profit centers for festivals and events. When the dispensing of alcohol results in frequent and severe problems, creating high risk, it may be in the best interest to eliminate the risk and devise alternative means of revenue production.

This strategy is important not only for the protection of participants at an event but also for the staff and volunteers who may be asked to perform risky work-related activities in preparation for the event. The risk-related tasks, if absolutely necessary for the success of the event, should be engineered in such a way as to eliminate the risk-producing portions. Changing the work procedure may effectively eliminate a risk. This can also be accomplished by contracting with professionals to perform dangerous duties that are not part of the routine responsibilities of your staff. Professionals who perform these tasks on a daily basis have both the extensive training and expertise to perform such duties with minimal risk to self and others. A common area of high risk is to ask staff members to perform work above the ground such as assembling temporary structures, laying wire or cables, and setting stage lights. Unless your staff is trained and accustomed to working high off the ground, it is best to contract with companies who perform this type of work on a routine basis. This is sometimes referred to as *engineering out* the risk.

Reduce the Risk Significantly

Reducing risk that cannot be eliminated begins with education, the introduction of safety programs, and fostering a safety-conscious environment. Risk occurrences that are of low frequency but high severity or of high frequency and low severity should be reduced to the lowest possible level of occurrence. If reduction of these types of risks cannot be achieved, these activities might have to be eliminated from the program. The publishing, dissemination, and continuous *enforcement of safety regulations* are important initial steps in reducing risk. Pre- and postevent reviews of the standing emergency management plan for the event allows for the adjustment and improvement of operating procedures based on new information and renewed perspectives. Risk reduction is also accomplished by *adjusting training to the level of comprehension* of staff, volunteers, and guests. Safety procedures must be accessible to each group in a meaningful way. Varying learning/teaching styles (visual, auditory, and activity-based methods) should be considered when developing training methods for each group. *Facility and equipment inspection* may require the intervention of local or state authorities trained to certify the safety of equipment that is placed in public service. This process must be portrayed in a positive light so that staff, volunteers, and contractual vendors develop a sense of shared responsibility and cooperation regarding these inspections and recommendations. Improperly maintained and worn out equipment must be identified and replaced. This requires *pre-event inspections of all facilities and equipment* as well as *daily inspections* prior to the arrival of guests. Regular *preventative maintenance* generally ensures against all but the most unpredictable and often unavoidable accidents. Prevention is an activity that by its very nature is continuous and without completion. This is perhaps the most important concept to be shared with all event stakeholders. Further consideration of particular risk-reduction strategies will be covered in separate chapters that address specific elements of events such as crowd control, concessions, and safety and sanitation.

Assume the Risk Partially or Totally

Certain risks exist whenever public gatherings occur. These risks may be inherent and unavoidable and are accepted as a part of doing business. It is advisable to develop procedures to address these occurrences so that their impact and costs are minimized. An occurrence of low frequency and low severity would fall into this category. The underlying principle is to *balance the level of risk with the benefits* of a particular aspect of the event. A fireworks show is a situation fraught with potential disaster. Understanding the risk and taking appropriate preventative measures during the planning and execution of the show, such as hiring a reputable company to produce and present the display, as well as enforcing all state and local regulations regarding the use of fireworks and set back areas, are appropriate measures that make the benefits of such a show worth the inherent risks. Assuming risk requires effective assessment, education, and preventative measures. Risk can also be assumed in strictly financial terms by budgeting for a certain level of loss within the financial strategy of the event.

Transfer the Risk to Insurers or Participants

Following the risk analysis and review undertaken by event organizers and prior to expending resources for a particular event, it may be decided that the level of risk associated with the event is acceptable but must be shared with other parties. Typically two transfer strategies are used. By incorporating the event into the umbrella insurance policy of your agency, additional insurance coverage for your event may be obtained. As mentioned earlier, this is desirable as insurance company representatives are trained to reduce and eliminate risk and often will provide organizers with many standards and recommendations to reduce the insurer's and the organizer's exposure to risk. Informing participants of the inherent risks of a particular event and enjoining them to sign hold harmless agreements or waivers is a second strategy used to transfer risk to others. While this effort does not remove the sponsoring agency from its legal responsibilities, it does hold some weight as evidence of proper preparation on the part of the agency.

Control

Relevant feedback through accident reporting, data collection, and analysis helps the event organizer to control risk in the future. A successful risk management plan should reduce the frequency and severity of loss in subsequent events. By *establishing loss prevention goals* on an annual basis the organizers position safety and risk management as a process open to improvement and a source of motivation for staff and volunteers. *Identifying additional training needs* well before an event, and *communicating a schedule of training opportunities* at the beginning of the event season will further focus attention on the need for continued improvement in safety considerations. By understanding where and why accidents occur and identifying effective practices to mitigate loss, the organization and the event will benefit by providing experiences for the public that are well managed and safe.

By considering risk management as a service provided to both the internal customer, comprised of direct staff members, volunteers, and other individuals within the larger context of the organization, and external customers including guests, sponsors, vendors, media representatives, one may develop a plan that satisfies the needs of all associated with the event or program.

Evaluation

Evaluation includes an analysis of several important factors and processes related to the event. All accidents and incidents should be documented using standardized reports completed by appropriate members of the event team. All reports should be entered into a database so that an overview of the level of risk-related incidents is quantified at the completion of the event. Any corrective actions taken during the course of the event should also be noted so that these changes will be incorporated into subsequent risk management plans. The training of staff and volunteers regarding risks should also be evaluated through surveys of those receiving the training and the examination of all actions taken by staff members during the event. In this way, the effectiveness of the training can be determined through the opinions and actions of those receiving the training. It is also recommended that a final analysis of the safety and risk management of the event be solicited from the local service providers including police, safety, traffic, and health officials. A review of all pertinent reports should also be conducted by the agency providing insurance for the event. Evaluation must be properly documented and combined with an implementation strategy that should be developed soon after the completion of the event so that the planning for the next event will benefit from the findings of the most recent operations.

Liability and the Law

This final section of the chapter provides an overview of some legal concepts that will aid in understanding the responsibilities of event organizers relative to civil and criminal law.

Understanding the most rudimentary aspects of liability and the law may help organizers to approach the issues of risk management with sufficient appreciation of the potential ramifications of a loss occurrence. This situation is predicated upon the fact that the event organizer assumes the following responsibilities in relation to their guests:

- The responsibility to provide adequate supervision
- The responsibility to provide appropriate and well-conducted activities
- The responsibility to provide safe and appropriate environmental conditions

Liability is closely related to the idea of responsibility in that liability means the level of obligation that one party owes another. In the legal world, this usually refers to your level of exposure to a lawsuit. If you are *liable*, you are responsible to another due to the relationship that you have with the other party. What this means in the realm of event management is that the organizers of an event have a responsibility to those who attend the event and those who involve themselves in the event in other ways such as volunteers, supporters, and employees. The organizers are liable for damages should anything happen to any of these individuals that would harm them or deny them their basic rights. The event organizers may fail to do something that they should have done (omission) or may do something that they should not have done (commission). In either case, if these behaviors result in injury or loss on the part of the visitor, the event representatives may be liable for damages. This situation is referred to as *negligence*, a legal term suggesting that the accused party had a legal duty to provide a certain level of care. Negligence can be described as failing to conform to acceptable standards of care resulting in some form of injury to another party if such behavior is determined to be the proximate cause for the injury. Loss, damage, or harm is characterized as *economic loss, physical pain or suffering, emotional distress, or physical impairment.*

Laws governing negligence are controlled on a state level and should be reviewed prior to the actual staging of a public event. The measure of negligence is sometimes equated to what is called the *prudent person* standard. *Prudence* means using good judgment, being wise and sensible. Any action of an individual or organization can be measured against what a prudent person would do in the same situation. A higher standard may be applied to event organizers, as the measure of prudence is that of a prudent professional. This suggests that individuals and groups who offer events to the public are expected to have professional training and judgment beyond that of the average prudent person.

Prudence includes the idea of *forseeability*, suggesting that a prudent person would anticipate certain situations that may cause harm to others. It is the duty of the event organizer to exercise foresight in creating a safe, well-supervised environment for the guests. This is why a risk management program is so important to the financial and institutional well being of an event-producing organization. The steps used to analyze and take action relative to risk has a direct effect in lowering the level of liability of an organization that provides activities and experiences for the public.

Summary

All of us in our daily lives make both conscious and unconscious adjustments to our behaviors due to our innate sense of risk management. When undertaking a project with the size and scope of a special event it is not sufficient to rely on the innate capabilities of individuals. The event must be considered as a living organism that must be protected from unnecessary risk and loss. This requires developing both a culture of safety amongst all those involved with the planning and implementation of the event. Risk is perceived and managed differently by different stakeholders requiring a plan that acknowledges and incorporates these diverse needs of all stakeholders into a comprehensive, effective, and manageable risk management plan.

Discussion Questions

1. How would you define risk management?
2. What are some potential losses associated with event management?
3. What are the four major mechanisms of a risk management plan?
4. How would you train your visitors to be aware of risk management issues at an event?
5. What precautions should be taken if alcohol is permitted at an event?
6. What is negligence and how is it related to standards of care?
7. What are the four major options in dealing with a risk?
8. How do severity and frequency relate to risk management?
9. Identify several control procedures that may effectively reduce future risk?
10. Why is risk management considered a fiscal issue in event management?

The following websites provide valuable perspectives on risk management, legal liability and appropriate standards of care:

www.aria.org, American Risk and Insurance Association

www.parma.com, FEMA site

www.sra.org, Society for Risk Analysis

www.riskworld.com

www.riskvue.com

www.nonprofitrisk.org

www.mcspotlight.org/mediaq/books/ritzer_excerpt.html

www.crowdsafe.com

www.factsontap.org

www.fipg.org

www.nhtsa.dot.gov

www.fda.gov

www.rff.org/crm_news/index.htm

www.fems.gov/emi/edu, this is a downloadable course on risk management for tourism and hospitality industries

www.esta.org, entertainment services and technology

1. Tarlow, P. (2002). *Event risk management and safety*. New York: John Wiley & Sons, p. 5.
2. Conrow, E. H. (2003). *Effective risk management* (2nd ed.). American Institute of Aeronautics and Astronautics, Inc., VA, p. 436.
3. Van Der Wagen, L., & Carlos Pearson, B. (2005). *Event management for tourism, cultural, business and sporting events*. New Jersey: Prentice Hall.

Section Three

Human Resource Management

This section includes chapters on developing a special events organization including paid staff and volunteers. You will also learn the importance of working with contractual employees and providing excellent customer service.

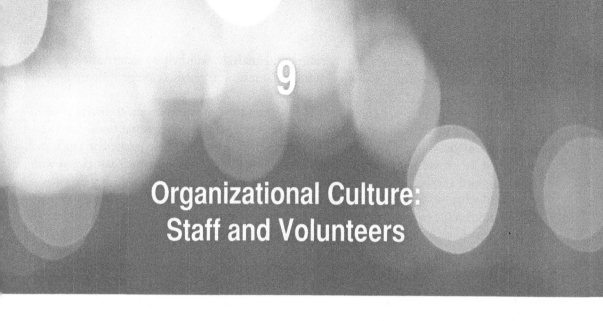

9

Organizational Culture: Staff and Volunteers

 It is generally wise to employ the fewest number of full-time permanent employees as possible.

Joe Goldblatt

Chapter Objectives

- Understand organizational culture
- Develop a process for event committee formation
- Differentiate between staff and volunteer responsibilities
- Describe effective volunteer management including recruitment, training, evaluation, and rewards
- Identify the principles of progressive discipline

This chapter examines the process of committee formation, the roles, relationships, and integration of full-time staff with an event committee, and important procedures necessary for effective volunteer management. Managing a special event is really about managing people, as the human resource element permeates all levels of event management. While financial resources create both opportunities and constraints to the scope and final status of an event, it is the people involved in the process who determine the level of success.

Understanding Organizational Culture

The first step in creating a successful event organization is to determine whether your event team, committee, agency, or whatever you choose to call it, is going to be primarily managed by existing paid staff members, by a community-based committee, or as a business-based board of directors. Understanding the current responsibilities and talents of your existing staff, through an environmental analysis, will help to determine what resources are available within your agency and what resources, in this case people, are needed from the outside.

When creating an event committee for the first time, it is important to invest time in creating a sense of organizational culture. These efforts should be directed toward answering the questions: who are we, and why are we working toward these particular goals and objectives? By providing the committee members with all relevant history associated with the event, and sharing a vision of the event's potential impact and future importance, a sense of identity, pride, and belonging can be nurtured in the group.

Oftentimes the committee is an extension of your existing agency and will likely adopt many of the characteristics of the larger organization. This is a positive development if your agency has the right personality to support an event-planning project. Ideally, an event committee should reflect the values of the agency and the demographics of the community that it serves.

Beyond the basics, event committee members should possess the organizational skills and community contacts needed to meet the event goals and objectives. Individual members should have a genuine interest in the type of event being planned and should bring a particular expertise to the committee. The scope and theme of the event will dictate the types of skills needed. Typically a committee benefits from members who may have expertise in marketing, volunteer management, entertainment management, concession and food service, facility and operational management, finance and fundraising, liability and risk management, or a particular expertise and set of experiences that match the type of event being planned (music, arts, historical enactments, and the like). In addition to task-specific skills, committees benefit from including individuals with a more general set of skills. These people may possess unbridled enthusiasm and optimism, an eagerness to get involved, and the ability to take on responsibilities and complete tasks. Political appointees and business leaders provide the necessary links to the resources needed from the greater community and should be welcomed and encouraged to become active committee members.

Once the group is assembled, it is paramount that sufficient time be spent in explaining the chain of command, the channels of communication, the time-management skills needed, and the resources available to accomplish tasks. Due to the deadlines and time limitations inherent in event management, it is important to develop effective working relationships very early in the process so that tasks may be assigned and the work may begin.

Creating a Task-Based Committee System

Effective leadership is necessary to support the formation of these working committees and to motivate all to establish SMART objectives for each committee. Reporting systems must be established so that committees understand the importance of timely communication and are aware of the procedures required in order to keep administrators and decision makers properly informed of accomplishments, challenges, and obstacles to success. General meetings of all those involved in the planning process are useful in order to continually communicate the big picture and to identify and reinforce the progress reported by each committee. Cross-fertilization of ideas through these general meetings helps to eliminate redundancies and allows for the sharing of solutions encountered during the process of accomplishing committee tasks. If time and resources allow, a web-based reporting system permits and encourages all committee members to track the efforts of other committees and will reinforce the need to share ideas and challenges while building a greater sense of group identity and purpose.

Most organizations make use of some form of *Robert's Rules of Order* in order to manage the flow of information and decision making needed for effective meetings. This set of parliamentary procedures was devised in 1876 by Henry Robert due to his need to run a local church meeting.[1] This guide is now in its 11th edition and is used by governmental organizations and many other groups that need to facilitate effective meeting management. The rules provide guidance for meeting attendance, voting procedures, the recording of official minutes of meetings, executive sessions, appointments, and resignations, and many other issues that typically arise in the course of holding meetings.

Strategic planning calls for all committee-related efforts to be linked with the marketing goals so that a synergistic relationship develops between the goals of the individual committees that will ultimately contribute to and support the marketing plan. Committee members must be mindful of the "message" of the event, as expressed through the mission statement or other guiding declarations of purpose. This is important when making decisions that impact the direction of the event or the perceptions of the event by other committee members and the general public.

Staff Involvement in Volunteer-Based Projects

Critical to the success of the event-planning group is its relationship with staff members who may actively participate in the process or may be called upon to provide ancillary or supervisory support to the group. Because volunteers hold such potential for an organization in terms of efficiencies and potentially beneficial expertise and service, a great deal of planning must precede the inclusion of volunteers in the event committee workforce. It is advisable to gradually introduce the volunteer element into your agency, selecting events with a limited scope so that the complexity of the event does not preclude the need to devote a great deal of attention to the initial formulation of your volunteer program. This means that full- and part-time staff must be involved in the assessment of the need for volunteers, the development of specific and complementary job descriptions, and the structuring of the volunteer force into the workflow of the organization. Included in this process is the need for existing staff members to fully understand the culture of their organization and their formal and informal roles within the organization. A review of written job descriptions and the actual job responsibilities of existing staff is necessary. Job responsibilities drift over time and may not match the written job description for a particular position within the organization. While keeping in mind any union-related issues, one must carefully craft volunteer jobs that actually will benefit the workplace rather than duplicate efforts and cause confusion for the paid staff. This is the clarification process of going from job descriptions to descriptions of the jobs. It is critical in supporting the buy-in process for existing employees. They must understand their roles in relation to the upcoming event-related tasks and understand precisely how a volunteer will add to the efficiency and effectiveness of the organizational effort. Providing the opportunity for staff members to more fully understand the responsibilities associated with their jobs is a very positive starting point for the development of a volunteer component for your agency.

In case anyone asks, you are technically initiating a human resource needs assessment relative to unmet challenges presented by the additional tasks associated with the planning and delivery of a special event. What is actually happening is you are returning a sense of control to your employees as they work through the process of volunteer development. Loss of control, or the perception of this negative outcome, is often the underlying reason for bad relations and dysfunctional working conditions between paid staff and volunteers. Volunteers come with enthusiasm and idealism that may have waned years ago in your paid staff. Volunteer workers can be seen as threatening by the more "established" members of your staff. The influx of ideas and energy associated with new personalities must be managed carefully. Volunteers must be positioned as resources that allow existing staff members the opportunity to strengthen their ability to perform their responsibilities and actually add a level of control to their jobs. Furthermore, volunteers must be seen as an asset rather than a threat for this arrangement to realize its greatest potential.

All that can be said about the inclusion of volunteers in an organization can be extended to interns. College students are required to have a guided work experience allowing them to obtain on the job training in an environment that is guided by professionals and evaluated by academic supervisors. In many cases students, particularly in the field of recreational services, must complete both an internship and a practicum in order to fulfill the requirements of the degree program. If an agency is sufficiently prepared, welcoming an intern into the organization can be a very positive experience for both the student and the staff. For more on internships see chapter eighteen.

Finally, you must consider the *opportunity costs* of assigning full-time staff to lead and manage an event based activity. Despite the fact that many recreational service providers enjoy fifty to sixty hour work weeks, the time and energy devoted to the demands of the event will mean a reduced amount of time spent on other important aspects of the agency's master plan for service delivery. Volunteers can help to reduce the opportunity costs associated with staging a special event. *Opportunity costs describe and quantify the loss of ability and resources to initiate activities or to continue existing activities based on the needs created by the resources dedicated to an event or other priority.* As we know, by redirecting personnel, funds, and equipment to a new special event, the opportunity to dedicate time and resources to existing programs may be diminished. Volunteers can provide ideas, labor, and other skills that reduce the demands on existing organizational resources without creating additional resource demands.

Overview of Volunteering

Volunteering is one of the most popular recreational activities in the U.S.[2] According to the Bureau of Labor Statistics, about 62.6 million individuals donated volunteer time between September 2012 and September 2013 (http://www.bls.gov/news.release/volun.nr0.htm). The majority of volunteer activity is of a short duration and is associated with a particular event. Short-term volunteer management requires a great deal of front-loaded planning and effort as the diversity of interests and the duration of the events require adequate preparation of the agency and the potential volunteer.

Volunteering is a necessary component of successful event management for a variety of reasons. Volunteer resources are critical to the effective operations of a special event as these events often extend beyond a normal workday to a full weekend or week-long series of activities. In its most basic form, volunteering meets the need to have warm bodies in place to perform a particular task at a particular time. Volunteers can more appropriately be considered a natural extension of the organizing agency. You have the opportunity to multiply your work force for a specific period of time in what are typically very public settings. For the successful event planner, however, volunteering must get beyond the basics. Volunteer activity must be viewed as a major opportunity for increased positive public relations for your agency. If your residents and guests have a positive perception of your agency based on their contact with your volunteer workforce, you are in a position to reach out to greater populations in a very constructive setting. Volunteers migrate from being external customers who have benefited from services provided, to being on the inside and participating in the creation and delivery of new experiences for the public. There is a definite multiplier effect to the goodwill generated by a well designed volunteer program. Volunteerism is a great opportunity for agency growth by not only expanding the workforce, but in challenging payroll staff to incorporate new personalities and talents into the makeup of the organization.

The Volunteer Coordinator

In the best-case scenario, an agency will have a trained professional who dedicates a portion of his/her work time to volunteer program management. In other cases, the volunteer coordinator may actually be a volunteer. The critical factor is the amount of training provided to this important leadership position. The volunteer coordinator should be communicating, not only the skills needed to volunteer for the agency, but also the personality, style, attitudes, and beliefs necessary to succeed with the agency. The volunteer coordinator becomes the face of the agency for the many volunteers who choose to offer their time and expertise. It is important that volunteers understand their responsibilities, but it is equally important that volunteers are provided some insight into the operations of the agency. This refers back to understanding the culture of the organization or the event. The greater the understanding of these important characteristics of the agency, the more inclined the volunteer might be in helping to achieve the goals of the project.

Volunteer management, like any other important aspect of resource management, requires thoughtful planning, group input, and a clearly identified set of objectives in order to fully realize the potential for positive results (see Figure 9.1). A *volunteer handbook* is a necessary tool that identifies organizational goals and objectives, as well as communicating the policies and procedures for programs and particular events.

As we know, policies provide an organizational perspective and the expected rules of conduct for the organization, while the procedures are the regulations that are used to implement these policies. The event operations manual will draw upon the guidelines found in the volunteer handbook as a baseline of expectations for volunteers.

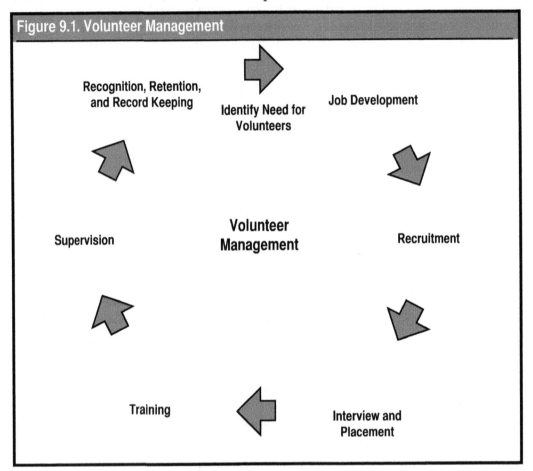

Figure 9.1. Volunteer Management

Volunteer Job Development

As described above, a well-planned volunteer program begins with an assessment of the existing work configurations within the organization. Identifying what is being accomplished by whom, and at what cost, is an important starting point. The answers to these questions might not match the actual formal job descriptions of the organization. This is not in itself a problem as long as it is adequately addressed and taken into account when determining the need for volunteers.

Staging an event is an appropriate time to introduce volunteers into an organization as the tasks associated with an event are easily identifiable and are limited by time and circumstance. The process has a beginning and an end and a finite number of necessary tasks. The actual details of the event being planned along with the present and anticipated responsibilities of payroll staff will determine the extent of volunteer assistance needed.

Volunteer jobs may address areas that staff cannot or are not interested in incorporating into their existing workload (see Table 9.1). Volunteers may also supplement staff to accomplish tasks that are best done in a shared environment due to the complexity of the work or time and resource restrictions. This may allow for a staff member to supervise a volunteer, providing job expansion for the staff member, and assistance in accomplishing their tasks. In the case of a special event, the feasibility of taking on a new event may be directly related to the inclusion of additional volunteer workers in order to address the challenges of the event realistically. Sufficient planning is required to analyze the event requirements in order to determine manageable *work units* that can then be assigned to staff and volunteers with adequate time and resources to accomplish the tasks.

Each volunteer should be provided with a job description specific to their position on the event management team. Detailed job descriptions must be developed in order to match volunteer skills and interests with the needs of the organization. In order to create a successful volunteer culture within an organization, the work for each volunteer must be meaningful and significant to both the volunteer and the organization. The job must have defined objectives and responsibilities so that the volunteer can experience success and closure, and the organization can measure effectiveness. The job descriptions should include responsibilities, required skills, time requirements, training needs, and lines of communication.

The characteristics of the event being organized will dictate both the need for particular skills and the assignment of relevant tasks. Despite the fact that many event related volunteer jobs are mundane, all are important to the success of the event. Each volunteer must understand that his/her efforts contribute to the success of the event. This suggests a need for job ownership and a sense of responsibility being imparted to the volunteer regardless of the duration or significance of the assigned tasks. Each volunteer should be encouraged to offer suggestions as to how their responsibilities and tasks may be better positioned in future events to more effectively accomplish the objectives of the job.

Volunteers will benefit from an orderly and predetermined means of regular communication and feedback prior to, during, and after the event. Being listened to and considered in the decision-making process will both insure a responsive and responsible volunteer workforce and will help to build organizational loyalty that will translate into individuals who return to volunteer in subsequent years.

Table 9.1. Typical Areas of Work for Event Volunteers

- administrative activities
- admission and gate control
- concessions
- entertainment and technical areas
- finance management
- gopher (go for this, go for that)
- information and customer service
- marketing
- operations and site management
- sponsor management
- ticket management
- volunteer management

Recruitment

The quality of volunteers for an event is directly related to the efforts made to creatively attract individuals who will make a positive contribution to the success of the event. An understanding of the human resources available in a community is a necessary starting point for the recruitment process. Are there *large businesses or corporations* within the region that value and encourage community involvement on the part of their employees? These businesses may also see benefits in becoming a corporate sponsor if the event satisfies public relations and community support objectives valued by

Volunteers can spell the difference between success and failure for many events.

corporate decision makers. If strategically positioned, this type of corporate involvement can easily become a win-win-win situation. A properly planned volunteer experience can be interpreted by the volunteers as a means of fulfilling professional and corporate goals, is supported and recognized by company supervisors, provides a high level of commitment and accomplishment for the event organizers, and provides tangible rewards such as civic and corporate pride and other forms of psychic income.

Every community seems to have its share of *civic organizations* that predicate their existence on community support and volunteerism. If their involvement can benefit both the event organizers and is perceived as beneficial to the club members, then there is a real possibility for a successful and effective relationship. Additional organized groups within the community should be identified and approached for volunteer resources. *Retired individuals* possess a wealth of knowledge and experience, based on their long working lives and often highly value the opportunity to give back to their communities. Many schools require *community service hours* on the part of their students. Involvement in an event that attracts their peers and is perceived as a cool thing to do may allow for the development of a young and loyal group of volunteers for the future. College-age students might find an event management internship or practicum to be a very valuable experience and should certainly be considered in the search for interested and qualified individuals.

Volunteer recruitment for a new event is time consuming but is time well spent, as future events will benefit from the early success of these efforts. The process cannot be accomplished in a few weeks as it requires a gradual building of interest on the part of the potential volunteers. If key stakeholders in the event are all given the task of finding ten or more volunteers though personal contacts, the number may grow exponentially. It is not sufficient to wait until the volunteer orientation meeting just prior to your event to determine if you have enough people. A process of identifying and enlisting volunteers should be seen as an ongoing effort for months prior to and after the event. Advocating for volunteer involvement for your event and your agency should be a continuous process. If volunteers feel valued, are provided clear directions and responsibilities, have the opportunity to enjoy themselves, and are recognized for their efforts, they will become the recruitment team for future years.

Interview and Placement

Most volunteer opportunities offer the possibility to select a job from a list of various tasks that need to be accomplished. This creates a rather unique interview scenario as the interview need not be job specific. What is being evaluated is the ability of the individual to fit into the organization in a meaningful way. While certain jobs require definite skills, the organization is generally looking for someone who is reliable, enthusiastic, willing to accept responsibility, and is realistic about their role within the organization. The agency is looking for that element of "good fit." Does the individual represent him/herself in such a way as to communicate the ability to work productively in a group setting? Is the motivation for volunteering clear to the volunteer as well as to the agency representative? This aspect of motivation is important in determining the appropriateness and level of their involvement in your agency's projects. It is also important to ascertain the level of knowledge that the potential volunteer has of the organization; has she/he been involved in other agency activities? Does they understand the mission of the agency and the objectives of this particular event? One must determine the strengths and weaknesses of the individual relative to their involvement in your event. In determining a good fit, it is also useful to know whether the individual prefers working on detailed cognitive projects or enjoys physical work. Do they enjoy working alongside other staff and volunteers or are they happier working behind the scenes in relative solitude? Do observable personality characteristics support the type of work that they have expressed an interest in undertaking?

Interviewing volunteers is also a sales job. Volunteerism has lost some appeal over the last few decades, and it is sometimes difficult to entice community members to get involved in a volunteer activity. The agency should be prepared to answer questions raised by the candidate concerning the job possibilities and the necessary responsibilities and qualifications for each position. Some volunteers, for whatever reason, really just want to use a two-way radio and get a free t-shirt. Again, understanding motivations can help to satisfy both agency and volunteer needs. It is also advisable to have information and materials about your agency and its programs, including the benefits of association with the organization, available to potential volunteers.

The interview should be the time to initiate a positive rapport with the candidates, to show appreciation for their interest in your organization, and to highlight the positive outcomes of their involvement. The interview should focus on the interests, aspirations, and availability of the volunteer. Have the candidates share their perspective on how they would manage a particular job for the organization. It is also the appropriate time to review the agency requirements outlined in specific job descriptions found in the volunteer operations manual.

Should the individual prove to be an acceptable candidate, an explanation of the procedures that follow the initial interview should be offered. This may include a second interview with additional staff members, and it may require a background or reference check. Any required training sessions and the timeframe for involvement should be discussed so that both parties are in agreement on the future direction of the process. If a printed job description can be given to the new volunteer it will increase interest and ownership in the commitment.

Training

Volunteers must be developed. They should be assigned to work with staff or senior volunteers who are capable of supervising their activities in a productive fashion by providing ongoing direction, evaluation, and feedback. Far too often an individual expresses an interest in volunteering for an event and is told to show up the day of the event and expects to receive an assignment at that time. This approach sends all the wrong messages to the volunteer: the job cannot be too important, the volunteer is not important, the organization of the event is last minute and probably crisis prone. If a volunteer orientation meeting is not held, or if proper training is neither valued nor required, a certain level of incompetence will become acceptable and will be reflected in the efforts and results of volunteer involvement.

An adequately publicized, organized, and well-attended orientation meeting sends a very positive, professional message to volunteers. That message is: who they are and what they are doing is very important to the success of the event and is greatly appreciated. A volunteer meeting is a time to build excitement about the event, to reach out to new volunteers, to brainstorm about the challenges that lie ahead, and is a time to review and inculcate the values and procedures that make yours an exceptional organization and event. The purpose of the orientation meeting is to integrate the volunteer into the workplace and create a sense of readiness and competence in completing tasks. General topics that should be addressed in the orientation meeting are included in Table 9.2.

Any necessary paperwork such as volunteer registration and waiver forms, insurance, and contact information should be completed at this time. It is also advisable to have all volunteers sign paperwork acknowledging that they attended the orientation session, received and read the volunteer manual, and have a reasonable understanding of the responsibilities of their involvement with agency activities.

Table 9.2. Volunteer Meeting Agenda

- Introduction to the agency and its representatives
- Explanation of the goals and objectives of the event
- Role and scope of supervision
- Rights and responsibilities of the volunteers
- A review of the volunteer manual
- Identification and explanation of the lines of communication
- Accident procedures
- Scheduling and attendance and absenteeism
- Dress code
- Performance evaluation procedures
- Progressive discipline policies
- Parking and access to the site
- Activities when off duty
- Exit interview procedures
- Recognition and celebration of accomplishments

Supervision

Volunteers are risky business and they are not "free." An agency may be exposing itself to significant risk and loss unless sufficient thought and time is given to the selection and training of volunteers. Volunteers, particularly for short term events, are relative strangers that an agency entrusts with its financial and physical resources and the anticipated enjoyment of its visitors. There is certainly the opportunity for theft, fraud, misrepresentation, and other obvious examples of malfeasance on the part of a volunteer. Of equal importance, and perhaps more likely to occur, is a loss of public perception, good will, and reputation that can occur due to poorly trained, disgruntled, or ineffective volunteers. Many times volunteers are in positions of greeting the public and creating that all-important first impression of your event and agency. This reality cannot be minimized when one is planning appropriate training and supervision of volunteers.

Organizers must discuss the arrangements necessary to ensure the appropriate supervision of all volunteers. Volunteer positions require different levels of expertise, have varying impacts on the safety and success of the event, and thereby require different levels of supervision. It is wise to develop a code to identify the level of supervision needed for each volunteer position to be included in the job description. This strategy should also be explained to the volunteer so that he understands the chain of command and the level of contact with supervisors that will take place during the event. A common complaint of volunteers is that when they are confronted with a problem or issue they do not know how to handle, they could not identify the correct individual to intervene and solve the problem. Volunteers must be aware of the level of responsibility and authority associated with their position. Volunteers must also be aware of the resources at their disposal in order to successfully complete their work.

In some cases, particularly those involving the interface between planning and technology, volunteers may be able to accomplish tasks prior to the event at their homes or regular places of business. It is important to establish reporting procedures so that the volunteer is apprised of time-sensitive deadlines and quality control issues. Reporting procedures must be clearly explained and adhered to by the volunteers and the supervisor.

If the volunteer is to work out of the agency office, there must be sufficient workspace (phone, computer, etc.) for the volunteer to accomplish the assigned tasks.

Delegation Nation

At the heart of volunteer management is the art of delegation. Delegation involves a realistic assessment of the needs of the organization, the time constraints of staff members, and the abilities of the volunteer workforce to take on particular responsibilities. Staff members must identify the highest and best use of their time, thereby also identifying those tasks that can be effectively delegated to volunteers. Volunteer coordinators should attempt to match jobs to individual capabilities, interests, and strengths. Combined with sufficient, specific training, the job requirements are then fully understood by the volunteer and the opportunity has been given to ask questions in order to clarify all aspects of the job.

Delegation is Intimately Linked to Evaluation

The volunteer must fully understand what a satisfactory job entails. Oftentimes the completion of a task is left to chance, and one person's opinion of a "good job" may not meet the expectations of the agency: "The cash drawer was only short by $10." This can only be avoided by clear communication of the necessary standards of the job. Evaluation of the volunteer's job performance should be tied to these communicated standards of satisfaction. Evaluation of volunteers, as in all situations, should be a process rather than a single event. This means that continuous performance appraisal is preferably combined with a post event evaluation. Feedback provided during the event encourages volunteers to do a good job, can allow for intervention to correct existing deficiencies, and leads to a greater chance for success for the volunteer and the supervisor, translating into a higher quality experience for the event participant. Periodic feedback also helps in establishing milestones for volunteers if their job extends over any length of time. It is natural to feel better about a job if progress and success can be experienced along the way. Consistent levels of communication with volunteers also raise the level of accountability on the part of the volunteer and can make them feel valued. Evaluation during the event does not, however, preclude a thorough post event evaluation or exit interview, allowing the organizers to gain a fuller perspective on the volunteer experience. Alterations to the job descriptions, resource allotments, and levels of supervision may be undertaken due to this valuable input.

A final and perhaps less tangible guideline for delegation is the ability of the organization to foster a sense of ownership, or buy in, on the part of the volunteer. Creating an environment of mutual trust, communicating the importance of their efforts to the success of the event, showing appreciation for and confidence in their abilities and commitment, and encouraging and acting upon volunteer input, all contribute to a sense of loyalty and good will. Through the delegation process, volunteers can exercise creative problem solving, further contributing to the quality of the event. Some volunteers thrive on a sense of accomplishment and should be made aware of chances for advancement to higher levels of responsibility based on successful completion of present assignments.

Progressive Discipline

Occasionally a volunteer does not perform to the required standards of the job. This is usually an unpleasant and sometimes difficult situation for a staff member or supervisor. Volunteerism, by its very nature, is a positive response to the needs of others. One would like to assume that both the motivations and commitment to the task at hand would ensure a positive experience for all. But we know better. If properly planned for, any needed discipline will be handled in a predictable, professional manner with minimum distraction or disruption to the positive energy associated with the event. This can only be accomplished if the issue of progressive discipline is discussed and planned for long before the need to enact corrective interventions.

The word *discipline* comes from the Latin *discipulus*, a pupil or follower. The concept is one of leading others and thereby nurturing a sense of follower-ship on the part of others. In this case, it is the need for individuals with limited knowledge and experience about your agency to be motivated to follow procedures set up to aid in the accomplishment of event related tasks. Discipline is not punitive but corrective, in that the effort is made to help individuals change behaviors and follow procedures that are related to the goals of the organization.

Progressive discipline is a necessary component of your volunteer handbook. Problem behaviors in the volunteer realm include issues such as the quality and timeliness of work performed, attendance, dependability, and generally unacceptable work, as well as behaviors such as dishonesty and a lack of sobriety. The ability to work with others and actually serve the public should not be assumed and must be addressed during orientation and training. Role playing and problem solving exercises can help volunteers to internalize desired behaviors. It is helpful if disciplinary action is based on the program that is already in place for paid staff. Decisions must be made as to the levels of discipline to be imposed and the desired behavioral changes required of the volunteer. The following procedures are generally used for full time employees. Due to the legal implications of any form of discipline for paid or volunteer staff, it is advisable for all supervisors to be aware of and incorporate a high standard of enforcement of agency policies and procedures.

When an incident occurs a thorough investigation of the reported infraction must take place and should include any and all witnesses, in addition to a statement from the volunteer. The *Just Cause Standard* requires that a supervisor determine that there is substantial evidence that an infraction was committed. The volunteer should be apprised ahead of time that a particular behavior is viewed as detrimental to the agency and could lead to disciplinary action. The policies must be fair and administered in a non-discriminatory manner, meaning that all volunteers should be treated equally, while accounting for any extenuating circumstances that might have bearing on the case. The volunteer must be given ample opportunity, in a nonthreatening environment, to fully explain and defend their actions. It is also advisable to allow the volunteer, as one would for a paid employee, the opportunity for representation during any meetings related to an infraction or the determination of disciplinary action as outlined in the Weingarten Rights clause of labor law. The degree of discipline must be in proportion to the infraction and be in the best interest of the operational and safety considerations of the agency.

Most policies allow for a supervisor to skip a step or two dependent upon the circumstances involved. It is always better and more effective to follow the steps whenever possible.

Infractions, as described in Table 9.3, are generally identified in terms of severity, including minor, moderate, and major infractions.

Table 9.3. Discipline Progression
Examples of Infractions Requiring Progressive Discipline
Minor: abuse of time, failure to show up at appointed time, dress code violations, discourteous behavior with staff or visitors, damage to equipment, general harassment, low work output or quality, minor safety violations
Moderate: non-cooperation, improper conduc, creating a disturbance, sexual or racial harassment, safety violations and other significant examples of misbehavior
Major: willful damage to property, theft, fraud, use of alcohol or drugs, fighting, assault, threatening, weapon possession, acts of violence, insubordination

In the case of a long-term volunteer commitment, you may find yourself in the unenviable position of having a volunteer who has broken several policies. This requires that each infraction have its own case development. This entails accurate record keeping so that a lateness problem, for example, has its own case history regarding the number of infractions and actions taken and is viewed independently from a second infraction involving other policies such as improper conduct or low-quality work output.

The only way progressive discipline is effective is if all actions are properly documented through the use of disciplinary action forms, letters sent to the individual involved in the investigation, accurate minutes from all meeting and investigative actions, and proper documentation of remedies used (see Table 9.4). Each document must contribute in a logical and chronological way to the overall proper administration of agency policies and procedures concerning progressive discipline. Any letter sent to the volunteer must include a factual exposition of events, behaviors, or deficiencies encountered, and a listing of rules and standards violated. Reference should be made to prior counseling or discipline, and the volunteer should be made aware of the nature and amount of improvement needed. The volunteer should be made fully and clearly aware of the consequences if improvement is not achieved.

If the only viable solution is to release the volunteer from service, it should be done with care, kindness, and clarity. In many cases, the dismissal of a volunteer causes the individual to harbor bad feelings toward the agency. This is sometimes unavoidable and could be indicative of the general disposition of the individual that might have led to the problems now being addressed. A dismissal meeting is not a time for analysis or debate. The meeting is held after the facts have been determined, counseling and discipline have taken place, and there is little or no chance for positive change. It is advisable to have another staff member present as a witness to the proceedings and to allow the volunteer to also have someone

Table 9.4. Volunteer Discipline Policy
Customary Steps in a Volunteer Progressive Discipline Policy
Counseling that is recorded Verbal warnings that are recorded Written warnings Dismissal Law enforcement intercession

present. If there are any questions about liability or risk, it is important to review the intended proceedings with your agency director or legal counsel. The charges and disposition should be presented verbally and should be supported by a written document that presents the same information.

You might have the individual sign a statement that she has read and understands the situation as it is presented. The signature does not indicate that the volunteer necessarily agrees with the termination but indicates cognizance on their part of the actions being taken. Use the opportunity of the meeting to collect any and all materials that belong to the agency so that the break in the relationship is immediate and final. Thorough and accurate documentation of the meeting is needed and might include having your witness attest to the accuracy of the report. There might be a need for communication with other staff and volunteers to acknowledge the results of the meeting without divulging confidential information about the individual. Being proactive, direct, and sensitive will help to thwart rumors and speculation on the part of other volunteers. This information regarding progressive discipline should be reviewed prior to a volunteer engaging in work with your agency and should be covered in sufficient detail during the orientation and subsequent training sessions.

Recognition, Record Keeping, and Retention

Motivation

Volunteerism by definition is offering assistance without the expectation of compensation. This does not mean that volunteers offer their time and expertise for nothing. Research indicates that volunteers typically get involved for a few important and sometimes very logical reasons. Research has identified many of the motivations for volunteering, but it is left to the Arts to capture what cannot be quantified. Consider the words of David Tamulevich and Michael Hough of the group Mustard's Retreat in their song:

Let's Hear it for the Volunteers

And it's one, two, three, hey!
Help them put the chairs away
If it wasn't for them we wouldn't be here.
Let's hear it for the volunteers.

Kathy is the one in the yellow pants
She loves the music, but she can't dance
But with her computer, now she writes grants.
Let's hear it for the volunteers.

Then there's Andy he works the sound
Thunderstorm's a coming, and he looks around
He all patched in but he's lost his ground.
Let's hear it for the volunteers.

It ain't for money, cause they work for free,
We're a great dysfunctional family.
Its all for the music and the company
Let's hear it for the volunteers!

Reprinted with permission of David Tamulevich

Researchers would call these *intrinsic and extrinsic motivational factors.* And while it is difficult to sing along with a research paper, here is what some scholars have found about volunteer motivation.

Henderson (1980) identifies three types of volunteers based on their motivation for involvement. There are certain volunteers who are motivated by *achievement.* They enjoy responding to a challenge and reaching a desired goal. Typically these individuals have experienced success in their lives and seek to reinforce competencies by accepting new and diverse challenges. There are others who are motivated by *affiliation,* the need to belong to and identify with a group. The value for them is in social interaction and relationship building and reinforcement. Finally, there are individuals motivated by *power.* This is not a negative factor if the realization of power is found in aiding others to achieve goals. This striving for significance can help the organization and the volunteers to meet their needs in a positive fashion.[3]

In reality, the motives are usually more complex than these, but they indicate the need for organizers to consider the fact that people are motivated by different reasons when offering their assistance. The better this is identified and understood, the more effective the volunteer effort may become. Demographics, socioeconomic status, and individualistic vs. community-based value systems may also play a role in satisfying volunteer motivations. It has also been noted that there are certain generational differences in the motivation to volunteer. Prior affiliation or identification with the event is also considered a strong factor when determining appropriate rewards and incentives for volunteers.

Farrell (1998) suggests that the intrinsic motivation for volunteering may be dependent upon the nature of the volunteer activity. Working from the earlier studies in human services, Farrell devised the *Special Event Volunteer Motivation Scale*, which resulted in the identification of four main factors when considering motivation to volunteer.[4] See Table 9.5.

Table 9.5. Special Event Volunteer Motivation Scale

Purposive – a desire to contribute and do something useful

Solidarity – a desire for social interaction and group identification

External Traditions – following family traditions of volunteering

Commitments – linking external expectations of the volunteer experience with personal skills related to the tasks

Volunteers often enjoy the rewards of working as a team.
Photo Credit: Deb Droppers Event Company

Additional research furthered this line of inquiry, confirming that community involvement as a means of positive contribution (purposive) and belonging to the community (solidarity) can be used as effective recruitment and retention strategies for volunteers. Less important were material incentives such as free tickets and other items. Long-term volunteers, with over five years of consecutive service to the same organization, were seen by Slaughter (2004) as being primarily motivated by doing something worthwhile that will benefit society, a desire to socialize and be a part of the community, to gain new skills, as well as being a response to external pressures and the expressed desire for tangible material gains.[5]

Understanding the underlying motivational factors that inspire individuals to volunteer is time well spent. Reward systems are most effective if they reinforce the basic needs satisfaction scenario of each volunteer. Based on the research presented, and with a little common sense, volunteer motivation may be grouped into a few categories. Reward systems may then be fashioned for a particular group of volunteers producing effective and meaningful rewards.

Rewards

Van Der Wagen (2005) suggests some nonmonetary rewards for volunteers that can be fostered through adequate planning and leadership. Job rotation allows volunteers to try different jobs throughout the course of their involvement with your event, which can be an exciting and fulfilling experience. Others may highly value the opportunity for involvement with celebrities. Some volunteers are content knowing that they are providing meaningful service to the organization and are content to receive verbal praise and the opportunity to develop relationships and friendships with other volunteers, staff members, and the public. For others the possibility of recognition in the media, free tickets, t-shirts, a certificate, or other types of rewards are very satisfying.[6]

Rewards can be classified as either material goods or activities. Items such as pins, certificates, souvenirs of the event such as event staff t-shirts or other clothing items, a video of the highlights of the event and other memorabilia are often greatly appreciated. Post event activities that are seen as rewards include a wrap-up party, which can combine recognition elements with an analysis of the event. A more formal recognition dinner or a presentation before the city council can also be a valuable form of recognition. Group building efforts are also an effective means of recognizing volunteer efforts and building a sense of camaraderie, an expressed motivator for many volunteers. All volunteers respond positively to a genuine and enthusiastic thank you. Positive feedback, during and after the event, goes a long way to solidifying a positive relationship between an agency and a volunteer. It is the feeling of appreciation that is the goal of any type of recognition. Verbal praise is both cost effective and very much appreciated. A letter to the volunteer on official stationery, or a letter of recommendation at a later date, is valued by individuals who seek to parlay their experience into an employment opportunity.

Record Keeping

A truly well-functioning organization will plan for and ensure that accurate records are kept of volunteer activity. This is frequently the case with organizations that use volunteers on a regular, repetitive basis. Volunteers typically sign in, record their hours, and are usually recognized on an annual basis for the number of hours that they have donated to the organization. Having a staff member or a volunteer coordinator to oversee this procedure ensures that volunteers are accurately accounted for. It is a little more challenging to achieve the same results during a short duration event with numerous one time volunteers. One might be inclined to think that as long as the jobs were completed and the volunteers were thanked, then all went well. The value of the volunteer experience goes beyond the accomplishment of a particular task during the event. Volunteers represent new customers for your agency. Their present involvement with your agency was not just helping at a swim class or tennis lesson but an actual chance to learn about and participate in the production of a special event. This public relations opportunity should not be minimized. Future support for the event and your agency can be enhanced by volunteer input. Furthermore, when calculating the value of your agency to the community, in addition to providing a high-quality event, the total number of volunteer hours accumulated during the event has a real economic value. Your agency has saved a significant and identifiable amount of money by using volunteers rather than an increased reliance on paid staff. The event is being offered at a great savings to the community due to the hundreds of hours of labor provided by the volunteers. When feasible, having standardized work shifts makes the record keeping process much easier to manage. The volunteers, in addition to their personal reasons for volunteering, always seem to respond favorably to the recognition of the number of hours or shifts that they worked. These can be kept from year to year quite easily, building a system for long-term volunteer recognition.

Retention

Volunteers will return to your event if the memories of their experience are positive. The reward systems described above help to create a tangible bond between the volunteer and the event. The perceived prestige, or coolness factor, of the event will also help to convince volunteers to return year after year. This sense of association with a successful event is a powerful retention tool and one that has additional benefits in recruiting new volunteers. If your volunteers were well treated, had a clear understanding of their responsibilities, were supported in their efforts, and felt a sense of accomplishment, they will tell others of the positive experience associated with the event. These positive feelings can be reinforced through off season contact by way of a newsletter, blogs, planning meetings for next year's event that are open to all volunteers, and by inviting volunteers to continue their association with your agency by volunteering or participating in other events or programs throughout the year. Again, this process reflects upon the motivational factors that create the desire to volunteer in the first place. Your agency and events can meet very real social, affiliative, and personal needs for members of your community.

Why Volunteers Don't Return

Volunteers may choose not to return to your event for many reasons, some logical and some that will remain a mystery. Their reasons may be a reflection on the management of the event, while others may be representative of changing interests or lack of continued commitment to your event. Competing interests from home and work may also challenge the commitment of a volunteer to your event. Organizers must be conscious of this but should also remain flexible in their approach to the type of help that the individual can provide. The event might lose meaning for the volunteer due to these competing interests or it might be a part of their natural growth and personal evolution.

If, however, the reasons for volunteer disassociation are the result of a negative experience, such as a feeling of a lack of appreciation, ambiguity, or confusion regarding their volunteer responsibilities or other organizational shortcomings, action must be taken to remedy the situation. This proactive stance, combined with an active recruitment program should ensure a continuing pool of enthusiastic and well-motivated volunteers.

Summary

Volunteering remains an important leisure activity for a significant number of our citizens. Despite a recent decline in overall numbers of individuals committed to the volunteer ranks, many schools and universities are including volunteering as a necessary experience for students. This type of civic involvement benefits not only the volunteer but builds community cohesiveness and pride. The economic implications of volunteer efforts are enormous. Many events simply would not be viable without an active and constantly replenished volunteer group. Volunteer management must be approached as an indispensible element of contemporary event management.

Discussion Questions

1. What are some areas of management associated with a special event, and how does this influence committee formation?
2. Why are volunteers so important to the success of an event?
3. What are some potential problems that might arise when incorporating volunteers into an organization that has existing staff members?
4. What are six tasks associated with volunteer management?
5. Identify four areas of an event that could benefit from volunteer involvement.
6. Why is a volunteer handbook important to the continued success of an event?
7. What are some potential sources for volunteers in a community?
8. Why is volunteer training so important to both the event organizers and the volunteers?
9. What are the keys to success in volunteer management?
10. List five means of recognition and reward for volunteers.

1. Retrieved from http://www.robertsrules.com/history.html
2. Lynch, R., & McCurley, S. (1999). *Essential volunteer management*. Downers Grove, IL: Heritage Arts Press.
3. Henderson, K. A. (September 1980). Programming volunteerism for happier volunteers. *Parks and Recreation*, pp. 61–64.
4. Farrell, J., Johnson, M., & Twynam, G. (1998). Volunteer motivation, satisfaction, and management at an elite sporting competition. *Journal of Sport Management 12*(4), 288–300.
5. Slaughter, L., & Home, R. Motivations of long-term volunteers: Human services vs. events. Retrieved from http://hotel.unlv.edu/pdf/MotivationsofLTvolunteers.pdf
6. Van Der Wagen, L., & Carlos Pearson, B. (2005). *Event management for tourism, cultural, business, and sporting events*. New Jersey: Prentice Hall, p. 179.

10

Contractual Services–Entertainment and Special Services

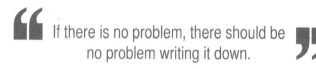

" If there is no problem, there should be no problem writing it down. "

Cash Edwards

Chapter Objectives

- Understand basic contract law
- Identify the benefits of using contractual service providers
- Enumerate the components of an effectively written contract
- Understand how to coordinate the services of other professionals

In assessing the strengths and weaknesses of your event organization, it is likely that you will find that certain skill sets are not within the repertoire of your staff or volunteers. In addition, there are many activities related to a successful event that you might choose not to take on within your organization. Fortunately, the growth of the service industry includes the existence of many specialty businesses that can adequately supply the service needs identified through your strategic planning process. Contractual strategies attempt to balance the resources and needs of the organizing agency so that the effective use of these resources and outside service providers results in the best possible product for your stakeholders.

Risk management, as described in Chapter 8, is an important consideration as you decide which activities to perform in-house and which are more effectively and safely done by outside contractors. Transferring risk to outside agencies through contractual service agreements accomplishes two important management tasks. The financial exposure to risk is reduced through inclusion of additional insured parties, and the level of competence in accomplishing critical tasks is raised through professional agencies that perform these types of tasks on a regular basis. In addition to risk factors, contractual relationships allow for a higher level of quality control by employing specialists in many service areas.

Contractual services may be used to provide expertise in the areas of overall event management, marketing, public relations, accounting services, construction, hygiene and sanitation, maintenance, entertainment, concessions, technical services including lighting, sound amplification and special effects, security, medical services, and traffic control. The specific characteristics of an event may include other necessary services that may be best accomplished through contractual agreements.

Recreational agencies often involve themselves on different levels in event management. Some events are produced solely by recreational service agencies that provide many of the resources needed to plan and produce an event. Recreational agencies may also co-sponsor events with other community agencies, and also frequently provide venues for outside producers to create a special event. For each of these situations, it is necessary that accurate contractual agreements be in place to identify the rights and responsibilities of each party.

What Makes for an Effective Contract?

An effective contract is one that is based on a solid understanding of the basics of contract law and is written in such a way that it is clearly understandable and enforceable.

The effectiveness of a contract is measured by whether it results in the parties understanding and performing the required action as specified in the contract.

Legal recourse provides a means of enforcing the conditions of a contract if an impasse is reached and a negotiated resolution becomes impossible.

Contract Law

In its simplest form, a contract is created when two or more persons promise each other to do something in return for something else. We enter into contracts frequently each day as a normal course of action. Trading desserts in the lunchroom could have been the first training many of us experienced in the art of negotiation and contract management.

Contractual relationships find their basis in the natural law of reciprocity. Natural law suggests activities that occur in nature and are not designed by written law or past practice. *Reciprocity* suggests that when one individual performs a task to the benefit of another, there is the expectation of a return action of equal value. One party reciprocates relative to the actions of the first party. It is considered a natural law because it occurs in nature without the need for specific training. It is the proverbial "I'll scratch your back if you scratch mine" scenario.

More formally, a contract is a legally binding agreement between two or more parties that imposes some kind of obligation or responsibility on each party. Contracts take many forms, from a simple exchange of words accompanied by a handshake, to a detailed multi-chapter document that might be indecipherable to the average college educated individual. Certain contracts for things like real property, goods in excess of five hundred dollars, or the agreement to be responsible for debt, should be put in writing.

Contracts are governed either by statutory law, common law, or private law. *Statutory laws* include all national, state, and municipal rules, regulations, and codes that govern behavior and are enacted for the betterment of society. These are sometimes referred to as ordinances or regulations. There are a number of state and local ordinances that may impact the planning and delivery of a special event. *Common law* is based on non-statutory precedents set by past court rulings and are enforceable in certain jurisdictions. *Private law* principally includes the terms of the agreement between the parties who are exchanging promises. Private law is the area of law that includes contracts and the rights and responsibilities of those who choose to enter into these types of agreements with other individuals or legal entities. The Uniform Commercial Code, used in nearly every state, is a body of statutory law that governs important categories of contracts. The main articles that deal with contract law are Article 1(General Provisions) and Article 2 (Sales). The purpose as stated in the General Provisions (Article 1 section 1-103) is to "simplify, clarify, and modernize the law governing commercial transactions; to permit the continued expansion of commercial practices through custom, usage, and agreement of the parties; and to make uniform the law among the various jurisdictions".[1]

Oral or verbal agreements, though legally binding, are subject to misinterpretation, modification, misunderstanding and fraud, and should be avoided in all but the most casual situations. If you can afford to lose the money or do without the provision of goods or services identified in your agreement, then a verbal contract will suffice.

Contracts set boundaries, identifying those items included in the agreement to the exclusion of any considerations not specifically addressed or implied by the language of the contract. If a contract is well written and clearly understood, all other processes or developments outside of the language of the written contract will not be considered. The answer to most questions involving a contractual dispute begins with a review of the exact language in the contract.

Contract Management

Contract management is a major component of modern business, addressing the level of specialization needed to accomplish complicated and highly specific tasks. Contracts typically include a set of components that not only address the exchange of things of value, but also anticipate and provide direction for the resolution of unmet expectations.

A contract begins with the identification of the needs of one party and the offering of resources on the part of the other party that can effectively satisfy these needs. When both parties communicate an understanding of this situation and prove to be capable of entering into a relationship, it is said that the parties have arrived at a *meeting of the minds*. This suggests that the parties are willing to enter into a mutually beneficial contractual situation with a general understanding of the possible components or conditions. These components may also include an agreement to refrain from doing certain things. This presupposes two important elements that define a legally binding contract. Both parties must be capable of entering into a contractual relationship. *Legal capacity* to enter into a contract is defined as being free from coercion, intellectually capable of understanding the conditions of the contract, and being of legal age as defined by state or local statute. The activity under consideration must be a *legal subject,* meaning that the activity or service sought must not be in violation of any laws. One cannot enter into a legally binding contract for goods or services that do not conform to acceptable social behavior as defined by federal, state, or local ordinance. You will not find the local drug dealer filing a lawsuit in a local small claims court for a deal gone bad, because illicit drugs are not a legal subject.

The meeting of the minds may include the process of offering the opportunity of providing services to a number of potential partners through a bidding process. Local agency regulations will dictate the procedures for the bid process. This could include procedures for writing the bid specifications, advertising the bid opportunity, a review process for the individual bids, minimum standards for bid acceptance, and negotiation of specific terms. Even if a bid process is not required, it is wise to solicit offers from several service providers prior to choosing a service vendor and entering into a contract.

The contract is an exchange of skills, goods, services, monetary instruments, or other items deemed to be of value to one or both parties. The *specificity of terms* of the contract is the most critical element in that the expectations for service provision and the allocation of the resources by the vendor are completely dependent upon the specific terms of the contract. An accurate description of the deliverables provides the service provider (*licensee*) with the basic information needed to determine the level of service or quantity of goods needed. The event producer (*licensor*), having already determined the level of service required, should be prepared to compensate the vendor at a fair market rate for the services or goods provided. The process might include a series of negotiations with *offers and counteroffers* before the final level of service and compensation is agreed upon. The exact needs of the licensor must include elements such as hours of service, location, product quantity and quality, and other pertinent items. The contract document encompasses the meeting of the minds, the specific terms or consideration, the conditions of enforcement, and the potential for seeking remedies, all of which are included in the body of the contract.

A contract must include the following information in order to be considered enforceable:

- *Identification of parties* includes the names, addresses, and other pertinent information that makes it legally possible to identify the individuals or organizations involved in the contract.
- *Conditions or terms of contract* identify what is being exchanged, when it will take place, a deadline for completion, and mutually acceptable criteria for determining a satisfactory completion of the contract.
- *Cancellation terms* describe how and when either party may remove themselves from the contractual relationship and what, if any, settlement will be necessary. This is also commonly referred to as an escape clause.
- The inclusion of the *signatures of both parties,* the *date of the signing,* and the inclusion of signatures of any *witnesses* to the agreement are necessary to confirm the terms of the contract. Signatures indicate an understanding of, agreement with, and commitment to all the material elements of the contract.

Conditions could arise through crisis, mismanagement, or deliberate dereliction of duties that produce a situation wherein the terms of the contract are not being met by one or both parties. This constitutes a *breach of contract,* which should be solved at the lowest level of mediation so that additional expenses are kept to a minimum.

Breach of Contract and Seeking Remedies

A *breach of contract* occurs when either party does not uphold its respective responsibilities as prescribed in the contract document. If one party feels that the contract conditions have not been adequately met, it may choose to seek some form of relief from the other party. This is known as an *election of remedies,* as the party chooses a strategy to recover damages for the breach of contract. The harmed party seeks to be *made whole* through a negotiated settlement of the differences between its expectations and the results of the services provided.

Enforcement of the conditions of the contract, in this case a negotiated solution, allows the delinquent party to set things aright by completing the contract as originally written. This is generally the preferred strategy if the parties have not experienced significant losses. If the harmed party has suffered any sort of loss, either in finances, time, reputation, or effectiveness due to the breach of contract, it may seek a *payment of damages* based on the assessment of the loss created by the breach. This requires a significant commitment of time and could be costly to enforce. A determination must be made regarding the cost/benefit results of this strategy. This means that an organization might determine that it would cost more to enforce the contract than it would to abandon the contract and find another means of completing the work.

Legal action could include seeking an *injunction,* preventing certain things from occurring or requiring a particular conduct by the wrongful party. Again, due to the legal expenses that are associated with this type of action, the desired outcome must be weighed against the costs.

If the harmed party feels that a termination of the contract is in its best interest, a *rescission* or canceling of the contract can be sought. This is typically associated with a settlement of all outstanding issues so that each party can move forward unencumbered by the failed contract. Another solution to a contract abrogation is *reformation,* the rewriting of the contract to conform to what both parties, or the court, feels is just and fair regarding the original intent of the contract. Breaches of contract are not uniform in severity or outcome and include *immaterial* or *partial breaches* and *material* or *total breaches.* A *partial breach* means that a section of the contract might have not been properly addressed but does not by itself void the entire contract. There is usually very specific language (the fine print) that addresses partial breaches and the effects of such a condition on the enforcement of the rest of the contract. *Total breach* renders the contract unenforceable and releases all parties from their obligations.

In cases involving significant sums of money or time-sensitive projects like special events, it is advisable to require the service provider to submit a *performance bond.* This is usually in the form of a percentage of the payment for the entire job. For example, if a company is going to supply the sound reinforcement for the event and will be charging $25,000, you may ask them to place $10,000 or more in your escrow account in case they don't provide the services according to the specifications of the contract. It is held in an escrow account as collateral to ensure a timely and accurate completion of the contract requirements. The contract language should identify the conditions of bond payment and the potential for forfeiture of the bond if the service provided fails to meet the conditions stated in the contract. If everything goes as planned, you would return the money with any interest earned while their money sat in your account.

Contract formulation and management is another means of safeguarding the resources and efforts of your organization in the production of your special event. We would all like to operate under the assumption that all parties are well meaning, well managed, and competent. Even if these conditions are present, there remains the possibility of unforeseen circumstances that can negatively influence the outcome of the event. Friendships can deteriorate quickly and might not be recovered if the expectations of a business relationship are not well planned, fully understood, and mutually agreed upon. A contract never can guarantee against all possible adverse conditions, but can, if properly executed, greatly reduce misunderstandings and provide predetermined solutions for many potentially catastrophic challenges that could arise. A festival or special event requires the organizers to conduct business with individuals and companies that are not part of the everyday routine of your agency. Contracts are a safe and fairly successful way to do business with a diverse group of service providers. This is particularly true if the event includes entertainment and the necessary technical support required of an entertainment venue.

A well-written contract helps to ensure an outstanding performance.
Photo Credit: deLisle

Entertainment Contracts

There are many urban legends concerning outrageous requests made by famous and not-so-famous performers regarding everything from the thread count of the sheets in the hotel room to the color of the M&Ms in the dish in the green room. A recent story describes a very famous female singer who requires all furniture, carpeting, and other elements of her dressing room to be completely white. This requires that the event organizers bring in new furniture, carpeting, and paint for the night or two that the artist is in residence. Due to the popularity of the performer and the sold-out audiences that accompany her concerts, the event organizers willingly comply with these somewhat extreme demands. Entertainment contracts present their own particular set of challenges. Many times, the elements included in the contract or the technical riders include unfamiliar terms and unique requests (see Figure 10.1).

Figure 10.1. Artist Contract

Wood Nymph
Music

Agreement for Artist Services

This agreement is made this_____day of _____, 20___ between Rhonda Larson (hereafter referred to as ARTIST) and _____ (hereafter referred to as PURCHASER).

PLACE OF ENGAGEMENT: _____
EVENT DATE & TIME: _____
REHEARSAL/SOUND CHECK TIME: _____

FINANCIAL ARRANGEMENT: Artist Fee:
All payments shall be made to Rhonda Larson in cash or certified check prior to performance.

Other Arrangements:_____
_____
_____

MERCHANDISE: ARTIST shall sell merchandise, including CDs, Sheet Music, and other program related paraphernalia. ARTIST shall provide sales personnel and collect 100% of the revenue received from these sales. ARTIST requests that PURCHASER provide a table located in an appropriate, public area for the sale of this merchandise.

RECORDING: Any audio and/or video transmission or taped recording of any rehearsal and/or performance by PURCHASER and/or any affiliated individual or groups associated in any way with PURCHASER is strictly prohibited

PROMOTION:
1. **Billing: Grammy Award-winning flutist *Rhonda Larson* in Concert**
   with Chris Rosser, strings, Tim Ray piano, Eliot Wadopian, bass, and Carolyn Koebel, world percussion. [*names of musicians to be listed as part of the billing.*]
2. **Description of music:** Performed with exhilarating precision and virtuosity, Rhonda Larson & Ventus' charismatic music merges the most soulful elements of sacred, Celtic, classical, folk, jazz, and world music, celebrating the human spirit.
   Rhonda Larson leads Ventus with her gold flute and a variety of ethnic flutes from around the world, and is joined by world-class musicians…[*please use names of each musician and their instrument*].
3. **Promotional Materials:** High resolution photos, bio, and other press available for downloading at: www.RhondaLarson.com/press.htm
4. **Please schedule interviews** through Rhonda Larson, (Rhonda@rhondalarson.com).

CONCERT:
A. Technical Equipment Requirements
   1. See enclosed tech rider for sound equipment, to be given to the VENUE-SUPPLIED sound Engineer assigned tour show
B. Program Contents
   1. We require the following to be printed in the concert programs:
      a. Program title: *: Rhonda Larson &Ventus in concert*
      b. Ms. Larson will announce her program selections from the stage. Please note that music titled will not appear in the printed program.

Figure 10.1. Cont.

   c.   All musician biographies, as available from www.RhondaLarson.com/press.htm

   d.   The following to be listed in the program:

       Please visit us at *www.RhondaLarson.com*, or write:
       Wood Nymph Music
       26 Hydelar Ave, Prospect, CT 06712

   e.   Please feel free to add any information you wish about your own organization.

FORCE MAJEURE: ARTIST's obligation to perform in agreed upon concert is subject to: detention or prevention by sickness, inability to perform, accident, means of transportation, Act of God, riots, strikes, labor difficulties, epidemics and any act or order of any public authority or any cause, similar or dissimilar, beyond the Artist's control. Provided Artist is ready, able and willing to perform, PURCHASER agrees to compensate Artist in accordance with the terms hereof regardless of Act of God, fire, accident, riot, strike or any event(s) of any kind or character whatsoever, whether similar or dissimilar to the foregoing events which should prevent or interfere with the presentation of the show. In the case where PRESENTER cancels this agreement for any other reason, any deposit made to secure ARTIST shall be nonrefundable.

SPONSOR'S BREACH: TThe terms and conditions of the Agreement and this Addendum are material and of the essence. Presenter's/Buyer's failure to provide the equipment and services required in the Addendum for Artist's appearance and proper presentation, shall constitute a material breach of this agreement by the Buyer. If the Artist does not perform due to the Buyer's non-compliance with the Agreement or this addendum, Artist and Artist's agent will suffer no liability and Artist will be totally compensated according to the terms and provisions of this Agreement.

Contact person and email address:_____

TECHNICAL RIDERS: The technical riders regarding sound equipmentand sound technicianrequirements are part and parcel to this agreement. Any and all changes to these riders must be discussed and agreed to in writing by Artist, and Artist Representative. **Please supply the name and email contact information of Sound Technician running show at least three weeks prior to engagement.**

Technical Riders read and accepted: (Please initial):_____

No income taxes shall be deducted from the stated Artist Fee; any income taxes withheld are considered a liability of Purchaser.

NOTICES: All notices, arrangements, and changes with this agreement shall be provided in writing and in a timely manner to the follwing:

AGREED

FOR ARTIST   **FOR PURCHASER**

By_____   **By**_____
     Artist Representative   Signature

_____   _____
         Print Name   Print Name

_____   _____
    Date   Date

Professional entertainers frequently spend days and weeks away from home, moving from one event to the next, and are at the mercy of event organizers and venue managers. For example, while the organizer might think it is fine to provide a musician with the same food that is being served at the event. Imagine having to eat that way every evening! Local groups might be happy to have a free meal before their show, but touring musicians, if they are seasoned professionals, identify the need to take care of their health and well-being while on the road. The objective for the event organizer is to provide the best product for their customers. This translates into providing an environment that will support an outstanding performance by the hired entertainment. Performers will always strive to give their all, but if they are subjected to a meal of chili dogs and beans before the show, you may be getting more music than you bargained for!

Entertainers appreciate being treated in a respectful and caring way. The artists' world is one of giving away their talents to strangers each night, hoping to be well received and then being ready to move on to the next event. It is certainly in the best interest of the event to meet the needs of the entertainer as well as possible. This is accomplished through the written contract and riders provided by the entertainer, the booking agent, or management group that handles the performer.

Entertainment contracts are about the details. Some contracts are quite challenging to decipher, including clauses such as *force majeure*! The reason for this legalise, despite the difficulty in understanding it, is to ensure precision as understood by the legal system. Ultimately in the event of a dispute, a contract is effective if it can be understood by a third party; usually this means a lawyer or mediator. It is generally easier and more efficient for the event organizer to accept a contract from the entertainment representative, as it will reduce the amount of information exchange that will inevitably take place over the course of the contract negotiations. The issuance of the contract is the first step in the negotiation process; everything that follows is negotiable.

The important fundamental elements in an entertainment contract are the identification of the location, and the specific date and hours of the performance. If the performer's schedule does not allow for a performance on the dates desired, the process usually ends at that point in time. If the presence of this particular performer is seen as critical to the success of your event, you may inquire if, by paying a premium, the entertainer is able to alter the schedule to accommodate your needs.

Interpreting and making necessary changes to the contract and having it reviewed by legal counsel is a time-consuming process. The artist management agency might be amenable to a *memorandum of understanding* or a *letter of intent* stating that both parties seek to enter into a contract for a particular service on a specific date. This type of agreement might hold the date for a specified length of time, allowing for a thorough review of the contract. This type of document is very useful if the details of the event are not complete. Unfinished details could include the approval of a budget, sponsor commitments, grant awards, or the setting of the actual date or time of the event. The performer might ask for a letter of intent if he needs time to schedule additional dates in the same region, or if other factors prevent executing a contract at that time. The letter of intent should provide as much information as possible and should include a final commitment date that allows both parties to work out the unfinished details but does not extend either party beyond a reasonable amount of time. Should all the details be worked out favorably, a letter of confirmation can be sent to secure the date. This could then be followed by a formal, detailed contract that addresses all pertinent issues relative to the performance.

Upon receiving a professional contract, you should set aside some time without interruption to review the document, taking separate notes on all the elements that are not clear or are questionable. A systematic approach to this initial review will help to identify any errors. A booking agency might be issuing multiple contracts for a particular tour and can unintentionally forget to change the dates on the template. This can result in a performer having to be in two different locations on the same night—someone loses!

It is your responsibility to find and make note of any mistakes, misspellings, or other conditions that could result in miscommunication or potential problems. Changes can be made to the contract by crossing out or adding words directly on the contract if this can be done without confusing the readers. All changes or corrections must be initialed and dated by both parties. This process will then be repeated by the management agency before the contract is complete.

In addition to contractual errors, there might be other elements that need modification. Some performers might request items that you cannot, for budgetary or legal reasons, make available. These conditions might not be deal breakers and should be discussed at the earliest possible opportunity. In the best of situations, the performer is only asking for treatment that allows them to lead a healthy existence while on the road. In the worst-case scenario, some groups will ask for extravagant items and will happily accept them if offered. Remember, everything is negotiable.

Performance Contract Ingredients

A complete *performance contract* will typically include most of the following elements:

1. Identification of Parties

The agreement must be between two legal parties who can be identified based on verifiable personal information. Note that states have different age requirements in order to enter into a contract.

2. Place of Engagement

This information should include the address of the venue, contact information such as phone numbers, email addresses, and emergency contacts.

3. Performance Date, Time, Length of Performance, Load-in, and Sound Check

It is important to verify days and dates with a calendar in order to identify any discrepancies that may exist. It is also important that sufficient time is allowed for the load-in of equipment and a sound check prior to the performance. This may be a bit tricky if the event features multiple performers on a back-to-back schedule. It is best to have a stage manager who is familiar with the requirements of this type of operation so that it is done in the most efficient manner, and a manageable amount of time is allotted for the breakdown of one group and the load in of the next. Any questions should be addressed with the performer prior to signing the contract.

4. Type of Performance

An explanation of the event should be supplied so that the performer has a general idea of the venue, the other acts, and the time frame of the entire event.

5. Technical Requirements

This clause refers to any additional technical riders for sound and lights or special equipment needed for the show. These items are absolutely critical to the performance and must be fully accommodated or met by substitute items that are approved in advance by the performer. It is strongly advised to provide the name and contact information for the local technicians so that the artist or agent can have direct and meaningful communication prior to the event. By allowing direct contact this removes the burden of interpreting the technical details by the event staff and allows for more effective use of your time.

6. Compensation, Deposit Dates, Final Payment Procedures

The fee proposed by the booking agent reflects the ideal for the performer. The negotiated fee must then be divided amongst the booking agent, management agency, road crew, and any other support mechanisms associated with the performer. You may always present a counteroffer to the fee included in the contract, particularly if you have real fiscal restraints on your entertainment budget. At the same time, it must be considered that musicians and other entertainers must negotiate their daily wages, oftentimes through an intermediary agency. Booking agents will usually take a lower fee within predetermined limits. Generally, a lesser paycheck is better than no paycheck. Arriving at a fee should be a win-win situation. If you truly value the importance of quality entertainment, you must be prepared to pay a fair price for the services provided. The artist's services cannot be thought of as the forty five to ninety minutes of time spent on the stage. That is the product that you are presenting to the audience, but it is only one factor in the production of the show. The best way to approach the negotiation of a fee is to fully understand the value of the performer to the anticipated revenue of the event. A top name performer may attract a larger audience and may bring a sponsor who would be very happy to be associated with a popular entertainer. If an attitude of trying to get a sought after performer for the best fee possible is adopted, all parties can reap the rewards.

Once a fee is agreed upon, a deposit date must also be determined. Agencies frequently use an early booking as an anchor date in order to set up a tour in a particular region and may require a deposit to be paid in advance. Also, the agent must be confident of the intentions of the event organizers. Other gigs may be turned down based on the contract with your event. It is also very important that the final payment procedure be clearly explained. No performer wants to leave a venue without getting paid. This would be similar to attending a movie and telling the theatre management that you will send the price of your ticket in the mail sometime next week. Despite the protestations of your finance department director, you simply should not even consider not paying a performer on the night of the performance. The agent or group leader is responsible for paying band members, road crew, sound engineers, and other support staff the day of the event. Delayed payments place many individuals in very difficult and unprofessional situations. Get all your entertainment checks cut and ready for the performers ahead of time. It is simpler to plan ahead than to manage a crisis the night of the performance.

7. Ticket Prices

This piece of information is important if the fee paid to the performer is based either partially or wholly on the number of tickets sold to the event. Accurate records must be retained of the number and types of tickets sold if tickets are sold at a premium for particular times or seatings. This is a difficult strategy to implement in outdoor settings and should be avoided unless the booking agent insists on some percentage of the gate. In general, it is helpful for the performer to have an understanding of the scale of the event, which is defined in some respect by the ticket prices.

8. Merchandise Policies

Many venues require the performers to pay a percentage of their merchandise sales back to the event organizers. While this is an acceptable practice, most performers would rather not share their product sales as it represents an additional revenue source for the performer. Typically the performer will adjust the price of their merchandise in order to reduce the impact of the product tariff, which can be up to 50% of sales at some venues. One must consider that ultimately your guests pay the difference in higher prices for the products that they purchase. You might want to calculate the net gain from the entertainment product percentage versus the profit made through additional concession and merchandise sales that may not occur if higher priced cds and t-shirts are purchased from the performer. If your organization is providing volunteers to sell the performer's products before and after the show, it might be more appropriate to require a fee for those services. But if you want to make the most favorable impact on the performer and booking agent, forgo the product percentage and make profits elsewhere. Building relationships with entertainment professionals will help the long term goals of the event. Entertainers and agents often share their experiences at conferences and workshops. Other potential performers who know that your organization is fair and reasonable will be more willing to offer their services for a reasonable fee in the future.

9. Cancellation Policy

Cancellations are the most stressful situations for both the promoter and the entertainer. Some agents will cancel a performer's date if a better offer comes their way. The better offer may involve a higher fee or a career advancing opportunity. It is important to review any cancellation language included in the contract. Typically the agency will seek to be released from a contract if thirty to sixty days notice is given. It is not easy to pull back on publicity, sponsorship benefits, and other acts that are dependent upon the performance of a headliner act. You can choose to not agree to a cancellation policy offered, or you could attach a penalty to the cancellation clause to discourage this type of behavior. The downside of offering a low fee to an artist is that it increases the chance of a better deal coming along. To reduce this risk, it is advisable to negotiate a fee that is satisfactory to both parties.

10. Force Majeur

French is such a beautiful language even when it's describing catastrophic, uncontrollable crises that cause the cancellation of your event. It wasn't a tornado—it was a *force majeur*. This clause relieves both parties from the original terms of the contract due to situations beyond the control of either party. If there is a power outage due to an electrical storm or an accident that interrupts power, it would be considered a force majeur. If power is lost because the contractual requirements for the sound, lights, concessions, etc. are greater than the available resources, that is a case of negligence and bad planning and is the responsibility of the event organizers.

The inclusion of a "rain date" in the original contract will keep the relationship alive, potentially reducing financial loss due to the cancellation of the original date. Before rebooking, the artist must consider all the costs associated with the rescheduling and determine whether the rain date will allow the promoter to recover the expenses associated with the show. In addition to the performance fee, this would include all logistical considerations from lodging, to sound and staging, and marketing expenses. Depending on the complexity of the event, frequently the best choice is to not rebook the event that year.

11. Insurance and Indemnity Clauses

There are so many possible scenarios that can result in damage, injury, and loss at a public event. Risk management requires that you consider the worst and work for the best. There must be an understanding of the responsibilities of the event organizers and the entertainment agency regarding liability and indemnification. The artist will want to know what type of insurance coverage exists for the event and whether the performer is indemnified for all but their own negligence. Event organizers will want to scrutinize the insurance provided by the entertainer or representing agency. What is important is that both parties understand their responsibilities and liabilities in this situation.

12. Partial/Total Breach Clauses

It must be determined ahead of time what constitutes a deal breaker for both parties. If a band is scheduled for two sets and only plays one, how will this be reflected in the final payment? By writing these issues down and reaching agreement prior to the event, it will be much easier to enforce all or part of the contract in the face of an immediate problem. It may seem like splitting hairs, but this approach provides both parties with guidelines to deal with difficulties that may arise.

13. Disputes and Attorney's Fees

Should a disagreement arise that cannot be settled and that negatively impacts one party or the other, it may be time to bring in the lawyers. The contract should acknowledge that this possibility might occur. There are several legal options at your disposal in the case of a partial or full breach of contract. Litigation is costly, time consuming, and usually very frustrating. Weigh the benefits of pursuing the issue prior to committing any resources. Four options are generally available in these situations. *Small claims court* is a fairly inexpensive way to recover small sums of money or damages related to a breach of contract. State law generally stipulates the boundaries for suing in small claims court. *Arbitration* is less formal than a court setting and makes use of a third party with experience in the type of dispute presented. Arbitration often has fewer restrictions on evidentiary procedures than an actual court case and allows for greater flexibility in scheduling and the adoption of resolution strategies. *Mediation* is another out-of-court strategy that allows for a settlement to be reached by a neutral third party, which is less of a binding decision and may provide guidance in settling a dispute. Finally, *litigation* carried out in a full court setting may be the only appropriate solution if the claim involves a large sum of money and the defendant lives in another state. Recovering of damages in this case is a long-term proposition that includes a multilayered process of depositions, hearings, and a trial.

14. Identification of Jurisdiction

This clause identifies the state that will hold jurisdiction should a dispute arise that requires legal action. This is important, as the laws regarding small claims, contract law, and other entertainment related issues differ greatly from state to state. The performer or management agency may be based in a different state than the location of your event. The jurisdictional authority for your contract must be clear to all parties.

15. Signatures and Dates

As previously mentioned, the inclusion of signatures and dates of signing for both parties indicates the understanding of and willingness to enter into the contract as described. Signing seals the deal.

16. Contract Riders

Contract riders are commonplace and are critical to both parties in the successful staging of an event. The riders explain additional requirements that are sought by the performer that are not identified in the performance contract. The majority of these requests are legitimate and should be honored. A careful reading of the riders will identify those items that have logistical worth from those that are personal indulgences.

17. Technical Riders

Technical riders provide the stage manager with the needed information to have the stage, sound, and lighting arranged for an optimum performance. Technical issues require technicians; identify individuals that have the training and expertise to interpret the needs of the performer and the ability to meet these needs in a cost effective manner. It is money well spent to hire a competent sound and lighting crew that understands stage operations and can deal with the inevitable last-minute crises that occur with live performances. Technicians are also experienced with interacting with engineers and other support staff that might accompany a performer. It is very comforting to watch two professionals work together to ensure that the technical aspects of a performance are perfectly tuned for the show. As tempting and cost effective as it may seem, do not use volunteers in this critical area of performance, even if they set up the microphones every week at church. Hiring professionals allows you to worry about other issues!

Technical riders should also include sound amplification requirements, stage dimensions and stage plot, lighting requirements, load-in and tear-down personnel needs, and any other items or activities needed to deliver the show to the audience.

Case Study: Hospitality on the Fly

Many years ago, while working as a student building supervisor for the recreation department located in the field house at the University of Connecticut, I was thrilled to be on duty the night that a big concert was being presented by the student government organization in the field house. The headline band for the evening was Fleetwood Mac. Despite having no experience in event management, I sensed that things were not quite right. Many assumptions were made by the student government organization, including the expectation that the building supervisor would take care of all the hospitality needs of the group. When the band arrived, their manager asked me for the key to their dressing rooms. I knew nothing about their dressing rooms and brought them to a locker room that was used by students and faculty. The manager, JC, screamed at me, stating that his band would not be using the locker rooms and would not perform unless better dressing rooms were made available. This was a vintage 1940s field house built before the days when student athletes and coaches had achieved rock star status. There were not a lot of options for dressing rooms. I was aware of, but have never been in, the coach's lounge that was tucked away in a remote part of the building. It was the only alternative, and as a 20-year-old confronted by an insistent adult and the expectations of a concert to follow, I made my move. The room had couches, a bathroom with mirrors, and seemed to be fine. The manager maintained an air of indignation but said the room would be "OK." Upon returning to the dressing room after the concert, I found the room filled with people, a bar was set up, and the air was filled with smoke from a non-tobacco substance; the after-party was in full swing. None of this was usually allowed in the field house as far I could remember, but once again, with no prior briefing, I was confronted with making an "executive decision"—I didn't say a word! At that point I was warmly welcomed into the room by the band, thanked for my efforts and rewarded with food, drink, and the bouquet of roses that Stevie Nicks (before she was a blonde) received at the end of the show. After their departure, I cleaned the room as best I could and left the windows open for the rest of the weekend. My girlfriend got the roses, I got a leftover case of beer, and I awaited being called in on Monday morning to explain the activities of Saturday night, and lose my job. Thankfully there were no repercussions, and I remained happily employed and wiser for the experience.

18. Hospitality Riders

This language addresses the issues of transportation, lodging, dressing room, and the pre- and post-performance space (known as the green room, although I have never actually seen a green one) requirements including the number of dressing rooms, the need for mirrors, bathrooms, food, and other personal items prior to and after the show. On stage requirements such as water and hand towels for each performer are also very important. An effective stage manager will supply things like water and towels as a matter of business, even if they are not included in the rider. It demonstrates an understanding of the needs of the performers and helps to form a supportive environment for your event. You might not be able to meet all the specific needs of the performer as written. Do not simply ignore those items and approve the rider as presented. Riders should foster additional communication between the contractual partners in order to fully meet the needs of both parties. Frequently a performer will ask for lodging in a particular brand of hotel. The reason for this is that they most likely have stayed in that brand previously and found the accommodations and service to be satisfactory. Understanding the motive is important in providing satisfaction to the performers. Unless they are major stockholders in the hotel chain, it is not really about the brand as much as it is about the service. Do a little research concerning their request, and if the closest hotel of that particular brand is in the next county, find out what it is about the chain that appeals to them (could be an exercise room or a breakfast buffet) and try to match those amenities with a sensible alternative that is within reason.

The rider is a communication tool to inform the event organizers of the real needs of the artists. Make note of the prohibitive items and negotiate a solution for each item prior to signing the contract. The expectations of the performers are presented in the contract and riders. If you do not mention any problems or do not make any alterations to the documents prior to signing, all conditions will be expected on the day of the event. Usually technical and hospitality riders are included with, and considered a part of, the performance contract. It is imperative that the information in the riders be distributed to those individuals who will be providing the requested services for review before the contract is signed. If this information is not shared with the relevant support staff, it can result in a multitude of problems. It is also imperative that a progress report be provided by those responsible for arranging the contract requirements. The day before the event is not the time to be solving contractual shortcomings.

Entertainment Areas

Careful consideration must be given to the scheduling of entertainment at an event. Entertainment is an integral part of many festivals, and expectations might be very high for the presentation of the artists scheduled to perform. The entertainers also expect things to run smoothly. Using the information provided in artist contracts and riders is the appropriate starting point for effective stage management. Some entertainers will be assigned to the main stage while others might be situated on auxiliary stages or might be wandering the grounds of the event. This needs to be communicated to the artist prior to the event.

Stage Management

An experienced and competent *stage manager* is critical to the successful management of the entertainment responsibilities of the event. Decisions regarding the operational logistics needed to coordinate the activities of technicians, agents, performers, and support staff are best made by an individual who understands the needs of each of these groups.

The stage manager will establish standards for the set up and break down of equipment and will identify tasks to be managed prior to, during, and after performances. The agreed-upon parameters established by the event organizers guide the stage manager to control the length of each performance and the transition time between performers. Adequate stage crew, talent handlers, and other personnel under the leadership of the stage manager can be the difference between a show that runs close to schedule or one that features lengthy dead space between performers.

Other stage management considerations include the following:

Load in. The stage manager, along with the artist representatives, should determine the equipment requirements of each band. The stage manager may determine what equipment if any, can be shared amongst groups and how many people are needed to accomplish the load in with the allotted time. It is a common goal to avoid delays between the staging of each band during an event. The stage manager must coordinate all load in activities with this in mind.

Sound checks. The public address (PA) system should be up and running hours before the performers have their sound checks. Even a small problem with a sound system can take a very long time to find and solve. Interference from other equipment such as lighting may cause problems with the sound system. Bad cables must be isolated and replaced, fuses might have to be replaced, individual pieces of equipment could be faulty, entire units may have to be traded out for backup equipment. Typically in an event with back-to-back performers, a general sound check is done prior to the beginning of the event, and line checks are offered to each of the performers directly before their performance. In this case, adjustments to the sound must necessarily take place during the first few songs.

Lighting check. Individual performers may have a specific lighting plan for their group as detailed in a technical rider. The governing rule for all technical requests is no substitutions should be made without the approval of the performer or their agent. All aspects of the lighting must be tested prior to the performance.

Stagehands. Despite the opportunity to be close to the performers, a stagehand's job is decidedly unglamorous and generally includes a great deal of continuous physical labor. Unless specifically assigned to provide hospitality, stagehands should not interact with performers except to ask pertinent questions regarding the stage plot or performers' needs.

Summary

A well-written contract and accompanying riders are living documents that anticipate and guide the fulfillment of the necessities of staging a successful performance. Negotiating and signing the documents is only the beginning. Fulfilling the contract requirements is a process, rather than an event, in that most of the work is done long before the show. Like so many other aspects of event management, the positive results are directly related to the amount of analysis and planning that precedes the actual event.

Discussion Questions

1. Why is it wise or necessary to contract for some particular services related to a special event?
2. What is the legal definition of a contract?
3. What are meant by the terms *legal subject* and *legal capacity*?
4. What is a meeting of the minds?
5. Why is the specificity of the terms considered to be the most important part of the contract?

6. What are three options in dealing with a breach of contract?
7. Why is the identification of the sound check time important to a performer?
8. What are some typical strategies in dealing with a performer's merchandise sales at an event?
9. What is *force majeur*? Why is this statement important to both parties in a contract?
10. What is a hospitality rider and why is it important to a performer?

1. Uniform Commercial Code. Retrieved from http://www.law.cornell.edu/ucc/1/article1.htm#s1-301

11

Customer Service and Satisfaction

 The trick is not to arrange a festival,
but to find people to enjoy it.

Friedrich Nietzsche

Chapter Objectives

- Identify the particular challenges of customer service at a special event
- Understand the elements of customer satisfaction that are important to the event organization
- Understand the elements of customer satisfaction that are important to the customer as represented in a hierarchy of needs
- Learn the critical issues in measuring customer satisfaction
- Identify best practices in achieving customer satisfaction

Customer service is the process of identifying, understanding, planning for, and meeting the needs or requirements of individuals and groups as they interact with your organization or event. "Customer satisfaction is a measure of how your organization's 'total product' performs in relation to a set of customer requirements."[1]

Customers come in at least two varieties. *Internal customers* are those who are involved in the planning and production of the event. This would include staff, volunteers, sponsors, contracted service providers, and others who support the operations of the event. External customers are those who attend the event and others who are not a part of the event management process or organization. *External customers* are those who consume the products, services, or experiences offered at your event. A secondary set of external customers includes those who choose not to attend the event but might be impacted positively or negatively in some way by its presence. It is important to realize that meeting the needs of both internal and external customers is important to the overall success of your event. Each group deserves appropriate attention and excellent customer service.

Customer Satisfaction

Getz (1997) tells us that the enjoyment and satisfaction of event visitors is the result of a mix of impressions and interactions of the guest with the setting, staff and volunteers, management systems, and program characteristics offered by the event. *Satisfaction* is the net result of the organization's understanding and delivery of quality services and the customer's expectations and subsequent experience of the event. Satisfaction is experiential, as both positive and negative encounters shape opinions.[2]

Researchers over the past twenty years have examined many of the variables that influence these factors in an effort to create adequate means of evaluating customer satisfaction. Customer satisfaction is an important contributor to current organizational success and may impact the future economic viability of your event. In the past few decades, the expectation levels of participants have risen due to heightened consumer sophistication and the incremental improvement of event standards. This implies that delivering quality products and services that meet the needs of your visitors is becoming more challenging over time due to heightened expectations. As we know, the event product is an experience that begins long before the day of the event and lasts long after the lights go out, which hopefully occurs at the end of the event!

The external customer has many experiences while attending an event or festival. Each event experience, from finding a parking place, to entering the venue, purchasing products at the concessions, watching and listening to entertainment, and whatever else is specific to your event, is an opportunity to meet or exceed the needs and expectations of your guests.

Getz, O'Neill, and Carlsen (2001) offer several strategies for identifying elements of satisfaction that also provide guidelines for measuring service quality. Opportunities for experiencing satisfaction are based on the temporal and physical aspects of the event. Getz et al. make use of a method referred to as *service mapping* in order to identify critical contact service points for the visitor. The authors divide the mapping of visitor experiences into an initial stage referred to as *approach and orientation* to the event and a second stage that encompasses *on-site experiences*. These delineations can be understood in the following time frames.

Pre-Event Impressions

Pre-event impressions are gained through contact with promotional materials. The accuracy and details of information provided, the choice of language used to describe the event, and the overall impression created for the event produces a distinct level of expectation regarding the benefits of the event. Technology, particularly the use of websites and social media, has increased the exposure to, and importance of, pre-event contacts for the potential visitor. Visitor expectations begin at this critical point and must be carefully planned to portray an accurate first impression.

The entry gate is the moment when the Pre-Event Impressions are compared with the reality of the event.
Photo from www.eps.net

Arrival

Arrival at an event is accompanied by a heightened sense of anticipation and an increased awareness of the signals sent by the physical environment. Expectations and preconceived ideas about the event are immediately and almost unconsciously compared to the activities unfolding before one's eyes. Positive first impressions include a sense of the buzz created by the event that becomes evident as one enters the venue. Crowd size, visual attractions, a well laid-out site plan, and clear directions and communications reinforce the anticipated benefits of the event.

During Event

During the event the customer further compares expectations to reality and creates a relationship with the event. Based on the motivations for attending the event, the visitor is either reinforced through experiencing desired outcomes or must realign desires with the levels of service and products that are available. Some events, for various reasons, do not meet expectations, while others may exceed expectations. Both aspects require adjustments on the part of the visitor.

Post Event

Post-event memories include positive highlights of the event but will also give weight to any negative encounters that take place. The interplay between these two factors will determine the overall evaluation of the event. If organizers view the entire experience as one of creating and sustaining a relationship with the customer, efforts will be made to stay in contact with visitors through newsletters, renewed contact prior to the next year's event, and special offers for repeat visitors. The post-event relationship is an important consideration in establishing the bond needed for repeat visitors.

It is a valuable exercise to identify all aspects of your event that can influence a visitor's perception of quality and feelings of satisfaction during these four time frames.

Getz et al. also offer five main elements in devising a service mapping strategy for an event in Table 11.1.

Table 11.1. Service Mapping Strategy

Organizers must:

1. Identify the process and actions required by the visitors in entering, experiencing, and leaving the event.
2. Analyze the number, location, and effectiveness of encounters with staff and volunteers during the event.
3. Inventory of all services provided in order to quantify service transactions.
4. Observe the behavior of the crowds at the event as this factor affects the visitor's experience at the event.
5. Describe the management systems and operations used at the event.[3]

Customer satisfaction, as we now know, is relative to the expectations that individuals have regarding the event. Expectations can be created and fostered through event marketing, through past personal experience with the event, and through the comments and recommendations of third parties who have some knowledge of the event. Expectations are dangerous as they directly affect the possibility for the participant to experience satisfaction, which is strongly impacted by these initial expectations. Overzealous marketing can create a *set up-to-fail syndrome* whereby the hyped expectations are not matched by the services provided. It is important to get the public's attention and to persuade people to participate in your event. However, this should be balanced by the practice of a strategic level of underselling that is complemented by over delivering the final product. Simply put, do not make promises that you cannot actually keep. To understand fully customer satisfaction one must consider the factors that create the customer's expectations as well as the elements that determine satisfaction.

What is Important to Your Customer?

People attend events and festivals for many different reasons. There are those who have some connection to the theme or product such as the type of music, food, or merchandise. There are others who are looking for new experiences, those seeking social contacts, repeat visitors who experienced some level of satisfaction with a previous experience, casual attendees who happen upon the event, and those who gave it no actual prior thought and just showed up. Attendees at your event probably include individuals from each of these categories and carry with them different sets of expectations. Expectations, or a lack of them, set the stage for the resulting levels of satisfaction expressed by the attendees. Due to the diversity of reasons that people choose to attend an event, and the multiple levels of service/experience that are encountered at an event, it is very challenging to achieve a high level of customer satisfaction for all participants.

Events represent a very special product that is of short duration, interacts with varying levels of anticipation, product knowledge and expectation, and requires satisfying the customer in an ever changing environment. Customers are looking for outcomes or benefits that meet or exceed their initial levels of expectation. The well positioned event organization will have a clear idea of what these requirements are through the use of exploratory research that may include focus groups of potential or past customers, surveys that identify the issues that are important to the community, or in-depth interviews with key stakeholders that clarify the parameters that will contribute to satisfaction. All of this information is valuable, particularly if it is prioritized in relation to the stated objectives of the event.

Service Quality

Event organizers are concerned with quality service, as it is the foundation of customer satisfaction. Dictionary definitions of quality include the idea of something being of a particular kind or grade, or the degree of excellence that a thing possesses. Quality is therefore a relative term in that it, like beauty, is in the eye of the beholder. Quality is generally established through the setting or acceptance of standards that guide the decisions and actions of service providers. The strategic planning process for an event is the appropriate place to begin the process of establishing service quality standards and the means to measure or evaluate performance relative to these standards. Success is achieved when the event offers products and services that possess characteristics that match the expectations of the anticipated audience. Understanding the audience is a critical first step in creating a high quality experience. The level of service and amenities such as comfort, hospitality, professionalism, and cost offered at an event must make sense to the visitor.

Edosomwan (1993) describes quality service as providing safe, error free performances, activities, services, and settings. It also includes service characteristics that are described as prompt, efficient, effective, courteous, reliable, trustworthy, and punctual. Quality service also suggests that correct and timely solutions will be found for problems that arise.[4]

Measuring Customer Satisfaction

Hill (2002) described the process of customer satisfaction measurement, or CSM, as having three main objectives. Included are *determining the customer's requirements, measuring the level of satisfaction reported by the customer,* and using past information to *understand the impact of past experience on current levels of expectations.*[5]

The *first objective* is to determine your customers' needs and requirements. There are many important factors relative to the customer feeling satisfied with an experience or product. Customers anticipate benefits that can be expressed through the realization of particular outcomes. In order to gather this type of information, past or potential new customers must be questioned as to what they would expect or require from attending the event. This can be accomplished through interviews or focus groups that elicit important details about the expectations regarding the event. This pre-event research might seem like an unnecessary burden, but it is worth the effort as it provides a baseline of expectations regarding the event. The important aspect is to look at your event from the perspective of the attendee rather than the organizer's viewpoint. What makes the event successful for the organizers might not equate with a high level of customer satisfaction. Another method of aligning your event with the expectations of the consumer is to include additional external and internal customers and stakeholders in the planning process. An open planning process will foster levels of communication that allow for the expression of anticipated benefits and required outcomes.

The *second objective* is to measure the level of customer satisfaction through the use of the list of requirements developed in the completion of the first objective. This can be achieved by providing surveys to attendees directly after the event. Identify a manageable number of stakeholders from the many groups that are involved or impacted by the event to gather this important information. It is also helpful to compare these results with other organizations that provide a similar type of event. This initiates the important process of *benchmarking* the event relative to the needs of your participants and the standards set by other events. You may also compare satisfaction with a particular event to the overall satisfaction that people report regarding your agency or other special events that you offer. In this way, you can determine whether the event matches the expectations for quality that you have established in your other activities.

The *third objective* aids in understanding the impact of past experience on the expected level of service for the event under consideration. Customers, as a matter of human nature, compare their present perceptions to similar past experiences. This is a form of benchmarking by the consumer that can greatly aid your organization in meeting the expectations of your customers. Achieving a consistent level of satisfaction across several of your events will help to develop loyalty on the part of your attendees.

With this information, event organizers can now develop priorities for continual improvement. This objective is determined by identifying discrepancies between the important needs or requirements of the customer and their stated levels of satisfaction. An overall determination of customer satisfaction is used to compare the general level of satisfaction from year to year. Despite changes in the specific requirements of the customers on an annual basis, this measurement can be used and tracked on a recurring basis to provide a satisfaction quotient for each event.

Finally, it is helpful to study the perceptions of staff and volunteers in relation to the requirements and levels of satisfaction reported by their customers. Service delivery is impacted by the perceptions and behaviors of both the customers, as well as the service providers. There must be a general consensus in terms of what constitutes excellent customer service if the expectations of the public are to be effectively met. This internal survey can identify weaknesses in the management of key resources within the event-management process.

Case Study: A Triathlete's Triathlon

Back in 1985, triathlons were not common community events. A group of 20-something-year-old athletes approached me in order to stage a triathlon in our community. I knew what a triathlon was but couldn't imagine participating in one and had no idea of the logistical demands in staging such an event. I agreed to the task on the condition that the athletes would provide at least five individuals with some experience in the sport to staff the organizing committee. It was a unique experience in that my role was to trust and coordinate the knowledge and needs of the athletes while providing logistical support in areas such as water safety and traffic management that lay outside their areas of expertise. I learned a great deal in our first year, regarding things such as numbering protocols, transition areas, safety procedures, and the particular needs of this unique type of athlete. The event was a success due to the fact that the needs of the triathletes were identified early in the process and they received adequate resources in order to meet their needs. The event attracted a national beverage sponsor, Bud Light, who saw the product link between a low-carbohydrate beer and low-fat athletes as an appealing target market. The sponsor aided in our attempt to cater to the needs of the athletes, resulting in a festive, very effective event that included sports massages after the event, lots to eat and drink, a reggae band, and a great sense of accomplishment on the part of the athletes and staff. Due to the novelty of the event at that time, it received excellent media coverage and was perceived to be a success by the participants, spectators, and sponsors. Despite my lack of experience, the event worked and continues today due to the input from the athletes who knew what was needed from the participant's perspective to make the event successful.

The lesson of the triathlon is to understand the needs of your potential customers through their active involvement in the planning and execution of the event. This can occur through interviews and discussions or through direct contributions to the planning of the event. Asking the right questions of the right people will greatly increase your chance to provide excellent customer service. Understanding the important criteria that will determine an acceptable level of satisfaction for the participants is at the heart of successful event planning.

The SERVQUAL Method

In support of the above-mentioned objectives, Zeithaml, Parasuraman, and Berry (1988) offered a method of measuring service quality that helps to identify areas of importance as expressed by the consumer. Five key dimensions are suggested in order to understand the consumer's perceived needs regarding the most important elements of service quality.[6] These dimensions are defined in Table 11.2.

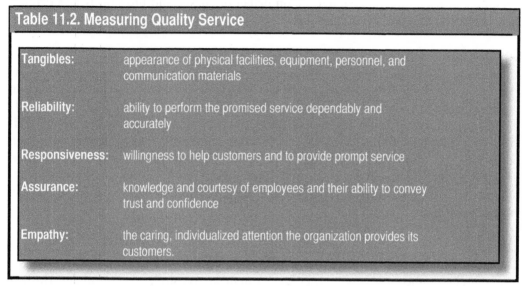

Table 11.2. Measuring Quality Service

Tangibles:	appearance of physical facilities, equipment, personnel, and communication materials
Reliability:	ability to perform the promised service dependably and accurately
Responsiveness:	willingness to help customers and to provide prompt service
Assurance:	knowledge and courtesy of employees and their ability to convey trust and confidence
Empathy:	the caring, individualized attention the organization provides its customers.

In studies performed using these criteria, reliability was consistently rated the most important characteristic, while tangibles, the physical resources, were generally ranked as least important. This model has been expanded over time to include ten dimensions that are of particular importance to event organizers. Event management can benefit greatly from using these guidelines for customer satisfaction and by assessing your organization's ability to address these important issues.

Physical Environment

The tangible elements of the event site are intimately linked to the feeling that a festival or event evokes for the visitor. Although research shows that tangibles are not rated as "highly important" to customers, it would seem that this would not hold true for special events, because the product, the festival or event, is so closely related to the venue. These tangible physical elements include the appearance of the venue and facilities, the staff, equipment, booths, printed materials, and other elements that create impact. As mentioned earlier, the five senses are critical to a positive physical experience of a special event. Each positive sensation can help to support the desired environmental effects or detract from the visitor's experience. Read more about managing your venue in chapter thirteen.

Reliability

The reliability of your event includes the ability to provide all visitors with a uniform level of service. This is particularly important in planning for the peak visitor periods of your event. Facilities and services should be designed to provide excellent service during the busiest hours of the event. Reliability also suggests that whatever it is that you are offering the public will be done right the first time according to performance standards appropriate for the event.

Responsiveness

Responsiveness to customer needs includes the ability to quickly and effectively address requests or problems. The organization must promote an attitude of willingness to answer questions, provide directions, intercede on behalf of guests, and proactively and deliberately contribute to a positive atmosphere.

Competence

A competent staff is evidence of proper preparation and a serious commitment to service. Many times, the first encounter with an event is the roadside signs and directions to the event and the volunteers who direct traffic and parking. Directions should be clearly marked, professionally presented, and of the appropriate size for the speed of passing traffic. If your volunteers display a helpful and effective demeanor, it makes an immediate and positive impact on visitors before they even get out of their cars. Incompetent, abrasive, or arrogant parking attendants send the wrong message and can leave a lasting negative impression. This standard of appropriate and effective behavior must be adhered to in all aspects of the event.

Courtesy

Courtesy suggests that the customer is highly valued and deserves consideration and respect. When someone is genuinely polite, it can make you smile, inside and out. The best souvenir of an event can sometimes be feeling good about oneself and the event due to the level of courtesy displayed by the event staff. *Continuous, contagious courtesy* should be a core value that is practiced by all representatives of your event.

Credibility

Credibility conveys a feeling of trustworthiness and honesty that allows a sense of freedom on the part of the guest. The reputation of the event is based on a trust that the best interests of the visitors are of the highest priority, and the inherent sense that the organizers guarantee that they are striving to provide an excellent experience for all.

Security

Event visitors must sense a feeling of physical security before any possibility of satisfaction can be experienced. Freedom from danger and risk is a basic human need that can be reassured through the communication of safety requirements for all event stakeholders. The enforcement of rules, the inspection of all physical elements of the event, the presence of security, health, and medical authorities all send a message of security to your guests.

Accessibility

The accessibility of staff and volunteers suggests that efforts are being made to reach out to guests in a proactive manner. This is achieved through proper levels of staffing at entrances and exits, the availability of accurate printed guides and schedules, strategically placed information booths, and knowledgeable staff members walking about the venue to provide assistance. Requiring all staff members to wear official event staff shirts or hats is a recommended means of identifying event service providers and is a very positive and effective way to communicate the value of accessibility to your guests. Accessibility has taken on a new significance in our current environment of accommodating special needs. Planning for and meeting the needs of individuals with mobility, sight, hearing or other restrictions can greatly increase the overall impression of the commitment of the event organizers in providing a universally satisfactory experience. Federal, state and local ordinances are a great starting point for making appropriate accommodations. It is also wise to include input from individuals with direct experience of these needs in your planning process.

Communication

Effective communication is all about listening and conveying a sense that you understand someone's issues or concerns. Being able to solve problems involves providing information in a way that is understandable to the customer, including directing them to other staff members who are better equipped to meet their needs. Staff members must be trained in the art of *effective referral*. Sending a guest to someone else for a solution can result in that person feeling dismissed and not valued, *or* they can feel that an extra effort is being made to provide the best solution to their particular problem. It all depends on the communication skills of the staff member or volunteer. Training can greatly enhance positive outcomes, particularly through role playing scenarios with feedback provided to the trainee. Personal communication is supported and enhanced by the effective use of signs, banners, programs, schedules, maps, and other printed materials that help to provide excellent customer service. Announcements from the stage or the PA system alerting guests to the schedule of activities and any other pertinent information is also critical to effective communications.

Empathy

The final element, and in some ways the most important consideration, is your ability to communicate that you understand your customer. Success in this endeavor is somewhat dependent on an individual's ability to personally understand the feelings or needs of another. A truly empathetic personality is the result of an approach to life that cannot be acquired through a few volunteer training sessions prior to your event. Those assigning staff and volunteers to particular tasks should seek to assign those individuals who appear kind and caring to assignments that would benefit most from these and other related qualities. Finding lost parents (children never get lost, but their parents do) requires a sensitivity to the fears of the individuals involved and is not best served by an autocratic personality type. Match your staff with their strengths, and all parties will benefit from their abilities.

Bridging the Gaps

The SERVQUAL model also provides the means to measure the gaps between the expectations of the visitor and the actual levels of service provided. This has immediate significance in impacting customer satisfaction. The process allows planners to identify and understand where service gaps exist within the organization, and between the organization and its customers. It allows for the prioritization of the gaps in terms of relative impact on quality of service, and in identifying the reasons for the existence of those gaps. The program is most helpful in guiding efforts to plan for service improvements by supporting the development of a program to close service gaps and implement processes to continuously review and refine customer service quality. By the 1990s, the model was condensed to five components identified as Reliability, Assurance, Tangibles, Empathy and Responsiveness.

What the Research Tells Us

Understanding the needs of your audience is the key to developing policies and procedures that will help to ensure high-quality services that support the goal of creating a positive relationship with your customers. Managing visitors is not an easy task due to the sometimes unpredictable character of special events and the varied expectations of potential participants. The relationship between visitors and your event is dependent upon perceptions and expectations regarding the venue, the quality of the product, the effectiveness of staff and volunteer interactions, the success of crowd management procedures, the impact of risk management strategies, and of course, the weather.

The value of planning for and executing evaluation procedures, according to Yeoman et al. (2004), is that the investment made in this type of data collection will help your organization to better focus future efforts. Results are studied to identify customer needs, highlight service delivery weaknesses, review operations, develop and revise an overall training program, and support the strategic-planning process in the future.

Additional research by Homburg, Koschate, and Hoyer (2005) indicates that customer satisfaction is directly related to the willingness to pay for services provided. Satisfaction has its greatest impact on a customer's willingness to pay at the very highest or very lowest levels of satisfaction. This means that low levels of satisfaction will elicit the least motivation to pay for a service, while very high levels of satisfaction result in a more open attitude toward willingness to pay. Moderate levels of satisfaction have the least effect on willingness to pay. Mediocre, middle of the pack experiences are simply not a motivator to financially invest in an event. Research also shows that the willingness to pay is more highly influenced by the cumulative or overall feelings of satisfaction about the event, rather than being the result of a particular incident or transaction. This reasserts the notion that continuity and reliability are once more indicated as important elements of customer satisfaction.[7]

Event organizers might consider charging a premium price for their events if there is a history of high levels of satisfaction with the overall event. High levels of customer satisfaction can result in strategic decisions that can increase the bottom line of the event, thereby allowing for investment in additional services that may further increase customer satisfaction.

Summary

The following list should serve as a guide in achieving excellent customer service. Your particular situation may stress some components over others, but a consideration of all of the listed elements will contribute to your success.

Best Practices for Customer Satisfaction

- Accurately define and communicate the goals of the event.
- Model your practices on similar successful events.
- Identify standards for operational excellence, communication excellence, professional excellence, and service excellence.
- Know your audience, particularly their expectations for quality service.
- Understand your event from the perspective of a visitor.
- Understand the elements of your event that communicate quality.
- Differentiate between the Crompton/Hertzberg (maintenance vs. satisfiers) qualities of your event.
- Conduct pre- and post-event quality and satisfaction assessments with multiple stakeholder groups including customers, sponsors, vendors, volunteers, and media.
- Use trained *secret shoppers* to gain detailed narrative impressions of their experiences at the event. Their notes will indicate those elements that made positive impressions and others that appeared to be less than inviting.
- Feel the event; how did staff or volunteers and other visitors influence your feelings as you experienced the event? What did you remember most vividly about the event and how did that affect your attitude toward the event?
- Think about these experiences and compare them to what the perfect experience would be. Implement procedures to improve the experience for others.

Discussion Questions

1. Identify internal and external customers in the event process.
2. What are the four opportunities to experience event satisfaction according to Getz?
3. How do performance standards relate to service quality?
4. How would you determine what the customers may be expecting from your event?
5. How would you go about measuring the customer's level of satisfaction?
6. Why is it important to survey customers, staff, and volunteers when trying to ascertain the level of service being provided for an event?
7. What are the five dimensions of the SERVQUAL method?
8. What does research tell us about the relationship between visitors and your event?
9. How would you go about trying to understand your event from the perspective of a visitor?
10. What is the relationship between customer satisfaction and willingness to pay for an event?

1. Hill, N., Brierley, J., & MacDougall, R. (2003). *How to measure customer satisfaction* (2nd ed.). Hampshire, England: Gower Publishing Limited, p. 7.
2. Getz, D. (1997). *Event management and event tourism.* Elmsford, NY: Cognizant Communication Corporation.
3. Getz, D., O'Neill, M., & Carlsen, J. (May 2001). Service quality evaluation at events through service mapping. *Journal of Travel Research*, vol. 39, p. 383.
4. Edosomwan, J. (1993). *Customer- and market-driven quality management.* Milwaukee, WI: ASQC Quality Press.
5. Hill, N., Brierley, J., & MacDougall, R. (2003). OPCIT, p. 7.
6. Zeithaml, V., Parasuraman, A., & Berry, L. (1990). *Delivering quality service: Balancing customer perceptions and expectations.* New York: The Free Press, p. 26.
7. Homburg, C., Koschate, N., & Hoyer, W. (2005). Do satisfied customers really pay more? A study of the relationship between customer satisfaction and willingness to pay. *Journal of Marketing*, 69(2).

Section Four

Physical Resources

This section leads you through site planning, concessions management, crowd management and safety, and how technology can make these tasks easier and more effective.

12

Site Planning and Selection

 It is not what you have, but what you do with what you have!

Lee deLisle

Chapter Objectives

- Determine the site characteristics necessary to support the goals and objectives of your organization
- Choose an event site that meets the needs of the stakeholders, visitors, and residents
- Understand the issues of vehicular and pedestrian access and egress
- Create effective entertainment areas
- Strategically place concessions at an event site
- Address site safety and risk-management concerns

The Minimum Daily Requirements

In event planning, there are certain elements that must be present in order for your event to have a chance at being successful. These are the minimum standards that must be met by organizers and are expected by your customers. Included are such amenities as safety features and sanitation stations, quality vendor services, accurate information services, adequate affordable parking with a sensitivity toward accessibility considerations, proper visitor flow, adequate seating and sight line to stages, effective sound and public address systems, and more. It is about safety, comfort, convenience, and accessibility.

Strategically Supporting Your Mission

The site chosen for a special event is as important as the activities presented. The site is the *tabula rasa*, or blank slate, to be filled with color, motion, sights, sounds, tastes, smells, and textures. Your work of art, the special event, is created and supported by the site you choose. The site must be selected and designed to meet the needs of the stakeholders, thereby achieving the goals and advancing the mission of the organization. Site choice can enhance the experience or can create conditions that limit the success of the event for organizers, sponsors, vendors, and most importantly, your customers.

Site planning is an integral part of the early strategic planning for your event. Event site development is analogous to park planning. The greatest minds in landscape architecture approached park development as a process of designing a series of outdoor rooms joined together in a way that invited visitors to move easily from one special environment to the next. This process also works well in designing the space for a special event or festival. The "rooms" will be determined by the theme or general character of the event, the anticipated crowds, and the types of entertainment or interactions envisioned. It is wise to analyze your proposed activities and determine the most suitable space for each element followed by a well-designed means of controlling and directing visitor traffic.

Marketing efforts can also be enhanced through thoughtful site selection and design. A site choice can support advertising efforts if the site can take advantage of the amount of traffic the area generates on a regular basis. As the site is prepared during the days and weeks preceding the event, increased interest and excitement can be generated for those passing by. In this way, a properly planned site can be effectively used in the marketing strategy and may help to lower advertising costs. By considering all aspects of the event during the site selection phase, maximum benefits can be realized. Many times, however, a site is chosen because it is the only one available that can meet the basic needs of the event. Nonetheless, every effort should be made to accent the strengths of the site and minimize the weaknesses.

Special events bring together potentially large groups of strangers intent upon enjoying themselves in a unique environment filled with things to see and do. Designing a space to take advantage of the five senses is an effective way to plan your environment. What is it that your customers will see, hear, smell, touch, and taste from the moment they arrive until the time that they leave your event? How can each of these experiences be maximized so that they reinforce the desired effect on the visitor? By combining information about the basic needs of the stakeholders with creativity and an acute environmental awareness, you have the possibility to design a memorable experience in a unique venue.

The site requirements are best determined through an understanding of the needs of external customers—sponsors, attendees, the media, residents, and the internal customers—staff, volunteers, vendors, entertainers, and corporate or governmental agencies that support the event. A thorough understanding of the needs of all significant stakeholders including the anticipated needs of the dominant demographic groups that will likely attend the event including families, young adults, elderly, etc., is called for. A site SWOT analysis will help to make the connection between the needs of your customers and the necessary levels and types of services and amenities to be provided. Systematically walk through the event as an attendee, entertainer, vendor, and volunteer in an attempt to envision the needs of each group. Site planning is about attention to detail and the significance of the details varies depending on their relationship to the event.

A detailed site plan is necessary. This can be initiated by using one of the many geographic visualization programs, such as Google Earth, to get an overview of the area to be used for the event. Depending on the clarity of the digital photography, the details of the site may be excellent or can be very grainy and lacking detail. Software programs allow for the inclusion of roads, buildings, commercial and food outlets, geographic features, and other points of interest that can aid in the choice of a special event site. Most municipal governments now have electronic files of all *aerial digital images* of their jurisdiction that can be plotted and printed on large-scale printers providing organizers with useful and accurate mapping tools. This information can also be accessed electronically and can be enhanced through *computer-assisted drafting*, CAD, to include the facilities and amenities of the event site.

A Site Plan Checklist

The following checklist of thirty seven essential site plan elements, organized alphabetically, will help you in preparing your event site. There are items that may be of particular concern to your event that are not mentioned in the next few pages, but the majority of standard site demands are presented.

1. Accessibility

Your site must be designed so that it maximizes the most efficient means of entering and exiting the area. It must also be capable of accommodating individuals with mobility restrictions by including specified parking and drop-off areas for disabled visitors and allowing for access to all attractions for those in wheelchairs or other modified means of mobility.

2. Accommodations

Although this is a term generally associated with hotel rooms, in event management all stakeholders must be considered when accommodating their needs on site. Accommodations include items such as sponsor hospitality areas, entertainers' facilities and other specific spaces required on site to meet the needs of visitors, contractors, staff, and volunteers.

3. Admission Gates

These areas must be designed to ensure safety and accountability in addition to being attractive, inviting gateways to your event. Accurately estimating the flow through your gates will help in determining the number of admission areas needed and the levels of staffing required at each gate in order to minimize congestion.

A well designed site plan aids both staff and visitors to have the best possible experience.

Downloaded from http://georgetown.patch.com/groups/summer/p/2013-smithsonian-folklife-festival-full-schedule-directions-and-more

4. Administrative Needs

Staff members will be expected to provide on-site administrative support in areas such as accounting, press relations, data entry, cash management, and other tasks. It is important that they be provided with an area that is sufficiently protected from the public activities so that meaningful work can be accomplished.

5. Children's Areas

If the goal of the event is to have visitors remain onsite for more than two or three hours, it is wise to have areas and programs designed to appeal to the youngest visitors. Attention span issues and the need for appropriate and engaging activities suggests that time and resources be dedicated to children's needs.

A children's area provides for fun and will usually result in your visitors staying a little longer at your event.
Photo Credit: Deb Droppers Event Company

6. Comfort and Safety

This is an overriding priority for event organizers. The event must be planned and designed for your customers. Sacrifices must be made in terms of efficiency and perhaps conventional thinking in order to provide the most comfortable and safe environment for your guests. There are always easier ways to provide services, but the emphasis must be on customer safety and comfort.

7. Communications

This is a multilayered challenge in that onsite communication must be designed to meet the operational requirements of the event and must also present customer information in easily accessible formats. The newest advances in wireless technology, as will be demonstrated in chapter fifteen, can greatly aid in this endeavor.

8. Concessions

Space for concessions must be organized in such a way that it maximizes exposure of the products and services to the visitor in a manner that is deemed equitable for those providing concession services and does not create negative crowding factors.

9. Crowd Capacity

Intelligent site design begins with understanding the scope of your event and providing sufficient transit and gathering spaces so that an optimum balance is reached between functional crowding and comfort and safety.

10. Destination Potential

A special event may become the catalytic activity in developing your area as a visitor destination. Cooperation between event organizers and the local tourism industry can create mutually beneficial results.

11. Dining Facilities

Many outdoor events anticipate their customers buying food at concessions and continuing to move about the event site. Providing adequate, shaded seating for dining will send a more positive message to your visitors and will increase concession sales as eating will become a more structured activity at the event.

12. Emergency Services

Local EMT service providers must be allocated space within the site that is convenient and strategically placed but does not bring undue attention to their presence. All such services must be linked to the control center of the event through communication devices.

13. Entertainment Seating Capacity

Seating must be allocated for the anticipated number of visitors for the premiere entertainment offered at the event. While this might result in empty seats during different times of the day, it is important that peak crowds be accommodated so that the maximum crowds experience the best you have to offer.

14. Entrances and Exits

All pedestrian walkways must be well marked and logically designed to eliminate bottlenecks. In the case of an emergency evacuation, or at the end of the last performance of the event, visitors should be able to easily find and make use of exits. The number and location of exits should be carefully planned to meet peak capacities.

15. Environmental Concerns—Green Technologies

Event visitors may be somewhat oblivious to the sights and sounds and smells of the event as they are an expected part of the experience. For local residents, who may have to endure these same sights, sounds, and smells for numerous consecutive days every year, it is important to understand the possible negative impacts. Every effort should be made to minimize or eliminate all environmentally unfriendly aspects of the event. See http://www.agreenerfestival.com/ for strategies for environmentally friendly events.

16. Groundskeeping

Prior to the opening of the event, efforts should be made to accentuate the positive natural elements of the event site. It is a matter of building on the strengths of the site and minimizing the weaknesses. Additional landscaping elements may be added to enhance the theme of the event.

17. Maintenance

Staff members should be readily available to perform any needed maintenance in an orderly and efficient manner. Work that must be completed during the course of the event should be accomplished in the least intrusive manner with great care to ensure the safety and comfort of visitors. This may require a temporary closing of a part of the venue. Barricades, signs, and security personnel should be used to inform and protect the public.

18. Maps

Site maps help to educate visitors about the many wonderful things for them to do and see at your event. Maps can also help to direct the flow of visitor traffic in order to reduce crowding and increase the enjoyment of the event offerings. You will help your cause by having site maps available online prior to the event so that interested visitors can study the layout of the event prior to their arrival. Printable formats will allow visitors to bring their own copy of the site map increasing the cost effectiveness of these types of investments.

19. Marketing Strengths

As mentioned earlier, site design must be included in the marketing plan for your event. The site should provide support to the marketing of the event and the marketing plan should help to highlight the amenities provided at the site.

20. Parking

Parking plans are critical to the success of the event and are addressed in great detail in chapter fifteen.

21. Pedestrian Flow

Site design can greatly impact the flow of visitors to your site and can help to create a positive environment within the grounds of your event. See Chapter 15 for more on the phenomena of crowding.

22. Permits

Permits help to ensure that organizers provide the necessary planning and resources to meet the demands of the scope of event. Permits support acceptable standards in many areas of event management from food handling, to electrical and utility services, road use and environmental concerns. The permit process should be portrayed as a necessary and very helpful aspect of event management.

23. Proximity

This is an important concept in site design as the spatial relationship of different elements of the event including parking, food services, and restrooms all will benefit from a thoughtful consideration of proximity issues.

24. Public Address System

Even if your event does not provide amplified entertainment, it is important to have a public address system and a backup power source so that important information can be transmitted to all visitors in a timely and effective manner.

25. Recycling

You will serve your event well to meet or exceed the local regulations regarding recycling activities. Innovative recycling practices are overwhelmingly met with approval and positive comments by event attendees.

26. Restrooms

Local and state sanitary codes will dictate the minimum number of restrooms and hand washing stations required for varying attendance levels at events. If financially feasible, try to provide more than the minimum and include at least one midday facility clean-out during the course of a daylong event. Restrooms are rarely a crowd pleaser, so once again attempt to exceed expectations for convenience and cleanliness. Be sure of proper lighting for evening events.

27. Risk Management

Site design must consider risk management in every aspect of the planning and placement of facilities and attractions on the property.

28. Room for Growth

When choosing a site for your event, it is wise to plan for the future by considering the possible need for expansion of the dimensions of the event in coming years. It is easier to justify expenditures to develop a site if it can be assured that the investments will be amortized over a significant period of time.

29. Security

Effective security is a combination of the implementation of an effective risk management plan, the proper assignment of identifiable trained staff and contracted service providers, and the overall perception of safety that is created by the visible indications that the event site is adequately staffed and under the control of the event organizers. While it is not wise to underfund this most important area, it is advised to incorporate as many perceptual supports to the security plan that may cost little or no money.

A shaded dining area is greatly appreciated by event visitors.
Photo Credit: Deb Droppers Event Company

30. Shade

From a health and comfort perspective, as well as the cold, hard realities of revenue production, it is not wise to subject large groups of people to prolonged exposure to the sun. The discomfort and energy sapping characteristics of being out in the sun too long have no possible positive benefit for your event. If natural shade areas are not present on your site, you must provide shaded areas under tents or other structures so that people can experience some relief from the sun and hopefully extend their stay at your event.

31. Signs

Signs help to direct people to certain locations, protect them from unnecessary dangers, contribute to the theme and mood of your event, and enhance the visitor experience by providing important information that allows them to become more deeply involved with the experiences provided by your event. Signs should reflect the quality of your event. They should be uniformly produced at the highest level of graphic quality that you can afford. Signs should be authoritative when necessary but should also communicate respect and provide a sense of welcome and appreciation to the visitors.

32. Sponsor Recognition

Depending on the agreement between your event and your sponsors, it may be necessary to create additional signs, banners, and other means of identifying and thanking sponsors. Like all other visual support materials, they should reflect the quality and integrity of your event.

33. Staging and Backstage Accommodations

Sufficient space is needed for the transport and assembly of amplification, lighting, and musical equipment. It is also very important that the entertainers be provided with comfortable, private space with a restroom, lighting, and mirrors. Your goal is to provide your customers with a great show. Take care of your performers!

34. Tents and Temporary Structures

These items have become an important resource for festival and event management. The venue environment can be greatly altered by the appearance and placement of temporary structures such as tents. Use a reputable company that provides high-quality products and assembles them on time.

35. Theme

Much of the effort to create the right feel for your event comes from the amount of planning given to the support of the theme of the event. All elements of the site should support the theme, from the type and appearance of the vendors, to the uniforms and demeanor of your staff and volunteers. Each year you should strive to incorporate more elements of your event into a deliberate, definitive support of your theme.

36. Utilities

Perhaps not the most interesting part of creating a memorable event, but the accurate estimation of utility services (electricity, water pressure, etc.) is critical to the operational integrity of the event. Insufficient power supplies can damage expensive equipment and jeopardize the financial viability of your event. When in doubt, get professional help and overestimate your needs.

37. Waste Management

One indication of a well run, mature event is the extra attention paid to issues like waste management and recycling. Positive, proactive policies and procedures help to solidify a positive impression of your event with visitors and other stakeholders.

Summary

Proper site planning and management creates the potential to have a highly successful, safe, and enjoyable event. The key to success in this area is to make use of the expertise of the many professionals in your area who may have experience in a particular aspect of managing the physical resources that go into an event site. Contact these professionals early in the process and incorporate their opinions and practices into your planning and management activities. Very few individuals have expert knowledge in all the areas of site management, therefore you will benefit greatly from the input of many individuals and businesses that have successful experience in the trades associated with physical site arrangements.

Discussion Questions

1. What are some minimum standards for site selection that must be met in order to create a successful event?
2. Provide an example of site selection contributing to the achievement of an event mission and goals.
3. How is risk management related to site selection?
4. How do signs contribute to the successful use of an event site?
5. How would you design an event space to accommodate future growth?
6. Why is shade an important consideration for outdoor events? How can this impact your revenue?
7. Why is a public address system critical to an event?
8. List three items that can be added to an event site to make it more attractive and inviting.
9. How is site planning similar to park planning?
10. Identify several amenities at an event site that you have personally appreciated or enjoyed.

13

Concessions: Bread and Circuses

 The meeting between Adam and Eve had been running quite smoothly until it was ruined by catering.

Fields and Stanbie

Chapter Objectives

- Understanding the importance of food strategies and food themes for your event
- Identify revenue strategies for concession management
- Describe the impact of using one or more professional vendors or community groups
- Identify the necessary ingredients for an effective concession contract
- Understand the importance of additional concessions such as merchandise, sponsor booths, and organizational promotions

In ancient Rome, the governmental leaders sought to control an ever growing population of non-Romans living in and around their great capital. In order to avoid unrest and revolt, the practice of providing entertainment for the masses was adopted as a political strategy to maintain peace and order. The concept of *bread and circuses* provided weekly entertainment along with food and drink in order to occupy the meager amounts of leisure enjoyed by the population. Gladiatorial fights, human sacrifice, animal slaughter, and the reenactment of great Roman military triumphs all reinforced the benevolence and power that was Rome. Each event was accompanied by food and sufficient drink to ameliorate the stress of a difficult existence. Although the fare probably did not include Caesar salads, the needs of the people were met with great quantities of food and drink.

Today the stakes are not quite so high. But in order to keep the peace and satisfy your customers at your next event, sufficient attention must be paid to the management of concessions. Cruise ships, the military, monasteries, sports venues, and festivals all understand the importance of serving quality food that meets the expectations of the customer. Stadium food, for example, has evolved from a cold hot dog and a warm beer to sushi bars, turkey foccacia sandwiches, Caesar salads, and microbrew beers. Our desire for unique and higher quality foods has risen over the past few decades, and it is important that event organizers accurately assess the expectations of potential customers.

Concession Strategies

The first step in developing a concession strategy is to understand the role that food will play at your event. Food may be the main attraction for events such as a lobster festival, pig roast, rib fest, or a medieval feast. In other situations, food may play a supportive role in meeting the comfort and convenience needs of attendees. It has long been recognized that having refreshments available at an event will often prolong the length of a visitor's stay. Whatever your particular situation is regarding the role of food at your event, be sure to have knowledgeable and motivated individuals working to plan and organize successful concessions that support your mission and meet your customers' expectations. Once the role of food has been established, a realistic assessment of the available resources to provide the food and beverage services must occur. Concessions have the potential to create sizable profits for an organization. The profit margin greatly expands with the volume of food sales, as the fixed costs do not generally increase once the startup is complete. Product costs will

The food can be the main attraction, especially at a pig roast!
Photo Credit: deLisle

increase but will be more than offset by the markup for each item sold. If trained volunteers can be used at the point of sale, overall profits should increase by way of reduced labor costs. A cost/benefit analysis of an in-house operation should be conducted to determine the return on investment for a concession program provided by the event organizers. If your organization has the facilities, personnel, and skills to provide the concessions, you must determine whether it is an area that deserves such an outlay of resources.

If the benefits of in-house concessions don't outweigh the costs, you should determine the local resources that might meet the objectives for food services at your event. Subsequent questions will include whether it is wiser to contract with one vendor to supply all the concessions, or is the event better served by having a variety of food types supplied by a number of different vendors. An increase in the number of vendors increases the communication demands between your organization and the vendors and multiplies the potential for problems. On the other hand, the failure of a single source concession can adversely affect the entire event. Your research into these and other important questions is most effective if you have someone with experience in the food and beverage industry providing information and initiating contact with potential service providers. Based on research findings, food served at outdoor fairs and festivals is perceived as significantly less healthful and less safe than food at other food preparation sites.[1] The challenges to a successful concession operation are determined by the relationship between product and service quality and the expectations of the customers.

Case Study: A Chilling Experience

I recently attended a fundraiser for a nonprofit organization that included a sit-down dinner followed by an auction of wonderful pieces of art and some great gifts. While dinner for 100 might be a lot for a home party, it should not be a particularly difficult endeavor for a catering service. Unless of course ... the meals were brought out unevenly with some guests finishing their meals before others were served the first course. Individual tables had a 20-minute discrepancy between one guest receiving a meal and the last hungry person at the table being served. And while it is polite to wait for everyone at your table to be served before beginning your meal, it was extremely impractical at this event. The food, when it did arrive, was not merely cooling down but was ice cold. It was uncomfortable for the guests to not make comments about the quality of the service; it was, in fact, unavoidable.

At a follow-up meeting of the event-organizing committee, the food committee praised the efforts of the caterers in that they were easy to contact, communicated well with the committee throughout the process, and met the vegetarian/non-dairy requests of some patrons and worked very hard. The committee also mentioned that some of the food may have been a little cold, but they were serving one hundred guests. The measure of success for the food committee was the relationship between themselves and the caterer, which apparently was pleasant and positive. These are valid observations, but they do not minimize the importance of other issues such as the timing of food service and the temperature of the food. No one eating the dinner commented that, although the food was of poor quality, the caterers seemed to be nice people. No decision has been made to offer the job to the same caterers at the following year's event. From the customer's viewpoint, and in the process of considering attending the event next year, undoubtedly some individuals will remember the poor food service and may opt to make other plans that evening. The lesson here is to realize that satisfaction means different things to different people. The food committee was willing to overlook, or was not acutely conscious of the problems with service and quality because they felt good, in fact satisfied, with the personal interactions with the caterer. The catering company had come with many positive recommendations from other community groups, creating positive expectations. The initial impressions created by these recommendations can predispose individuals to think highly of a vendor or service provider to the point that shortcomings may be ignored. The long-term reputation of the event can be negatively impacted in this type of situation. There is a better way.

What would you do if you had to make a decision about using this caterer for another similar event for your organization?

How can this type of problem be avoided in the future? Like all other aspects of a special event, it is necessary to set performance standards for each element of service. In the case of the cold food and untimely service, the food committee and the event organizers would be better served by making a specification sheet identifying the expectations relative to the timing and temperature of the food being served. If the caterer does not meet the expectations, the resultant actions will be based on agreed upon contractual obligations rather than personal feelings and predispositions.

The following questions regarding the provision of food and beverages will help to clarify the decisions that need to be made regarding the choice of food and beverage service at your event.

What facilities are available on site to provide food services? Your venue may have full service kitchen facilities, or may lack basic utilities such as water and electricity. The limitations of your site are an important factor in determining the level of food services that can be provided. Generators, water tanks, portable sinks, and other equipment will be necessary in remote or poorly served locations. A lack of proper facilities would suggest that the job should be contracted to a business that can supply all the necessary facilities and can meet the service demands of your event.

What are the overall dimensions of the event? Is the intention to create a multiday event attracting thousands of visitors? Can your organization handle the demands of the crowds at the maximum or peak periods? It is critical that you properly estimate the food needs for your anticipated crowd. Depending on the scale of your event, you might need to look beyond the local concessionaire resources to adequately meet the needs of your visitors.

What is the time scale of the event? Will the event last many hours, including a traditional mealtime? If the answer is yes, efforts must be made to supply more than snack type foods. Depending on the clientele that attends your event, the food menu and service configuration will vary. If you wish visitors to extend their stay beyond mealtime, you must provide palatable, healthy, and attractive food alternatives for your visitors.

Vendors should be equipped to handle peak periods of attendance at the event.
Photo Credit: Deb Droppers Event Company

Will attendees be allowed to bring food and beverages to the event? Some events encourage attendees to bring food, allowing for minimal efforts on the part of the organization in providing support in this area. It should be noted, however, that concessions provide a significant boost to event revenues. If revenue production is an important objective for your event, you may want to limit carry-in food and beverages. There are also safety considerations in allowing visitors to carry coolers, containers, bottles, and other items that can pose a risk to other attendees. This is a greater point of consideration if alcohol is allowed at the event.

What are the legal ramifications and responsibilities of using outside vendors instead of an in-house operation? Using vendors or caterers who are professionally disposed to provide food services allows your organization to transfer some of the liability to a third party contractual service provider. This reduces, but does not eliminate, the organization's responsibility for the safety and quality of the food and beverages served. Loss of reputation through poor products or service is another risk factor that must be considered when hiring outside service providers. An organization can best protect itself from liability and loss by formulating very clear policies regarding food and beverage service that are clearly communicated through the vendor contract. All state and local ordinances regarding food preparation and service must be acknowledged and adhered to by all parties.

Elements of a Food and Beverage Contract

Depending on the objectives of your event, selecting a caterer or concessionaire can have a significant impact on its success. Your expectations must be clearly enumerated and communicated to the potential vendors through a written contractual agreement. Make use of the contract to gather as much information as possible concerning the operations and products of each vendor. It might be one of the few times to communicate with a vendor prior to the event.

Some general considerations that must be shared with the potential vendors include your perception of the role of the vendors in the success of the event. If the vendors are a main feature of the event, careful attention must be paid to the link between the theme of the event and the types of food served. If the food and beverage is of secondary importance, there must still be an expectation of quality products and service. Typically, a set of bid specifications or other form of communication of the expectations for food and beverage service should be made available prior to any consideration of potential vendors. A specification sheet will effectively eliminate vendors that do not meet the programmatic needs of the event. Selection criteria will then be established so that vendors can meet the standards for the event and will understand the rationale behind selecting or rejecting particular applications. Having this information readily available helps to avoid misunderstandings, eliminates the possibility of a vendor taking a rejection personally, and presents a highly organized, professional image for your event.

Vendors likewise will have questions regarding the intentions and earning potential of your event. A professionally run concession will want information regarding the past performance of the event including attendance, gross income, number and type of vendors used, guidelines concerning exclusivity of products, and other items of importance to the potential vendor. More detailed information may be provided explaining the layout of the event, the proximity of the concessions to the performance areas, the scheduling of entertainment, and competition between scheduled programs and food sales. For example, if visitors have to leave a performance area in order to obtain food, it will have an impact on sales. Likewise, if some roaming vendors have access to seating areas while others are in static locations, this, too, will impact sales potential. This will also be perceived as an unfair advantage for some vendors. The previously discussed issues such as event scale, timing, and available facilities are also important to the potential vendor and should be communicated through the specification sheet and reiterated in the actual contract.

The Concession Contract

Based on a review of food and beverage contracts from many sources, the following information captures the critical requisites for a practical vendor contract. Additional items may be added to address issues specific to your event.

Identification of the Parties

As detailed in Chapter 10, a legal contract must be between two or more legal entities engaged in a legal activity. At the time of contract negotiation, the vendors should produce paperwork documenting their existence as a vending or catering business. Records should be kept of all the pertinent background information of the business. The actual name of the owner of the vending business, whom may not be the individual signing the document, must be included in the contract. This name should match that of any insurance or other legally relevant paperwork.

License to Do Business and Temporary Permits

Prior to the finalization of the contract, the vendor should produce its license to do business in the state or other relevant jurisdiction. Most municipalities also require a temporary vendor permit prior to operating a concession. The business license and temporary permit have fees associated with them that are considered costs of doing business and should not be deducted from any fees charged vendors by the event organizers.

Health Certificate

The concessionaire must have a valid certificate from the health department insuring that their facility meets or exceeds the standards set by local and state health authorities. The vendor must show evidence of proper food handling training for all employees. It may be advisable for the organizing committee to review health department records for evidence of past violations or failure to adhere to set standards by each potential vendor. Health inspection reports are considered public information and can be obtained through your local health department. It is also prudent to check with the local Better Business Bureau for any indications of less than professional performance in the past by any of the potential vendors.

Insurance Information, Liability, and Indemnification Statements

Along with a legal identification of the vendor, it is necessary to ascertain that the business is in possession of all mandated insurance needed to operate a concession business. Your organization or governing body might also have minimum requirements for insurance, additional coverage for the event, and an assumption of risk on the part of the vendor. The vendor might be asked to accept full responsibility for damages to persons or property arising from their occupancy and use of the facility and sales of their products. Vendors should supply evidence of insurance including *per-occurrence coverage, product liability coverage,* and a *general aggregate limit* in accordance with the requirements of the event organizers or their representatives. If the event takes place in an area that might impact other private businesses, such as during a street fair, the adjoining businesses may have to be extended coverage by the vendors. The specific language of the agreement must reflect the requirements necessary in your locale. Do not waive any of these requirements based on personal opinions, past relationships, or the desire to be overly cooperative and friendly. If an incident occurs, all the necessary paperwork must be available in order to protect the interests of the event and your stakeholders.

Fire Marshal Requirements

In addition to food-handling and storage regulations addressed in the permitting process, vendors must make themselves aware of, and adhere to, the state and local fire marshal regulations. These regulations control cooking, heating, ventilation and air conditioning, the use of tents, allowable type of flooring in cooking areas, the number and placement of fire extinguishers, the need for sprinkler systems or other fire control systems, and set-back dimensions between kitchen and food preparation areas and the public.

Selection Criteria

Once the minimum safety and health standards have been determined through interaction with the regulatory agencies, you might want to restate the selection criteria used in choosing vendors for the event as a means of reinforcing the original expectations for food and beverage service. The selection criteria reminds the vendor of the event objectives and gives the vendor the opportunity to officially and legally agree with these terms and conditions. Experienced vendors will recognize the value of these regulations and will work to cooperatively meet all required specifications. New vendors need additional attention and should be encouraged to contact both the event organizers and all regulatory groups as often as needed to meet the standards. There are however, less scrupulous vendors who will cut corners and not invest in the safety of their employees or customers in order to save some money. Enforcement of the selection criteria and vigilant monitoring of the concessionaires will help to identify these rascals and give you full justification in revoking their privileges.

Description of the Event

A description of the event should include dates, location, a general explanation of the purpose of the event, admission fees, attendance estimates, and the number and types of vendors to be allowed at the event.

Length of Festival

Quantifying the scope of the event allows for a realistic assessment of the resource requirements for the vendor and sets the parameters for service provision expectations for the organizers.

Hours of Operation

Vendors will be expected to be open for a definite number of hours during the event. Generally speaking, most vendors are expected to be open any time the event is open to the public. This can be altered to meet specific needs of the events, such as a cooking demonstration, or it can accommodate limitations expressed by the vendor or scheduling needs determined by the event organizers.

Proposed Menu and Prices

The product menu is a critical element in the vendor selection process. Organizers must address the objectives of the event that are to be met by concession sales. The quantity and quality of food and beverages offered at the event must be made clear to all parties and must be adhered to throughout the event. By reviewing the menu, the organizers are able to control the mix of items to be sold and can identify products that might require additional monitoring due to storage or cooking requirements. An in-depth review of the menu will help to identify items that are slow to prepare and serve or that can create health or environmental issues. It is also important to review pricing strategies, as some menus might not match the characteristics or demographics of your event.

Inclement Weather Procedures and Dates

Both the organizers and the vendors must agree to procedures addressing a weather delay or a postponement of the event due to inclement weather. The obligations of both parties regarding any dates chosen as make up dates must be made clear; for example, is the vendor required to participate on the rain date? Changes to fees and payments can be negotiated if the event is cut short by bad weather. Whatever is decided regarding this unfortunate but inevitable situation, it is important that the ground rules are clearly written and enforceable.

Set-up and Breakdown Times

All vendors must be aware of, and adhere to, the times designated for these activities. Vendors should be in place and ready to serve by the time the gates open and should not be putting equipment away or reducing their services until the event ends and the public has departed. This is important as a safety consideration and also helps to maintain a professional customer conscious atmosphere at the event.

It is advised to schedule these activities in shifts so that all vendors are not trying to deliver the equipment or take it away at the same time. Parking permits may be provided for a predetermined number of service vehicles for each vendor site.

Financial Considerations

The financial management of the vendor relationship is obviously a critical issue to both parties. There are many strategies available in order to collect revenue from the vendors in the form of booth fees or a percentage of gross sales.

Booth Fees

Booth fees can have a premium attached for particularly valuable locations such as corner sites or those nearest the more populated areas of the venue. Additional amenities such as increased electrical supply, nearby access to running water, additional square footage, or double booths also warrant higher fees. If a tiered approach is considered, the value of the additional items must be validated by vendors. You might think that a booth near the restrooms or directly near the entrance or exit is convenient, but experienced vendors have their own ideas of the best spots at the site. Get some input from trusted vendors before undertaking a complex fee based allocation system. Having a set fee or a tiered fee approach is definitely the easiest on the event organizers. This can be combined with a first come, first served, or a right of first refusal for returning vendors, in order to allocate the preferred spaces. You can accurately estimate your revenue from booth rental providing a reliable economic indicator prior to the event.

Percentage of Sales

This method can result in greater revenue if it is properly organized and monitored. The most controllable means of accomplishing this is to require all sales to be transacted by tickets sold by the event organizers at designated areas within the venue. Profits are then shared on a percentage basis with each of the vendors, depending on the number of tickets they turn in at predetermined times during the event. Allowing the vendors to return a percentage of their cash sales to the organizers often results in organizational revenue that might not reflect the actual sales amount at the booth. Again, you must be aware that all vendors might not be completely honest in their dealings with you. Hope for the best, but plan for the worst!

Materials Supplied by Your Organization

It must be made very clear as to what items the event organization is providing. For example, electrical service may be limited to a 110 volt, 15 or 20 amp service per vendor; this may affect the type of equipment and the variety of food provided by a vendor. It is important for the organization to be able to estimate the peak requirements for electric-

Case Study: Selling Spaces

Recently a local art fair reviewed its revenue sources and determined that more money could be realized through increased vendor space sales. The existing policy was that the participating vendors were required to turn in 15% of their revenue at the end of the event. This meant that if the booth sold $5,000 of product over the course of the event, they would be required to provide the organizing committee with approximately $333. The problem arose in that there was no inventory control system that would allow the event organizers to validate the number of items sold. It was essentially an honor system.

After some discussion, the event committee decided that a set booth fee, based on an average percentage payment by the vendors in previous years, would be used in the upcoming edition of the event. Oddly enough, all of the vendors who typically turned in very low amounts each year chose not to participate in the upcoming event. Others asked if they could expand their booths by purchasing additional space, realizing that it was a fair price. Despite one's best wishes, the honor system is not a best practice when it comes to managing vendor revenues.

Typically, a deposit amount is required at the time of application with full payment and a performance bond such as a disposal deposit should be required long before the staging of the event. Deadlines must be adhered to, as some vendors will attempt to hold a booth on deposit while waiting for more lucrative contracts to come through.

ity that can occur when all aspects of the event are underway, including entertainment, lights, cooking equipment, and more. Insufficient current is a showstopper, as it can affect the quality of sound reinforcement, can cause damage to all types of equipment, and can trip overload breakers, effectively shutting down electrical service. Options for additional electrical service, typically a 220 50 amp service, can be provided and can be accompanied by a higher fee paid by the vendor. Other issues that must be clearly explained include the provision of other utilities such as clean water, wastewater disposal responsibilities, shelters, and dining facilities, and any other amenities that are provided at the site that can impact the concession operations.

Materials Supplied by Vendor

Many headaches can be avoided if an accurate listing of all materials that are to be supplied by the vendor is included in the contract. All materials, supplies, personnel, and equipment used to prepare, cook, and serve food are generally included in this section. Additional items may include provisions for handling tickets, coupons, or cash depending on the arrangements for revenue sharing established for the event. It should also be noted if generators or refrigeration units are to be used, as this can affect the rental fee for a particular vendor. Noise abatement standards must be explained and enforced for motorized equipment used by some vending units.

Vendor Service Management

While this might seem a bit overwrought, if your objective as an event producer is to provide the highest quality experience for your customers, then it is important to know that your contractual service providers have given sufficient thought and planning to the delivery of services at your event. A written plan that describes the number of employees to be used at the event by each vendor, the shifts for those employees, and any other details that demonstrate proper preparation and planning for the allocation of resources is a beneficial document for organizers to review and retain. This should be attached as an addendum to the contract. Many contractors might complain about this request. The burden can be reduced if you provide vendors with a scheduling template, allowing them to fill in the needed information and attaching it to the contract. Vendors must then be held to the projected service plan. Spot inspections will help the organizers to assess compliance with these requirements.

Method of Food Preparation

This information is important for the organizers to understand exactly what will be taking place at the vendor's booth. Are items precooked and heated on site, are they prepared and packaged offsite, and is there a need for high temperature cooking equipment that produces smoke and potentially unpleasant odors?

You must be able to determine whether the food preparation and serving procedures will result in an extended transaction time. The length of time between placing an order and the actual reception of the product will affect service quality and can result in long lines and unhappy customers.

On-Site Managers and Contacts

The vendor must provide a list of on-site managers for each day of the festival. This allows for a rapid resolution of problems and allows organizers to interact with vendors in a predictable manner. Additional contact information, emergency numbers, and other information that can help you avert a crisis should be included. Experienced vendors will understand the need for this type of information to be provided to the organizers.

Disposal Procedures

Depending on the availability of municipal services, the management of wastewater, sewage, solid waste, and recyclable materials must be explained and agreed upon. A very busy booth is no excuse for overflowing garbage cans or the careless treatment of environmentally sensitive materials. It is important to remember that all aspects of your event, including waste disposal, send a message regarding the quality of your organization and the concern you have for your visitors' experience.

Weapons

Vendors must be informed about state and local regulations regarding the possession of firearms. Many states have quite liberal laws regarding concealed weapons that might not match the laws or sensibilities of your community. Obtaining additional information from your local police department, legal counsel, and your insurance company is recommended in order to limit/ban any firearms on your event site.

Cleanup Deposit

Acknowledging the reality of human shortcomings, it is wise to hold a bond or deposit to cover the expenses of post-event cleanup if vendors should fail to properly clean their sites. Standards of cleanliness must be communicated to the vendor so that the expectations of the organizers can be understood and met. Failure to meet clearly defined standards of cleanliness should result in forfeiture of the deposit.

Limitation of Cash On-Site

The vendor management plan described earlier should include language limiting the amount of cash that vendors may have at their booths. This condition can reduce the occurrence of theft and any associated violent acts.

Maintenance of the Premises During and After the Event

Busy is good! It is not an excuse for the vendor booth to appear messy, disorganized, or unhealthy. Cooking areas must be kept clean, waste must be properly disposed of, serving areas must be immaculate and accessible, and the general appearance of the vendor booth must reflect the professional care and quality of service reflective of the entire event.

Lodging Guidelines

Vendors may be on site for several days or weeks. In an effort to reduce expenses and maximize profits, some might choose less than acceptable lodging strategies. A designated RV and camping area can be identified that is far away from the public areas and has sufficient utilities to keep the place from looking like a shanty town. Specific regulations regarding dress, laundry, curfew, and noise regulations must be communicated and enforced if this type of arrangement is offered. It is better to make a deal with a local motel to offer a reduced rate for your vendors if a certain volume of reservations can be promised.

Appropriate Dress

If your event has a particular theme, you might want all vendors to fit into your scheme. If not, you will want to insist that all workers who are in sight of the public dress professionally for the event. Many vendors use shirts or uniforms as a means of advertising their business, and that is to be commended. You might want to at least rule out particular modes of dress that would compromise the image of your event. If this is left unspoken, you can expect the worst!

Naming of Booth

Consider the impact of signs on the overall atmosphere of your event. Limits on the size and composition of vendor signs can play an important role in the feel of the event. Do neon signs and bulb-lighted carnival-type signs fit with your event? Would your event be better served if all vendors had standardized signs created by your organization?

Photos of Tent, Booth, or Trailer

Many questions concerning the appearance and appropriateness of a vendor's business can be resolved by requiring vendor applicants to include a recent photo of the booth, tent, or vehicle that will be used at your event. Be sure that the event day set up closely resembles the photo submitted. If their booth does not substantially match the photo you can, and might have to, revoke their contract and refund their fee.

Exclusivity Rights for Products

Vendors are very interested in having exclusive rights for the sale of their particular product. The variety of offerings is increased and the potential profits for individual vendors are enhanced if product exclusivity rights are enacted in the contract. Particularly large events may warrant two or more of the same types of products being sold, but attention should be paid to the proximity of similar products in order to support sales by each vendor.

No Sales of Other Items

Vendors must limit their sales to the list of menu items that is included as an addendum to the contract. Any violation of this agreement can result in shutting down the booth or disqualifying the vendor from future involvement in the event. Inclusion of this clause helps to further reinforce any exclusivity rights provided.

On-Site Supervision of Vendors

Vendors generally move from one event to another during the festival season and do not dedicate too much time to contract management. Many vendors may bend the rules in order to save money or to reduce their workload. This erosion of standards cannot be tolerated, as it can jeopardize both the safety and enjoyment of your visitors and the quality of your event.

On-Site Inspections

In addition to those required by state or local ordinance, inspections are an important part of contract enforcement. If vendors are met at the gate at the time of set up and no further contact is made throughout the event, the vendors will surmise that that the contract conditions are not enforced, inviting violations, safety hazards and increased risk for your event. Periodic visits, particularly during peak times, reinforce the expectations of the event organizers and serve as a training exercise for new and veteran vendors. *The contract sets the level of expectation for your event, while the interactions during the event reinforce these expectations.* A written review of vendor performance that is shared with each vendor is an effective way to educate all vendors and to eliminate those that do not meet your performance standards as set out in the contract.

Surrender of Premises

Vendors must agree to make their on-site premises available to organizers at any time. This allows for periodic unannounced inspections of product and delivery services. In order to facilitate a cooperative environment, the event organizers should make any inspections as reasonable and unobtrusive as possible. The vendor must also agree to remove everything from the site within a specified timeframe. Occasions do arise when vendors would like to delay departure for several days if they are traveling to another event in the area and need to bide their time between events. It is best to not become involved with these extraneous needs but to enforce departure periods in a strict manner.

Audit Rights

If the financial arrangements of the event include some form of revenue sharing between the event organizers and the vendors, you might want to include a clause that would allow for the review of the business books relative to the time of the contractual relationship. Hopefully this would not be necessary, but if discrepancies arise, it is best to have a previous understanding and agreement identified in the contract to address post-event financial issues.

References in the Past 12 Months

Vendors should provide a list of current references who can describe the quality of services recently provided by the vendor at events of a similar size and duration. Responsible vendors who are good business people will be very willing to provide this information, as it will support their desire to be selected for your event.

Default and Termination of Agreement

All well-constructed contracts provide termination or escape language. This language describes the terms and conditions that lead to and permit termination of the contract for both parties. This section should also describe what steps can be taken by each party to be made whole should a partial or full breach of contract take place. Means and methods of conflict resolution, mediation, arbitration, and the initiation of a lawsuit should also be addressed.

Festival Authority

A statement should be included defining the rights, responsibilities, and authority of the event organizers regarding all actions to be taken regarding security, crowd control, the enforcement of event, and local regulations concerning sanitation, health, hours of operation, and the cessation of activities due to events such as weather and other unforeseen circumstances.

Signatures and Dates

The contract is not accepted as a legal document until is signed and dated by both parties. This should not take place until all the details of the contract are identified and fully understood by both parties.

Merchandise and Souvenirs

Merchandise, if properly managed, can greatly add to the positive perception regarding the event and can contribute to the future marketing effectiveness and longevity of your event. For some events, such as art fairs, the buying of merchandise is central to the experience of participating in the event. *Souvenirs* are a way of taking a part of the event home, allowing for the reliving of the experience, and a positive reinforcement of the choice to attend the event. Merchandise is an effective means of creating brand recognition for your event. At some point in the mid-1970s, t-shirts became a sought-after item at festivals and events. A commemorative t-shirt tells others that you were there and are happy to be associated with the event. It acts as a walking advertisement for the event and is frequently accompanied by personal testimony about an enjoyable experience. There are very few instances like this where an individual will pay to advertise and promote your event!

Other items that identify the event such as video/DVD recordings of the event, CDs of the performers, works of art, or craft items all serve to support the actions of the visitor and reinforce and reward the participant. Decisions must be made concerning the rights and control of such merchandise as the event organization should be positioned to gain the greatest benefit from these types of items. Vendors can bring merchandise items that are not on their proposed sales list in an effort to unload things that they have not sold at previous events. This might include items that are of poor quality, inappropriate for your event, or can pose a health or safety risk. These *contraband items* typically cause more problems than they are worth, which might explain the need for the vendor to try to get rid of them at your event. Should you see attendees with items such as unauthorized pieces of clothing, fireworks and sparklers, glow sticks, and other toys that are not authorized for sale at the event, it is wise to ask where they were purchased and immediately intercede at the point of sale. It is best to confiscate these items and return them to the vendor at the end of the event.

Your mix of vendors might also include local groups that seek to contribute to your event. Because they are usually not professional vendors, extra attention should be paid to these groups.

Community Organizations as Vendors

Many community events are confronted with the possibility of having local service organizations participating as vendors. This can be a mixed blessing. If appropriate to the objectives of the event, it is wise to involve as many local organizations as possible. This generates increased marketing of the event, can bring in more local attendees, and is a sign of cooperation and goodwill for the local community. Many events rely heavily on the local service groups for their particular signature food offering at the event. The downside comes when others learn of the financial gains of the service organization and want to become vendors in the future. Most service groups are not in existence to run food concessions and only take it on as a means to support a good cause or to make money at the event. Additional resources will need to be dedicated to working with these groups to ensure that quality products and services are provided in a healthy and acceptable manner. It might be prudent to have some groups offer prepackaged items or those that do not require extensive cooking or on-site preparation. In this way, the group can contribute something to the event and potentially bring in some revenue without creating unnecessary liability for the event. These types of issues must be dealt with in an extremely diplomatic fashion as the appreciation of local involvement must be demonstrated and managed successfully.

Summary

Incorporating the above-listed elements into a concession contract will greatly enhance the communications between yourselves and the various vendors that will be doing business with you. Professional vendors appreciate the order and predictability that are the result of timely and effective communications. You might be aware of other issues that affect the vendor/organizer relationship. Any such items should be properly identified and addressed in a written concession contract.

Discussion Questions

1. What is the first step in the process of developing a concession strategy for an event?
2. What on-site elements are considered when determining a concession strategy?
3. What are the risks and benefits of using a single vendor for concession services at an event?
4. What is the purpose of the permitting process for food concessions?
5. How could the length of a festival impact your food service contracts?
6. What is a recommended system for charging a vendor who runs a concession at an event?
7. What are two reasons that it is important to know the proposed menu of a vendor before accepting its application?
8. Why is it advisable to require a cleanup deposit to be paid by all vendors?
9. Why is it be a good idea to have vendors submit photos of their booth with their initial application?
10. What other types of concessions might be appropriate at a festival?

1. Yeoman, I., Robertson, M., Ali-Knight, J., Drummond, S., & McMahon-Beattie, U. (2004). *Festival and event management*. Amsterdam: Elsevier Butterworth & Heinemann, p. 176.

14

Event Safety: Traffic, Crowd, and Parking Strategies

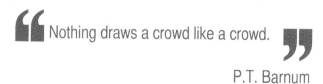

Nothing draws a crowd like a crowd.

P.T. Barnum

Chapter Objectives

- Identify general safety considerations in event planning
- Describe crowd characteristics, crowd management, crowd control
- Understand traffic as a supply-and-demand issue
- Understand how to create and implement a traffic-management plan
- Develop a pedestrian management plan
- Develop a parking management plan
- Understand the importance of evaluation and debriefing

General Safety Considerations

Allocating the necessary resources to ensure the safety, comfort, and well-being of your visitors is a primary responsibility that requires careful analysis and planning. Conducting an *environmental scan* to assess the safety needs of your event will have a positive impact on all facets of your event planning and operations. This environmental scan can be done as a part of a safety feasibility study that should be completed during the initial phases of the strategic planning process for the event. The resources needed to address the concerns of stakeholder groups regarding potential transportation challenges presented by the event must also be identified. This process will determine the viability of existing resources to handle increased demands in vehicular and pedestrian traffic associated with your event. Changes to present capacities, including rerouting traffic, closing roads, reconfiguring lane directions, posting signs, and positioning personnel for the day of the event should be identified and included in a communication plan to be shared with officials and the public well in advance of the event.

This assessment for customer and environmental safety should also include a consideration of the general and specific supervision of all event activities. *General supervision* addresses the overall supervision strategy for the event and includes the placement of event staff and security personnel in key positions, as well as assigning others to move about your site. General supervision is coordinated by a command center that assigns, monitors, and receives information from the appropriate staff members. General supervision is the first line of intervention should a crisis develop.

Specific supervision is a increased level of monitoring visitors in areas that require a greater level of supervision. Traffic crossings, backstage areas, food preparation areas, mechanical operations, and amusements such as rides, require assigned staff to be present at all times the public is on site. Specific supervision requires trained personnel to ensure a level of expertise that meets acceptable standards for each activity or area. Planning for staff assignments must take into consideration the need for both types of supervision during the event.

General Safety Checklist

In addition to traffic and pedestrian safety issues, there are many other areas that impact visitor safety that must be identified and included in a safety-management plan (See Table 14.1). Your event might include some or all of these areas in addition to items that are particular to your event that warrant consideration in the safety assessment process. Included in this would be any geographic elements such as open water or other natural elements that require additional planning and procedural development.

Crowd Management and Crowd Control

From an economic impact perspective, attracting nonresidents to an event can be a key strategy in determining the success of your event. On the other hand, an influx of visitors might also bring increased levels of crime or the perception of this type of activity to your community. Visitors might also feel a decreased sense of security when attending large festivals and events, particularly in unfamiliar urban settings. The experience of crowds and the phenomena of crowding play important roles in the overall enjoyment of a visitor at an event. Planning for the arrival and integration of large numbers of people into an event setting is an important consideration in the overall task of event planning.

Abbott and Geddie (2000) provide an understanding of this important topic by differentiating between crowd management and crowd control. *Crowd management, defined as the facilitation, employment, and movement of crowds,* considers the role of crowds in the planning of the event. Important considerations in creating a crowd safe environment include the allocation of resources and the appropriate training of crowd management personnel, the creation of scenarios to foresee crowd issues, and the ability to gather and evaluate data in order to constantly improve crowd conditions at events.

Table 14.1. Safety Checklist
1. First-aid and emergency response procedures
2. On-site safety procedures
3. Communication and control measures
4. Crowd management and crowd-control strategies
5. Federal, state, and local permits, codes, and regulations
6. Instructional signs for visitors
7. Entrance and egress procedures
8. Food- and beverage-handling practices
9. Accident reporting procedures
10. Security and public safety interventions
11. Tent safety codes and assembly procedures
12. Severe weather forecasting and evacuation procedures
13. Seating strategies
14. Media relations
15. Public address announcements
16. Special needs populations
17. The use of participation waivers on tickets
18. Sanitation, waste management, and recycling policies and procedures
19. Hazardous materials management
20. Machinery and equipment operation guidelines

Crowd control differs in that it involves creating specific procedures to handle a crowd that is creating a threat to the safety of others. Crowd control requires that organizers work through scenarios prior to the event in order to develop a plan that can be implemented on a moment's notice. Effective crowd management should reduce, but will not eliminate, the need for crowd control. Inadequate crowd management can lead to negative, destructive, and litigious outcomes.[1]

Crowd Characteristics

Crowd characteristics include a consideration of the numbers of people that attend an event, the density or spatial parameters of the gathering (what we commonly refer to as crowding), and the behavioral attributes of the group. Estimating crowd size and applying those figures to the dimensions of the venue are fairly straightforward exercises that will help in establishing an effective management plan. Increases in density, however, can evoke unpleasant feelings among visitors, who will at some point seek relief from those feelings. Therefore, understanding crowd psychology is a critical and challenging step in creating an effective management plan. See Table 14.2. Festivals, sporting events, parades, concerts, and fairs all attract different types of visitors with particular needs and expectations. Event organizers also have expectations regarding crowd density and associated behaviors. Individuals react differently to crowds based on their personal expectations and past experiences. Some folks seek the excitement of a crowd, while others will make great efforts to avoid crowds. Crowds themselves behave differently dependent upon their demographics, their motivations, and the environmental issues particular to the site. Environmental issues include such things as weather conditions, time of day or night, evidence of security personnel and control measures, the use or misuse of time, the presence of alcohol, site-specific causes of crowding, and the character or personality of your event.

Table 14.2. Attributes of a Crowd

- Crowds create a form of equality of status amongst themselves.
- Curiosity causes crowds to grow.
- Crowds move in the direction of an attraction or source of curiosity.
- Crowds become denser until safety is threatened.
- Stagnant crowds seek discharge or release in order to break existing patterns.

Tarlow, (2002)[5]

Case Study: That Mozart Concert was a Riot!

I can't recall ever hearing of a major disturbance or riot at a classical symphony concert. Although centuries ago, some classical music concerts did create problems and even violence due to the radical nature of new music, it's the wrong mix of music and attendees to create a mob mentality today.

I do recall a Grateful Dead concert at the Yale Bowl in New Haven, Connecticut, in the 1970s where young people who did not purchase tickets were literally scaling the walls to get into the stadium. The police rushed in and engaged the people outside the stadium in a battle. The paid attendees inside the stadium crowded the upper reaches of the venue peering over the walls to watch the battle between the uniformed police and the tie-dyed "attackers." It had all the drama of a siege on a medieval castle and was itself worth the price of admission. Of course, the concert crowd sided with the young people and cheered each time someone made it up the wall. Others inside the venue attempted to help those trying to charge the gates, adding to the chaos. Only when the band started to play did those inside the stadium return to their seats to enjoy the concert. Many outside the stadium were injured or arrested in the mob scene that took place. Many variables came together to create an unruly and potentially dangerous crowd situation. Social conditions regarding a general lack of respect for authority and the need for individual expression were at an all-time high in the early '70s. The band attracted many who were on the fringe of socially compliant behavior. The prevailing social conditions of the time were accentuated by the ever-present concert staples of alcohol and illicit drugs, further fueling the crowd to root for the "hippies."

Over the next decade, many rock festival settings and indoor concert events resulted in mayhem, injuries, and deaths. Today's concertgoers have a variety of music types to choose from, but might still encounter violence as has been experienced at concerts in major urban areas in the past decade.

Event organizers might seek to escalate levels of excitement and interaction amongst visitors through music and other forms of entertainment. Crowds themselves create excitement that can be gratifying or can lead to panic and irrational or antisocial behaviors. Crowding has been the subject of many research studies as it relates to the visitor experience. Crowding is identified as a major impact on the social experience of a visitor (Wickam & Kerstetter, 2000), and might be a negative influence on the quality of a visitor's experience at an event.[2] Hui and Batteson, (1991) cite the need for a satisfactory level of perceived control on the part of the visitor when confronted with a crowding situation. This suggests that the visitors' feelings are more positive if they sense or perceive that there are high levels of control in their environment. This is important for event organizers, as many cues that suggest crowd and environmental controls can be planned for and included in the procedures that are a part of the crowd-management plan.[3] Others, (Eroglu & Harrel, 1986; Foxall & Goldsmith, 1994), contend that crowds do contribute positively to a visitor's experience, particularly if a large crowd is anticipated and viewed as a positive indicator of the quality of the event. This level of crowding is referred to as *functional crowding*, as the appropriate density of a crowd contributes to the enjoyment of the event.[4] This information is important when considering the scale of your event and will affect marketing, site design and layout, and other crowd-related resource issues.

The Psychology of Waiting in Line

David Maister (2005) wrote an insightful online article (davidmaister.com) on the psychology of waiting in lines. Maister sees satisfaction as dependent upon the perception one has of an experience when compared to his/her original level of expectation. If an experience is deemed better than expected, then one will experience satisfaction. Conversely, if an experience does not meet expectations, then dissatisfaction is the end result. This may be stating the obvious, but it has real implications for those waiting in lines. Here are a few of his findings and a few suggestions that can help in planning and managing lines at your events:

- **Unoccupied time seems longer than occupied time**. The folks at Disney learned this lesson a long time ago as they saw the wisdom of having costumed characters interact with families waiting in line for the attractions. If lines are inevitable at your event, find a way to occupy your guests' time. Some amusement parks now allow for a reservation to be made based on your arrival time to the line and the anticipated time that you would be at the front of the line. You can return to the line at your designated time and experience a potentially shorter wait.
- **People want to get started**. Make the wait a positive part of the event experience. If you have sufficient staff/volunteers, have them bring event materials to the line such as entertainment schedules, maps of the site, and menus. Be available to answer questions and engage the attendees in a positive way. In this way, you are initiating a positive event experience while your guests are still waiting in line.
- **Preprocess waits seem longer.** The process of getting to the event and the sense of anticipation can make waiting seem interminable. The waiting to get into the event,

whether it is in a traffic line or a pedestrian line, can set the stage for the overall impression of the event experience. Front load the positive experience for the visitor by making lines as enjoyable, interactive, and as short as possible.

- **Uncertain and unexplained waits seem longer than known finite waits.** If you can provide information as to the cause of the backup and how long people will have to wait, most people will feel as if they are being attended to in a positive way.

- **Unfair waits are longer than equitable waits.** If one line is waiting while other lines are moving at a more rapid pace, something is wrong with the process. People want to be treated equally, particularly when they have an investment of money or discretionary time in the process. Line monitors can help to move people in a predictable and equitable way.

Long lines require some people to take things into their own hands...
Downloaded from http://www.bayd.info/pictures-5461-why_wait_in_line.html

- **The more valuable the service, the longer people will wait.** A simple cost/benefit exercise is in play as visitors are willing to devote their personal resources of time, money, and patience in order to reach their goal of experiencing your event. Pre-event marketing and a very welcoming entrance gate to your event will sustain the willingness to make such sacrifices.

- **Solo waits feel longer than group waits.** Most individuals do not attend a special event to feel isolated. If visitors do arrive alone, make efforts to extend a welcome and interact with them to bring them into the spirit of the event. Enthusiasm is contagious.[6]

Crowd Management

Every aspect of your event that influences visitor behavior impacts crowd management strategies. The theme of your event will draw a particular crowd type that may present problems in managing behaviors that are typical of a certain demographic group. The choice of venue will influence safety both inside and outside the event. The selection of particular entertainment and concessions will attract and stimulate the crowd to varying degrees. Event organizers must determine the movement of visitors throughout the event site. Areas that have the potential for overcrowding must be designed and monitored to prevent functional crowding from becoming a negative experience. This has to do with the density of the crowd and the anticipated time that individuals choose to stay in one place.

Overly effective marketing efforts can overload the carrying capacity of the venue if unexpectedly large crowds come to the event. From soccer stadiums to nightclubs, concert venues, religious gatherings, and even promotional events at major retailers, the mere threat of overcrowding can cause panic, injury, and death. Many big box stores have on several occasions experienced dangerous crowd behaviors resulting in injury and death by offering credit vouchers for a select few who manage to be the first to enter a new store during a grand-opening celebration. It is not uncommon for shoppers to line up days before the release of a new product in order to be the first on the block to own a new gadget. Recently these makeshift events have resulted in theft, vandalism, and fighting. A new twist on marketing-based events comes from Sony, who employed a technique referred to as mayhem marketing. According to Fruin (1993, 2002), mayhem marketing deliberately causes a public disturbance, increasing public curiosity and causes the crowd to grow significantly.[7] The City of Boston was confronted by such an event and had to send 12 police cars and additional officers to Copley Square to control crowd chaos created by the release of the newest version of the Play Station by Sony and Best Buy. The situation was exacerbated by the fact that the retailers had overhyped the event and did not have an adequate supply of the product for the size of the crowd of shoppers. Retailers, like other event producers large and small, must properly plan for and manage their crowds. Crowd Dynamics, a consulting firm, provides services to aid in the management of large crowds in unique environments. Recently they developed and event-planning software incorporating capacity analysis, risk assessment, testing of management plans, and automatic production of the written event plan (see www.crowddynamics.com).

Adequate security and control efforts must be estimated in order to meet the requirements of the size and personality of the crowd. Identifiable uniformed security personnel must be strategically positioned at the site and may be augmented with plainclothes officers to provide additional supervision.

Some Specific Considerations for Crowd Management

Stakeholder activities such as sponsor giveaways and the decision to allow alcohol at an event present additional challenges. The design and layout of the site, including the number and placement of entrances and exits in order to handle peak traffic times, and the elimination of bottlenecks within the flow of the site, can reduce crowding. Seating arrangements that promote order and avoid a rush to the best seats is advised. A command and control center that coordinates communication with all personnel should be strategically situated to provide visible and logistical support to crowd management. Communication systems that support the interaction of event organizers and the security and safety personnel are necessary. Additional communication procedures providing information to visitors through signs that can inform, instruct, or direct visitors, and public address systems that can provide immediate contact with all visitors are necessary considerations when formulating crowd management protocols. Bathroom facilities that are safely positioned and that prevent long lines or other causes for frustration will contribute to the sense of mutual respect that should be fostered at the event. Well lighted and supervised parking that allows for controlled egress in the case of an emergency or evacuation provides another level of safety for visitors.

The development and implementation of ticketing strategies that control the flow of traffic through the gates for the duration of the event will help in the allocation human resources during the critical times of the event. Consideration of the time of year chosen for staging the event will also impact the planning process for crowd management.

Important security guidelines for a crowd management system according to Berlonghi (1994) include an analysis of the risks associated with the event accompanied by an assessment of security needs based on the risk analysis. In addition, a well organized scheduling of event components and staff assignments providing for adequate and appropriate supervision at all times is needed. The careful selection and training of personnel, based on written job descriptions for each position, will ensure that staff members understand their responsibilities as well as the limitations of their authority.

The sheer number of variables inherent in event production suggests that crowd management is of primary importance to organizers. The initiation of the assessment and planning process for crowd management should begin in the very early stages of event strategic development.

Crowd Control

While riots in crowded elevators are not common, most crowded situations have the potential for getting a little crazy. Providing a safe environment that contributes to the enjoyment of visitors is the goal of a crowd-management program. Crowd control describes the actions taken when a crowd is becoming unruly or out of control.

Abbott and Geddie (2001) analyzed crowd control from three distinct stages. The *pre-crisis stage* is the time for managers to consider the preventive tactics that can eliminate many negative conditions before they occur and will also identify actions to be taken in an emergency situation. Training, appropriate staffing levels, intelligent site design, and other standards related to crowd management must be identified and communicated prior to the event. Training should include mock exercises for such things as fires, altercations, riots, and emergency evacuation strategies.

The *crisis stage* involves the implementation of crisis control procedures developed in stage one. This is in essence a problem-solving activity that is carried out under the duress of an emergency situation. It is essential that all those who might intercede in such a situation have a predetermined set of possible actions that can be taken in coordination with other emergency and safety personnel. This is particularly true for volunteers who might not normally encounter the types of situations or behaviors that can occur in a crisis moment. All actions taken during a crisis should emanate from the written protocols and training that preceded the event. Documentation in the form of incident and accident reports and supervisory summaries of responses taken during a crisis will help in defending the actions of the event organization should the whole thing end up in a lawsuit.

Finally, a formal review and evaluation should take place in the *post-crisis stage.*[8] Actions and improvements to the crowd management program should be informed by data and observations made during the event. This type of integrated approach to crowd management and control provides the right information to the right people and will instill a sense of control and confidence in your staff and volunteers. It will also facilitate the cooperative efforts of professional safety and security officers in carrying out the objective a providing a safe, nonthreatening, and comfortable experience for all visitors and stakeholders.[9]

Traffic, Pedestrian, and Parking Management

Traffic, pedestrian, and parking management are crucial elements in the design of a festival or special event. The best programming in the world will not compensate for a poorly designed or managed plan for the moving of people and vehicles to and from the event site. Long lines, inadequate parking resources, and a lack of clear directions create frustration and will certainly affect the initial and long-term visitor perceptions of your event. Fortunately, traffic engineering professionals have created a one-stop, all-inclusive guide for special event planners that covers every imaginable scenario that might arise in the planning, implementation, and evaluation of a traffic management plan. The full text, offered free of charge on the National Highway Administration website, is entitled *Managing Travel for Planned Special Events* (http://ops.fhwa.dot.gov/publications/fhwaop04010/toc.htm). This 400-page document recommends policies, regulations, planning and operations processes, impact mitigation strategies, equipment and personnel resources, and technology applications used in the advance planning, management, and monitoring of travel for planned special events. It is a complete guide, covering all categories of events and is presented in an easily understandable format offering the best practices and standards in traffic management. In addition, the NHA offers supplemental printed materials and holds conferences dedicated to traffic management at planned special events.

It's All About Supply and Demand!

Traffic management is a strategy to address a supply and demand situation. According to the NHA, transportation resources, including roadways, private and public transport, and parking areas, are finite resources that have a maximum carrying capacity. Under normal conditions, the demand for these resources is met by the existing configurations of public and private transportation spread over multiple destinations. A planned special event increases demand in a particular location for a predetermined length of time. Unplanned events, such as an accident or other emergency, also may increase demand on transportation resources and requires the immediate intervention of additional traffic control personnel and the rerouting of traffic. Unlike other supply and demand examples, it is not always possible to increase the supply of possible routes and resources in order to meet the increased demands associated with a planned event. The end result of traffic demands that exceed the capacity of the roadway without compensatory adjustments in supply configurations is *congestion*. Congestion generally occurs at times of peak usage or when significant changes occur in the balance of demand vs. carrying capacity.

Planned special events create a unique situation in that they increase traffic loads and can also decrease available resources due to road closures necessary to stage events such as road races, parades, and street fairs. Festivals and events also create additional trips to and from a specific location impacting existing transportation systems. The demand from a special event frequently magnifies weaknesses and limitations that exist in the local transportation system. Particular routes might be used beyond capacity during the beginning or end of a one day event. Public transportation might not be able to carry the increased demand for ridership without modifications to the existing routes and timetables.

Event organizers must be proactive in identifying present capacities, projecting anticipated loads associated with the event, and formulating and implementing strategies and technologies to improve traffic flow and ensure safe travel. Creating effective traffic management strategies is a multi-layered endeavor that must identify all relevant stakeholders and provide a means of communicating advisory information and travel options to each group. Special events attendees can expect a certain amount of delay associated with an event and local residents may devise strategies to avoid the routes that lead to the event as they go about their normal business. All potential roadway and transportation patrons must be considered in the traffic-management planning process.

Creating a Traffic Management Plan

The establishment of a traffic management plan is an extended process of determining how traffic, parking, and pedestrian activities will be coordinated on the day of the event.

This process encompasses all phases of strategic planning from the research and program planning stage through implementation, day of event procedures, and post-event evaluation. It is prudent to initiate the process by conducting a feasibility study of the event and its anticipated impact on the local traffic patterns and carrying capacities. Understanding the potential level of additional traffic generation allows for the identification of various methods of bringing visitors to and from the site. A *modal split* refers to the percentage of visitors that will make use of different means of accessing the site. The modal split can include the use of private cars, local public transit, shuttle buses, bicycles, and pedestrian access.[10] Understanding this split helps in allocating adequate resources for each mode of travel. In nonurban settings, the majority of visitors will come in private cars. This might require additional parking facilities both on and off site, creating a need for a shuttle service from outlying parking areas. Incentives can be created that encourage carpooling by reserving convenient parking for cars carrying more than two passengers. A drop-off area near the entrance to the site can allow cars to unload passengers before moving to parking areas, reducing the need for shuttle services. Each event site has particular opportunities to best manage access to the event. Through the recognition of the particular characteristics of your event, such as starting and ending times, market potential for local and regional visitors, the modal split, and existing road and parking capacities, event planners can develop a strategy that takes advantage of site strengths and minimizes the shortcomings inherent in the event site. Time spent planning for the most efficient use of the resources available will result in a more effective overall traffic and pedestrian management plan.

Traffic Management Plan Goals

The goals of an effective traffic management plan are to *achieve predictability, ensure safety,* and *maximize efficiency,* which together will result in the best use of the resources dedicated to organizing and directing the traffic flow during a special event. See Table 14.3.

The overall benefits of an effective traffic management plan include minimizing any negative effects that the event might have on the normal traffic patterns of the area impacted by the event. For those traveling to the event, the traffic flow and parking strategies must provide the visitor with a safe route to access the site with the least possible delay. In addition to travel convenience, the plan should accentuate safe driving practices and reduce the perception of annoyance and the emotional reactions to this type of frustration. A well-planned traffic management plan can contribute to the overall impression of the event, the organizers, and the host community. This can persuade visitors to return to the area for other events, adding increased value to the area as a visitor destination. The traffic management plan should be directed toward supporting the overall goals of the event including social and economic goals.

Stakeholder Input is Needed

These goals and benefits can be best realized if the event organizers identify and include the pertinent stakeholders in the planning process from the onset. Traffic issues af-

Table 14.3. Goals of A Traffic Management Plan

Achieving Predictability
- Perform a multi-modal travel forecast.
- Define the area and transportation system components impacted.
- Conduct analyses of parking demand and traffic demand.
- Identify and correct roadway capacity deficiencies.

Ensuring Safety
- Accommodate pedestrians accessing an event via a network of safe walking routes.
- Minimize pedestrian/vehicular conflicts.
- Provide unimpeded access routes for emergency services.
- Prevent congestion-induced secondary incidents.

Maximizing Efficiency
- Use all available resources and excess transportation system capacity, including road and transit capacity.
- Enhance transportation system operations.
- Deploy incident-management strategies to respond and clear traffic incidents.

Reprinted courtesy of the FHA[11]

fect event organizers, event attendees, local governments, safety and public works officials, public transportation providers, local and regional agencies, and residents and visitors who are not attending the event (See Figure 14-1). All road users must be considered in the management plan. The most efficient means of achieving this objective is to hold a sufficient number of well-advertised traffic planning committee meetings, making sure to invite all professional groups and residents who will be impacted by the event. Each stakeholder should provide a representative for all traffic planning meetings in order to explain their particular involvement and concerns with the upcoming event. In most communities, the local or regional law enforcement agency directs traffic control procedures. Safety is the primary concern of law enforcement agencies but is not the only concern for event organizers. Safety should never be sacrificed for convenience or public relations, but there are many situations that are better served if safety concerns can complement other customer satisfaction elements. It is the role of the event organizer to ensure fair and informed representation is provided to all involved with the event. Special attention should be paid to local residents, as their feelings about the event can impact the perceived success of the event. Unhappy residents can actively seek to terminate the event if traffic congestion, noise, and restricted access to the area are seen as negative results of the event. Local business owners might experience a drop in business due to the anticipated traffic demands and might also seek relief from future events. Event organizers must coordinate the needs of all stakeholders through a communication process that begins with meeting notifications and permit applications.

Establishing a timeline and keeping the interests of all those involved in a proper perspective is required. The desired result is to have all stakeholders understand and approve the traffic management plan and be willing to allocate the resources needed to implement the plan. Event organizers must also consider the costs that will be reimbursed by all cooperating agencies as well as the expenses that must be absorbed into the event budget.

Key Components of the Plan

According to Dunn Engineering Associates, authors of the National Highway Administration report, the vital components of a traffic-management plan for special events include developing the following elements found in Figure 14.1 and Table 14.4.

In addition, the authors recommend the development of a scenario-based contingency plan that can accommodate changes to the plan during the actual event. Unforeseen circumstances and unexpected incidents frequently occur in traffic intensive situations and

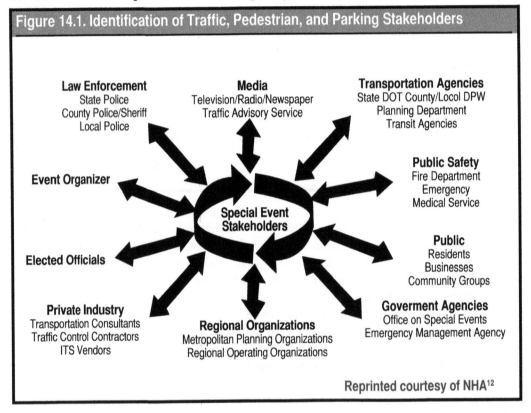

Figure 14.1. Identification of Traffic, Pedestrian, and Parking Stakeholders

Law Enforcement
State Police
County Police/Sheriff
Local Police

Media
Television/Radio/Newspaper
Traffic Advisory Service

Transportation Agencies
State DOT County/Locol DPW
Planning Department
Transit Agencies

Event Organizer

Public Safety
Fire Department
Emergency
Medical Service

Special Event Stakeholders

Elected Officials

Public
Residents
Businesses
Community Groups

Private Industry
Transportation Consultants
Traffic Control Contractors
ITS Vendors

Regional Organizations
Metropolitan Planning Organizations
Regional Operating Organizations

Goverment Agencies
Office on Special Events
Emergency Management Agency

Reprinted courtesy of NHA[12]

must be incorporated into the planning and training procedures. The most effective approach is to plan and manage this information on an hourly basis as the dynamics of the event will change throughout the course of the day or weekend of the event. This is particularly true of an event that has gradual arrivals throughout the day and a definite closing time. The demands on the traffic-carrying capacity will be greatest at the end of the event and may be complicated by nightfall and the state of the visitors at the end of the event. Fatigue, a rush to get home, a lack of familiarity with the local traffic patterns, and possible alcohol consumption can all influence visitors as they leave the venue. A traffic plan can-

Table 14.4. Key Components of a Traffic Management Plan
• Pedestrian access plan • Traffic flow plan • Traffic control plan • En-route traveler information plan • Traffic surveillance plan • Traffic incident management and safety plan Reprinted courtesy of NHA[13]

not rely on a single approach to the event but must acknowledge and address the changing nature of the event.

In the case of major events that attract large numbers of people, it is advisable to hire a traffic consultant with experience in managing event traffic to help develop the traffic management plan. An experienced engineer can see around the corners, literally and figuratively, to predict outcomes that might not be readily identifiable by local authorities. A professional engineer can also act as mediator between the competing concerns of the stakeholders regarding safety, mobility, and the reliability of the local transportation matrix.

Detailed Considerations of a Traffic Plan

A traffic management plan must be event specific. Making modifications to a preexisting standing operational plan is an appropriate starting point for the development of the event plan, but each plan must address the particular characteristics of the event and the demands on transportation resources. There are many characteristics of the event that should be considered in the development of the plan. The date, time, and location of the event will provide the framework for the analysis of access routes and available parking facilities. Summer events have the potential of attracting larger numbers of attendees, as good weather, annual vacations, and local tourism attractions can be positive influences. Weekday and weekend traffic patterns usually place different demands on local traffic systems and must be accounted for in the management plan. Day and nighttime scenarios create differing demands for directional signs, safety procedures, and the lighting of parking and pedestrian crossing areas. The type of event plays a role in the exact timing of peak traffic loads. Location variables such as urban, suburban, or rural settings will also present specific challenges to the traffic plan. Traffic demands vary if the event is a temporary venue, such as a park or fairground, with open admissions throughout the hours of operation over a period of several days. Multiple gates allow for the dispersion of entrance traffic over a larger geographic setting. The event may provide for non-specific departure times that allow attendees to leave when they please, prior to a predetermined closing time. This is in contrast to a fixed venue with a specific starting time that requires tickets with either general admission or reserved seating. Concerts, sports competitions, and other performance-based events involve starting and ending times that create increased vehicular and pedestrian traffic at identifiable periods before and immediately after the event.

The intended market audience for events might be limited to the local community or might be targeted on a regional or national scale. This information will impact the traffic plan, as a larger target market will include event specific traffic from diverse directions, on an increased number of roadways, all converging on the site during an established time frame. Marketing efforts will also influence the number of anticipated attendees having obvious implications for traffic management strategies.

Event Categories and Characteristics

Every event is unique due to its setting, theme, and attractions, its resource demands, and impact on the local community. Using data provided by the NHA plan, it is possible to identify events based on five general categories that allow for better planning of traffic-management concerns.

Traffic and Special Use Permit Process

Permits serve many positive purposes for event organizers. A properly designed permitting process forces the organizers to begin to think about the traffic management plan early in the planning stages of the event. Permits frequently require detailed information regarding the type and character of an event, the venue location, and the impact of the event on a number of stakeholders. See Table 14.5. An adequate review of the permit requires a substantial amount of preparation time as evidenced by the submittal dates for events permits often being six or more months before the event. Special use and traffic permits require organizers to think carefully and prepare a thorough analysis of the needs and impacts of the event. Submission of the permit begins the process and is generally followed by requests for additional information and the need for one or more meetings with local representatives of the permitting authority.

Table 14.5. Types of Special Events	
Characteristics	**Planned Special Event Category**
	Discrete/Recurring Event at a Permanent Venue
Event Location	• Fixed Venue
Event Time of Occurrence	• Single day, Night/day, Weekday/weekend
Event Time and Duration	• Specific start time, Predictable ending time
Area Type	• Metro, Urban
Event Market Area	• Local, Regional, Statewide, National
Expected Audience	• Known venue capacity
Audience Accommodation	• Cost, Ticket, Reserved seating, General admission
Event Type	• Sporting and concert event at stadium, arena, and ampitheater

Table 14.5. (Cont.)

Continous Event

Event Location	• Temporary venue, Park, Fixed venue
Event Time of Occurrence	• Single/multiple days, Weekends, Multiple weeks
Event Time and Duration	• Continuous operation
Area Type	• Metro, Urban
Event Market Area	• Local, Regional
Expected Audience	• Capacity of venue not always known
Audience Accommodation	• Free/cost, Ticket/ticketless, General admission
Event Type	• Fairs, Festivals, Conventions/expos, Air/automobile shows

Street Use Event

Event Location	• Streets
Event Time of Occurrence	• Single day, Weekends
Event Time and Duration	• Specific start time, Predictable ending time
Area Type	• Metro, Urban, Rural
Event Market Area	• Local, Regional
Expected Audience	• Capacity generally not known
Audience Accommodation	• Free, Tickets
Event Type	• Parades, Marathons, Bicycle races, Motorcycle rallies, Grand Prix auto, Dignitary motorcade

Regional/Multi-Venue Event

Event Location	• (Multiple) Fixed venue, Temporary venue, Street
Event Time of Occurrence	• Single/multiple days, Weekends
Event Time and Duration	• Specific start time, Predictable ending time, Continuous operation
Area Type	• Metro (Typically), Urban, Rural
Event Market Area	• Local, Regional, Statewide, National
Expected Audience	• Overall capacity generally not known if continuous events or street events involved
Audience Accommodation	• Free/cost, Ticket/ticketless
Event Type	• Sporting games, Fireworks displays, Multiple planned special events within a region that occur at or near the same time

Table 14.5. (Cont.)		
	Rural Event	
Event Location	•	Fixed venue, Temporary venue, Park
Event Time of Occurrence	•	Single/multiple days, Weekends, Tourist season
Event Time and Duration	•	Specific start time, Predicting ending time, Continuous operation
Area Type	•	Rural
Event Market Area	•	Local, Regional
Expected Audience	•	Capacity of venue not always known
Audience Accommodation	•	Free/cost, Ticket/ticketless
Event Type	•	Discrete/recurring event, Continuous event

Used with permission NHA[14]

The *special event permit* is a *planning tool* in that it requires detailed thinking and accurate projections of the impact of the special event on the host community. The permit acts as a *communication tool* used to transmit critical information between various jurisdictions as well as ensuring that all involved have given adequate notice of any proposed changes to the normal transportation patterns. The permit serves as a *financial tool* by requiring the organizers to consider the costs associated with the allocation of the necessary resources to meet the demand of the event. Depending on the needs of the event and the demands placed on the impacted systems, permitting authorities will suggest or insist on certain procedures to mitigate or alleviate the demands on the local transportation system. This can include the need to change major and minor aspects of the event if other strategies are not possible. Permits might also require the organizers to submit an event site plan, estimates on attendance, additional information regarding the history of the event, including any past traffic-related problems, a traffic flow plan, a traffic control plan, a parking plan, and an emergency evacuation plan. Evidence of providing notice of the event to affected property owners and residents is generally required and is best accomplished by inviting residents and business owners to a series of well advertised public meetings. The permit process may also require a hold harmless agreement for the transportation agencies and a certificate of insurance for the event.

Personnel

Special attention must be given to the assignment of personnel to traffic, parking, and crowd management responsibilities. There must be experienced personnel at all levels of this operation. The use of volunteers is unavoidable but must be supported by adequate training and supervision. Table 14.6 provides the recommendations of the National Highway Administration regarding the responsibilities and levels of expertise needed in these crucial areas.

Table 14.6. Transportation Personnel		
Event transportation services	Operate shuttle bus	Experienced personnel
Active traffic and pedestrian control	Manage traffic and pedestrian flow	Experienced personnel
Passive traffic control	Monitor barricades and other traffic control devices	Volunteers
Parking operations	Guide vehicles through parking area access point	Experienced personnel/ volunteers
Vehicle parking	Direct cars to parking spots	Experienced personnel/ volunteers
Operations monitoring	Monitor parking area occupancy levels	Experienced personnel/ volunteers
Operations monitoring	Observe traffic and pedestrian operations	Experienced personnel/ volunteers
Quality Control	Collect performance evaluation data	Experienced personnel
Crowd Control	Prevent overcrowding and vehicular/pedestrian conflicts	Experienced personnel
Event patron assistance	Disseminate directions at mode transfer points	Volunteers
	Provide support at shuttle bus stations	Volunteers

Used with permission NHA[15]

Communication

An event of considerable size should include a command and control center staffed by trained personnel with the capability to communicate with all levels of supervision throughout the event site. This communication must extend to all event staff, volunteers, and outside agencies that are present to support the safety of the event environment. Communication strategies must also include the ability to immediately contact the attendees through a public address system, electronic signs, and other means of mass communication. It is imperative that all communication devices used by the various agencies on site be tested for cross communication and procedural synchronicity.

Shuttle Service

A continuous shuttle service using local transport resources including coach buses, public transportation, and school buses is an effective way to alleviate congestion in the immediate area of the event. Shuttle buses can transport people to and from satellite parking areas, public transport hubs, and employee parking areas with a minimum of hassle and inconvenience. If the shuttle service is predictable and well managed it becomes a positive element in the visitor experience rather than a reduction in the personal control and freedom of movement that visitors have come to expect during leisure activities. All elements of the shuttle program should be directed toward quick and efficient access for the riders, a sense of reward for using the service, and a general feeling that the service enhances the safety and comfort of the event attendees.

A well-designed pedestrian access plan functions not only as a planning tool but is used to provide information and directions to the visitors prior to and during their time spent at the venue.

Pedestrian Access Plan

Getting to the event on foot should not be a walk on the wild side! Pedestrian access should be designed for the safety, efficiency, and convenience of individuals walking to the event, those being dropped off at the event, individuals transferring from public transit, and those arriving from adjacent parking facilities. The solution to this exercise is to identify safe walking routes with sufficient carrying capacities that minimize interactions with vehicles. The pedestrian access plan should minimize crowding by planning the routes based on the maximum usage that may occur during the event. According to the NHA guidelines (see Table 14.7), the plan should include a routing component, consisting of sidewalks or paths between street intersections and a *crossing component*, consisting of infrastructure or other vehicle control measures that allow pedestrians to cross a street safely. The planners must consider the use of temporary overhead bridges, road closures and traffic rerouting, mid-block supervised crossing areas, and access for disabled individuals that meet ADA standards in the formulation of the plan. Sufficient personnel must be allocated in order to meet the demands of the pedestrian traffic ensuring safe and expedient arrivals and departures from the event site.

Table 14.7. Pedestrian Access Plan Checklist

- Show recommended pedestrian access routes.
- Show pedestrian bridges and tunnels.
- Indicate special pedestrian crossing tactics (e.g., street closure or mid-block crossings)
- Show shuttle bus route, direction of travel, stop locations, and loading and unloading areas.
- Show vertical connections between infrastructure levels (e.g., stairs, escalator, elevator, ramps).
- Show designated pedestrian crossings at street use event venues.
- Indicate special regulations.
- Highlight pedestrian access routes and crossings suitable for disabled event patrons.

Used with permission NHA[16]

Parking Demand Analysis

I have to admit I generally don't appreciate detailed schematic drawings as a means of communicating information; I typically just gloss over them when I am reading. The detailed flowchart shown in Figure 14.2 created by NHA presented here is so well designed and easy to follow that I am including it despite my own predisposition against these things. This schematic aids in determining the necessary processes and decisions relative to the parking needs for your event. This begins with on-site parking, which is the most desirable solution requiring the least amount of additional resources. The areas available for parking must be quantified in terms of the number of spaces available. This is relatively easy if the area is striped for parking, but if not, you can use an estimate of 150 cars per acre. If the amount of space available exceeds the anticipated number of cars, congratulations, you are all done! If, however, your on-site space does not meet the anticipated demands, which is usually the case, you must determine the offsite possibilities. The offsite facilities must consider the distance to the site and the possible need for shuttle services. If the site can be used, the same process should be used to determine the carry capacity of the additional lot. This process should be repeated with any other sites to be used in order to meet the anticipated demand at the peak times of the event. So, give the chart in Figure 14.2 a try. Follow the centerline of diamonds answering the questions along the way, and you will arrive at a better understanding of the parking requirements for your event.

Implementation Plan

An implementation plan details the actions required to put a traffic management plan into effect on the day of event. Its purpose is to (1) define personnel assignments that indicate the roles and responsibilities of individual traffic-management team personnel on the day of the event; (2) describe a scenario-based, operations *game plan* at the management level; and (3) communicate instructions and organize personnel at the field level.

While the traffic management plan indicates *how* traffic, parking, and pedestrian operations will be managed, the implementation plan describes the *what, when, and where* in terms of personnel and equipment resource deployment needed to execute traffic management plan provisions. See Table 14.8.

Evaluation

Like all other aspects of event management, the traffic, pedestrian, and parking procedures will benefit from the establishment of performance objectives and the evaluation of the effectiveness of the plan. Because these elements are directly related to visitor and general public safety factors, it is imperative that the procedures be subject to continuous evaluation during the implementation of the event. Changes in the conditions of the event due to weather, a traffic accident or other emergency will require immediate and effective changes to the existing plan. Immediate feedback is necessary to determine whether the contingency plans are creating the desired effects. All problems experienced before, during, and after the event must be documented so that they can be studied in more detail during the debriefing exercise.

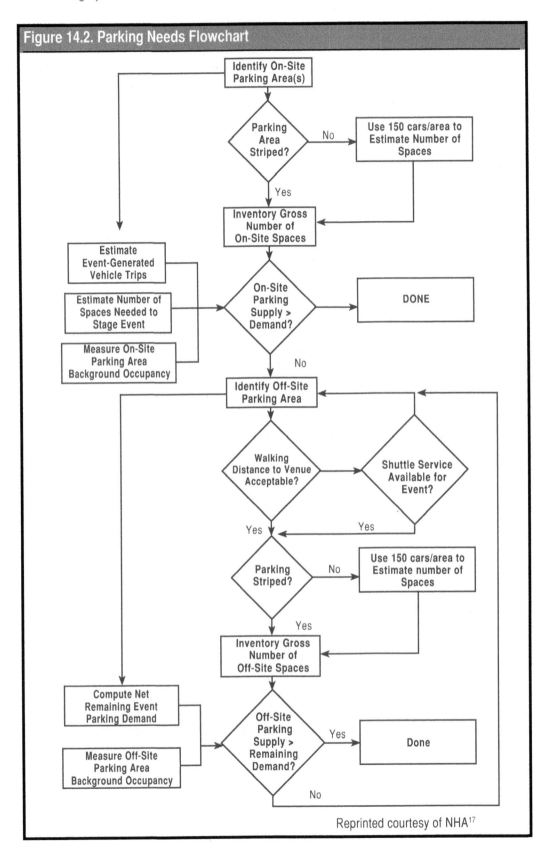

Figure 14.2. Parking Needs Flowchart

Reprinted courtesy of NHA[17]

Table 14.8. Site and Parking Plan Checklist

Element	Provision

Event patron parking areas	• Highlight free, pay (state rates), and reserved (permit) parking areas
	• Indicate lots where tailgating is permitted
	• Show specific parking area access points and state restrictions
	• Indicate number of entrance/exit lanes (or servers) at each access point
	• Designate lots by a number or letter and provide lot-specific directions
	• State time parking areas open, particularly if time varies by parking area
	• Discuss features of each parking area (e.g., paved, staffed, lighting, security)
	• State estimated walking time from each parking area
	• Indicate connecting pedestrian access routes
	• Show overflow parking areas, state distance from venue, and indicate criteria for operation (e.g., sell-out)
	• Indicate parking areas for motorcycles
	• Indicate parking areas for recreational vehicle (e.g., overnight parking)
	• Furnished map of available off-site parking areas
	   • Include Information on street regulation (e.g, one or two-ways) and connections to freeways and major arterials
	   • State on-street parking restrictions
	   • Specify private parking area regulations (e.g., egress control)
	   • Indicate location of entrance/exits points to off-street parking areas
	   • Indicate rates if available
	   • Show restricted off-site parking area (e.g., residential neighborhoods, etc.)

Gate access Information	• Indicate gate names as shown on event patron areas • Show VIP (e.g., official guest/sponsor) parking areas
VIP Information	• Show credentials pick-up location • Show hospitality areas
Shuttle bus route and stations	• Display shuttle route and all stations • State cost and emphasize free services

Table 14.8. (Cont.)		
Drop-off/pick-up sites	• Show access points and circulation lanes for transit/taxi/limo/shuttle service • Show exclusive bus lanes • Show transit/express bus station • Indicate general drop-off/pick-up site where turnaround is permitted • Indicate valet parking drop-off • Show disabled drop-off/pick-up site	
Other parking areas	• Show express/charter bus parking area • Show limousine parking area • Show media parking area • Show venue employee parking area	
Disabled parking areas	• State specific location (e.g., first row) of disabled-only spaces in general areas • Indicate number of spaces available	
Other considerations	• Show aerial map • Promote advance purchase (permit) options • Indicate tow vehicle (e.g., illegal parked) pick-up area • Emphasize new provisions (e.g., new parking areas, etc.) • Present map in grid format for easy reference • Prepare maps for different venue events if parking plan varies • Draw map to scale • Show private property • Display landmarks • Indicate municipal fireworks viewing areas	

Reprinted courtesy NHA[18]

Post-Event Debriefing

A post-event debriefing that focuses on the travel management plan should take place prior to the overall wrap-up meeting for the event. It is advisable to invite members of traffic and safety agencies that participated in the event, as they most likely have conducted their own evaluation of the event and may provide valuable information for the event organizers. The meeting should review what took place at the event in comparison to what was anticipated. This allows for an adjustment of assumptions and expectations for the future. Further analysis should determine which elements of the plan were effective and which need refinement for future events.

Summary

Whether the event is a one time only happening or an annual occurrence, the evaluation and debriefing process can contribute toward proactively improving travel management for all planned special events occurring in a region. To be beneficial for future planned special events, the results of the evaluation should be documented and made accessible to interested parties. See Table 14.9. In the case of a one-time-only event, the evaluation may show both general and specific insights, which can be used for other future planned events. For recurring events, a file providing the cumulative benefits of lessons learned will help sharpen the traffic-management plan developed for each new occurrence. It is also important to remember that with recurring events, slight changes in circumstances will require modifications to the plan.

Table 14-9. Sample Performance Objectives

User Class	Performance Objective
Event patron	• Minimize travel delay to/from the event • Minimize conflict between pedestrians and vehicles • Minimize travel safety hazard • Minimize impact of traffic incidents • Disseminate accurate, timely, and consistent traveler information • Increase automation of traffic control • Maximize site access service flow rates
Non-attendee road user	• Minimize travel delay on major thoroughfares, freeways, and major arterials • Minimize impact on commuter and trucker travel time reliability • Maintain required parking and access for local residents and businesses • Maintain unimpeded access for emergency vehicles
Transit user	• Maintain schedule travel time • Maintain transit bus dwell times • Maintain required transit station parking for non-attendee transit user

Reprinted courtesy NHA[19]

Discussion Questions

1. Differentiate between general and specific supervision.
2. Identify four major areas of concern in providing a safe and secure environment for an event.
3. Differentiate between crowd management and crowd control.
4. List four characteristics of crowds that can help in developing a management plan.
5. Why are visitor demographics important to crowd management?

6. How does supply and demand affect traffic management?
7. What are some strategies to alleviate congestion before, during, and after a large event?
8. What are the key components of a traffic management plan?
9. Who are the stakeholders in a traffic management plan?
10. Why are permits important to the planning process?

1. Abbott, J., & Geddie, M. (2001). Event and venue management: Minimizing liability through effective crowd management techniques. *Event Management*, Vol. 6, p. 260.
2. Wickham, T., & Kerstetter, D. (2000). The relationship between place attachment and crowding in an event setting. *Event Management*, Vol. 6, p. 168.
3. Hui, M., & Bateson, J. (1991). Perceived control and effects of crowding and consumer choice on service experience. *Journal of Consumer Behavior*, Vol. 18, p. 174.
4. Eroglu, S., & Harrel, G. (1986). Retail crowding: Theoretical and strategic implications. *Journal of Retailing*, 26(4), pp. 346-364, & Foxall, G.R., & Goldsmith, R.E. (1994). *Consumer psychology for marketing*. New York: Rutledge.
5. Tarlow, P. (2002). *Event risk management and safety*. New York: John Wiley & Sons, p. 90.
6. Maister, D. The psychology of waiting in lines. Retrieved from http://davidmaister.com/articles/5/52/
7. Fruin, J. (1993). The causes and prevention of crowd disasters. Crowdsafe Library. Elsevier Science Publishers. Retrieved from http://www.crowddynamics.com/Easingwold/Acrobat/Fruin%20Causes.pdf
8. Abbott, J., & Geddie, M. (2001). OP. CIT. p. 260.
9. See Crowdsafe.com
10. *Managing Travel for Planned Special Events*. Retrieved from http://ops.fhwa.dot.gov/program_areas/sp-evnts-mgmt.htm)
11. IBID Table 1-5
12. IBID pg. 63
13. IBID Key Components of A Traffic Management Plan
14. IBID p. 45
15. IBID 8-4 Day-of-Event Personnel Resource Requirements
16. IBID From NHA Tables 3-24
17. IBID Parking Demand Analysis
18. IBID Site and Parking Plan Checklist
19. IBID Sample Performance Objectives

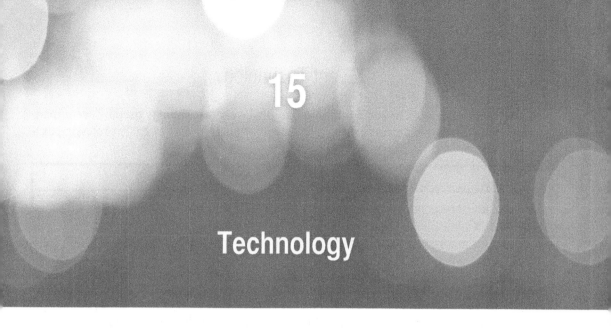

15

Technology

 What new technology does is create new
opportunities to do a job that customers want done.

Tim O'Reilly

Chapter Objectives

- Discuss the role of technology in event management
- Identify tools that assist in planning and organizing your event
- Explore professional development websites
- Understand some basics about event website development
- Implement task sequencing applications
- Identify traffic and crowd management technologies

Trying to capture the current status of technological innovations is like taking a picture of a quick flowing river. The photo only captures the river at a particular moment, while the river continues to flow. Once again, the most up-to-date ideas about the use of technology, social and otherwise, are being offered in this chapter, fully recognizing that these ideas and practices might well be obsolete and replaced by newer technologies before the book makes it to the bookstore shelves. Nonetheless, technology currently provides us with many tools to enhance the planning and implementation of special events and deserves our attention.

Event Technology

Research completed in 2005 indicated that the level of technology used by event managers was fairly nonexistent at that time. The data collected from over 2,000 professionals is found in Table 15.1.

Table 15.1. Technology Use in 2005
41.38% of respondents report using database software
24.14% of respondents report using spreadsheet software
20.69% are using a paper-based system for management and record keeping
3.45% use some form of business management software
10.34% use other types of software tools[1]

Since the publication of the first edition of this text, there has been exponential growth in the variety and sophistication of technological tools available for effective event management. A more recent survey conducted by The Active Network and the Event Marketing Institute of over 500 companies that utilize events in their strategic plans illustrates not only the rapid growth of the use of technology in event planning but also informs us of the areas considered to be most important to event organizers when using new technologies (see Table 5.2).

Table 15.2. Top Event Industry Concerns
1. Improving Event ROI (return on investment) = 90%
2. Improving the Attendee Experience = 88%
3. Expanding Customer Engagement = 83%
4. Driving Higher Quality Attendance = 79%
5. Improving Measurement of Key Performance Metrics = 72%

Downloaded from http://www.red7media.com

The same report also tells us that only 23% of event producers and marketers have a specific budget to address event technology. So, as it was ten years ago, there remains a gap between the continual growth of all forms of supportive technologies and the ability of organizations to make best use of these opportunities.

Table 15.3 shows a brief list of possible uses of technology in event management. Several of these will be explored in greater depth in this chapter.

Table 15.3. Applications for Mobile Technology for Event Management	
Twitter	Webinars
Facebook	Online meetings
Pinterest	Customer relationship management
Tumblr	systems (CRM)
YouTube channels	Constant Contact
Flikr	Virtual events
Meetup	Event management software
Ustream.tv	Room scheduling software
Peer-to-peer marketing	Registration software
Intelligent badges and scanning	Exhibition software
Photo sharing sites	Customer relations software
Cloud technologies	What's next...?
Digital lights and staging	

How many of these tools would you be comfortable using to plan an event?

The benefits of increased use of technology can serve both the internal operational goals, including achieving organization goals more efficiently, collecting data through electronic registration systems, budgeting, inventory controls, performance production elements, and many other aspects of the management challenges of the event. External goals such as strengthening brand recognition for your event, increased marketing reach, reducing marketing costs, and attracting and retaining audience members can be greatly improved through emerging technologies. Eventmanagerblog.com offers ideas on useful materials for web-based event tools.

Social Media

The most evident effect of technology in the last decade is the development of social media. Consider that it took television thirteen years to reach fifty million users, while in nine months Facebook connected with 100 million users.[2]

Contemporary event planners are compelled to create a social media strategy when planning the roll-out of an event. Social media are tools to help reach the goals of the event. The tools should not be the focus but should be strategically employed to support the operational goals of the organization. From this perspective, your social media plan must also have goals and objectives that can be measured.

What must be remembered in any business setting is that technology is a tool, a means to an end, not the actual goal of using the technology. Social media has been launched as a fun, convenient way to stay in touch with friends, share photos, follow friends and stars, provide painfully minute details about our whereabouts and feel connected to a greater sense of community.

Tables 15.4 and 15.5 from Active Network provide both a strategic framework and specific tactics to make a social media campaign an effective tool in event management.

Table 15.4. Social Media Strategy
• Establish the organization as a thought leader.
• Establish the organization as an education leader.
• Increase the organization's (or event's) visibility in search results.
• Increase the number of new attendees.
• Increase the return attendee rate.
• Increase the spending of returning attendees.
• Gather more information about attendees/customers—education needs, spending plans, etc.
• Expand the reach of the event/organization through the advocacy of attendees/customers.
• Expand awareness of the event to grow niche audiences.
• Build community.
• Drive more traffic to specific parts of the event—or specific exhibitors.
• Make the industry more aware of everything your organization offers.
• Extend the reach of the conference to an at-home audience.

There are a number of *software programs* that provide guidance in general project management strategies and tasks that are applicable to event management. Additional software packages that come in a suite of office tools as standard equipment on most computers include such things as spreadsheets, word processing, data storage, desktop publishing, and other business management tools.

"The most important thing to remember as you ramp up your social media efforts is that you're trying to build relationships. You're talking with people, not at them. Think ping pong, rather than archery." [3]

Project-management tools include prepackaged kits that can help in developing timelines, progress charts such as Gantt charts, site plans using CAD and other geo-software design products, and databases with qualitative and quantitative analyses. There are many other tools that might not be computer based but qualify as technological aids and have the potential to support event management. These include communication devices, electronic signs, and changeable message boards, cameras, and other recording devices, weather detection devices, GPS systems, electronic interactive kiosks, alternative power sources, and numerous personal organizer devices.

Software programs and services offered by online companies can provide solutions for event registration, centralized information storage, calendars, communication links, and other event and conference-based services. Text messaging and other instantaneous means of communications can help event organizers to make full use of the prevailing technologies in getting the word out about an event and creating a buzz.

Table 15.5. Social Media Tactics

- Build your profile on your chosen platform. Use those keywords.
- Make sure your social channels are integrated with your website.
- Start following the people who are talking about your industry or product.
- Start commenting on blogs, LinkedIn posts, Facebook, etc. Just add your two cents.
- Start making posts of your own. Your voice should be authentic, transparent, and engaging. Don't push your goals too hard yet. You're trying to build a following.
- Share your content. Why hide it behind member-only walls? Could it do more good shared?
- Don't over post or under post.
- If your platform supports it, schedule "chats" or start a discussion group.
- Know when to get out of the way. If your audience wants to move a conversation in a specific direction, let them.
- Always respond to negative comments. Tell us how you're addressing the issue.
- Think collaboration. What could your audience help with? Socializing topics or speakers for your event? Features for a new product? Social media is like having a free focus group.
- Help attendees engage. Launch a game. Introduce people. Connect exhibitors and speakers with attendees.
- Make a point to meet your followers at industry events. Plan a "meet-up" for everyone.
- Congratulations, you've started building a community!

Educational websites provide both theory and practical applications that assist in the planning and delivery of special events. Of particular note is a site by Julia Rutherford Silvers offering a multidisciplinary approach to event management entitled *Event Management Body of Knowledge EMBOK* (www.juliasilvers.com). Rutherford has authored or contributed to eighteen books on event management, twenty-three articles and other publications, and four videos for the George Washington University Event Management Certificate program. Her website provides valuable information by developing a taxonomy, or categorization, of all the important elements of event management. This detailed approach offers the experienced event organizer the chance to enhance his/her management strategies through the inclusion of additional areas of expertise that are generally overlooked by most event managers.[2]

Festival and event professional organizations also maintain very helpful websites that provide services free of charge. Many represent membership-based organizations providing education, training, networking, conventions, idea sharing, certifications, and other means of support for event planners. Several of these types of organizations are listed at the end of this chapter. The oldest of these deserves mention here. The *International Festival and Event Association* (www.ifea.com) has been around for fifty years and is considered the premier membership organization for event professionals, with chapters and affiliates on five continents. The Association has an extensive member networking system, offers over seventy-five publications, articles, dvds, and videos available from the online bookstore, and very useful templates of working documents that can be downloaded, modified, and used for your event. These generic templates include examples of contracts, vendor guidelines and agreements, press releases, emergency plans, sponsorship proposals, and volunteer training programs. Whether your job involves one event per year, or you are totally immersed in event planning year round, the IFEA is a great source of information and professional development opportunities.[3]

A second noteworthy association is ISES, the *International Special Events Society*, a professional membership organization dedicated to the education, advancement, and promotion of the special events industry (www.ises.com). ISES brings together professionals from a variety of special events disciplines including caterers, meeting planners, decorators, event planners, audio-visual technicians, party and convention coordinators, educators, journalists, hotel sales managers, and many more professional disciplines.[4]

Both IFEA and ISES offer job search and job-posting opportunities through their career centers. Both organizations also support professional certification programs, offering the Certified Festival and Event Executive and the Certified Special Events Professional, respectively.

The Importance of the Internet

The Internet can help you find *special event management companies* that can provide varying levels of support and marketing for your events. These companies include full-service planning and management firms, as well as organizations that can help you to enhance your use of technology through website development and search engine enhancement strategies.

The predominant form of internet marketing is currently the use of sites such as Face Book, Twitter, Instagram, Pinterest and others that allow for consumer driven marketing. One must remember that all of these can support a marketing pan but are not a substitute for strategic planning.

Website development has become a skill set that is easily accessible through packaged software that does not require the reader to understand or use html language codes. The proliferation of additional social network and video upload sites has greatly increased the ability to market events to specific demographic groups. Producing a website for your festival or event can open new avenues for marketing, advertising, sponsorships, and the dissemination of information to the public. Website design is not so difficult, especially if you find a college kid to help get you started!

Back in the early days of web design, most websites were static pages that presented varying levels of useful information, which invariably were not updated in a timely fashion. As the Internet evolved, more interactive sites arrived, providing multiple layers of information, communication with site operators, and the ability to purchase products from the site, providing for a more consumer-based orientation. These are positive developments for event organizers and potential customers. One can now visit a festival website and check out the schedule of entertainment for the upcoming year as well as link to the band's websites to hear music or view their products. You can register to be a volunteer, buy tickets in advance, reserve a campsite, or book a room at a sponsoring hotel, study a map of the site, learn about the history of the event, and receive news from the event organizers by registering for email updates. Potential visitors receive an enormous amount of information while event organizers can create a list of individuals who have expressed an interest in the event and can be reached by email.

The most recent development is the use of event specific apps to keep event attendees up to date on the activities of an event or meeting. The National Recreation and Park Association uses an app for its annual congress to highlight the daily schedule of the conference.

Research by Cox and Dale (2002) identifies important aspects of web design that contribute to customer satisfaction. They found that website effectiveness is dependent upon such attributes as clarity of purpose and design, offering reliable information, accessibility and download speed, the ability to interact with the site, purchase products, confirm orders, choose from multiple services, and the opportunity to learn more about the products or services offered by the organization.[5]

If straightforward research doesn't draw you in, try the website appropriately named Web Pages That Suck (webpagesthatsuck.com). This *via negativa* is a fun way to learn from the mistakes of others. Through a series of self-confessional checklists the user can identify design flaws in a website and attempt to make the necessary corrections so that the site is more effective. The site also identifies the worst web designs of the month and year. Most often, the faults cited involve design issues that made the site difficult for the end user.[6]

The lesson is that websites are not shrines to the builders but should be created to provide services for the customer. Apparently this message has not become a universal standard for web design quite yet. A useful exercise is to have several staff members and others access your site as if they know absolutely nothing about your organization or event. The effectiveness of the site can then be determined by the amount of information and the level of service provided to the new visitor. Some questions to ask yourself in the development of a web page might include: How will people feel or react to the home page—how do you want them to feel? What do you want people to do when they arrive at your homepage; how easy is it for them to accomplish these tasks? Each page of a website should be based on a storyboard. What is it that you want to accomplish, to relate to your visitors by creating each specific page? Depending on the goals of your event, a well-constructed website can offer many strategic advantages for your event.

Web-based marketing is an important element in getting your event known by a larger audience. It must invite and capture the attention of new users if your goal is to persuade the visitor to actually come to your event. As sites become more sophisticated, there is the possibility to include video clips from past events, audio messages from event organizers, messages from performers personally inviting visitors to the event, and the option for site visitors to share their ideas and opinions about the event through a blog format. These advances in web design require a vigilant webmaster so that the quality of the site is not jeopardized by the amount of information that must be managed. The worst thing a site can do is to provide the reader with inaccurate or out-of-date information. A website, like a special event, is all about the experience and should be managed accordingly.

Optimizing Web Presence

A factor that is growing in importance due to the proliferation of websites is the ability to optimize your site in search engines. One important factor is the use of keywords to increase site traffic and to make your site search engine friendly and easily indexed. Web ranking is determined by the location of keywords in the site and the frequency with which these keywords appear on the pages. Other factors in search engine placement include how often the site is accessed by web users and how well a site links to other sites with similar types of information. Ways of improving search engine ranking is to focus on words that appear on your pages that will help the search engine to include your site in the results. Usually two-word phrases are helpful. For example, if your keyword is *festival,* the results will be too broad. By including the words *world music festival* or *wine festival,* there is a greater chance that your site will be ranked higher for those types of searches. Do not make the mistake of including keywords repetitively on your home page, which is a form of spamming, as this is identified by the search engines and is discounted in the search process. Keywords must appear in the html title tag to be most effective. Use your keywords high up or early on your page to gain the best advantage. Search engines do not read graphics and are put off by multiple tables; be sure to have important keywords that describe your site in a prominent position on the home page. It is also important to have html hyperlinks to other pages in your site, as they often contain important information about your event. In most cases, is it more timely and cost effective to have a trained web technician address the listing and ranking strategies for your website. There are, however, many sites available that can both educate and guide you through the technical aspects of effective web design and search engine submissions. *Google AdWords Keyword Tool* provides a list of relevant words or phrases related to the type of event or product for which you are attempting to establish a web presence.

Current developments in search engine dynamics include news organizations and other commercial enterprises paying to have their sites show up high in search engine results. This strategy might, over time, make it more difficult for smaller agencies to effectively use many search engines. Given the development of the Internet over the last decade, if search payments become the norm, creative solutions will be found to combat the overcommercialization of the Internet.

A Case in Point

We are reminded of the quote by Ben Franklin: "Imagination is more important than information," and he didn't even have his own website.

Mobile Communication Devices

A very practical research study conducted in Sweden in 2005 (Lexhagen, Nysveen, & Hem) examines the use of mobile communication devices in the management of a music festival. The authors identify the challenges in attempting to communicate with all event staff regarding changes in the event plan that may occur once an event has begun. The three-day festival attracts around 55,000 visitors and offers music on nine different stages, hosting seventy different artists. During the prior week, a restaurant and bar festival is held, and an amusement park is set up adjacent to the festival. During this ten day period, an estimated 300,000 people visit the site. The possibility of delays and other problems are immense given the scope of the event. Event organizers provided wireless devices to event staff that allowed them to access information including live video feeds from five cameras positioned on the site, maps of the site identifying all the important features, message-sending capabilities (SMS), a menu with general information about event schedules, and a section with information about each event staff member with wireless access. The staff information section included a photo of each staff member and a listing of his/her role and responsibilities for the event. Each device user was given proper training prior to the event.

The researchers studied this event to determine the effect of ease of use of the equipment, the perceived usefulness of the equipment, and the positive attitudes and intentions of the staff members to actually make use of the equipment. While the results were mixed, it was deemed important that efforts be made to identify and strengthen the willingness of staff members to use technology in their roles as supervisors in an event setting.[7]

With the mobility of present technology, it is an interesting proposition to consider the effectiveness of wireless technology in the planning and staging of festivals and events in the future. Wireless mobile guides and other platforms can be made available to event visitors and interactive services can enhance the visitor experience.

Other Relevant Techno-Marketing Ideas

Depending on the goals of your event, you might want to consider marketing strategies that can also be sources of additional revenue for your event. The production of a DVD of your event is a possible way to create a souvenir-based product that will reinforce the positive visitor experience and can be used to reach nonattendees in preparation for the subsequent year's event. Likewise, a CD recording or downloadable tracks of performers at the event is a real possibility but involves detailed and sometimes cumbersome negotiations with performers, agents, and record companies. It is worth investigating these possibilities, but both of these options require a great deal of planning, negotiation, and commitment to the entire process, from scripting the product to final production and distribution. The long-term positive results of this type of enterprise can be significant and should be considered by well-established festivals and events that are trying to move to a higher level of visibility and significance.

Ticket-scanning programs can help in identifying and producing more detailed information about the attendees to your event and can help to create effective database support for mailing lists, sponsorship efforts, and fundraising strategies for the future. The use of this type of technology also helps in tracking gate activity at the event that can aid in the future management of crowd and traffic-flow issues.

Traffic Technology

Technology certainly has an important role to play in the safe management and monitoring of pedestrian and vehicular traffic. Traffic monitoring systems can include tools such as surveillance cameras, electronic message boards, radio messaging, weather sensors, and wireless communications that can link individuals with information from multiple sources both within the event site and outside affected travel zones. Any resources that can be employed to provide visitors and nonvisitors with additional information regarding traffic flow and congestion and inherent safety issues should be considered for your event.

Technology can be integrated into the planning, marketing and staging, and evaluation of most types of events. It is time well spent to delve into the possibilities of enhancing all aspects of your event through technologies that are presently available.

Summary

Event management has entered a very exciting period due to the advancements made in the past fifteen years in the area of technology. Operational and logistical demands have been supported and simplified through the use of relevant technologies. Perhaps the greatest impact of new technology is in the area of marketing and public relations. Event organizers can reach out to potential customers and support the attitudes and behaviors of existing customers through the use of Internet-based technologies. Students today are well positioned to contribute greatly to the further expansion of these efforts as they keep pace with the technological innovations that seem to be created on a daily basis.

Discussion Activities

1. What are some possible reasons for the decided lack of technology in the event management profession?
2. Name three professional membership organizations that support event management professionals.
3. Find three web-based event management companies and compare the services provided by each.
4. Locate two sites that evaluate websites. Compare the criteria used by each.
5. Analyze three festival sites using the criteria found in question three.
6. List five important elements that should be included in a festival website.
7. Find two examples of project-management software available on the Internet.
8. How can mobile technology be used to enhance event safety?
9. List three technological aids to traffic management.
10. How can social networking websites enhance event marketing?

1. Retrieved from www. planmyfestival.com
2. Retrieved from www.eventmarketing.com/research/
3. Retrieved from www.activenetwork.com/news-and-events/active-press-releases/2013/active-network-unveils-social-media-playbook
4. Retrieved from www.ises.com
5. Cox, J., & Dale, B., (2002). The quality factors in web site design and use: an examination. *International Journal of Quality and Reliability Management*, 19(7), pp. 862–888.
6. Retrieved from www.webpagesthatsuck.com
7. Lexhagen, M., Nysveen, H., & Hem, L. Festival Coordination. (2005). An exploratory study on intention to use mobile devices for coordination of a festival. *Event Management*, Vol. 9, pp. 133–146.

Section Five

Toward a Positive Future

Chapter 16 illustrates the importance of assessment/evaluation prior to, during, and after your event and provides suggestions for the various areas of your event that might benefit from evaluative review. The final chapter can be read at anytime during the use of this text. It describes the current situation relative to pursuing a career in event management.

Chapter Sixteen

Evaluation: The Path of Enlightenment

Chapter Seventeen

Career Opportunities in Event Management

16

Evaluation:
The Path of Enlightenment

 Other than that, Mrs. Lincoln, how did you enjoy the play?"

Ford Theatre Customer Service representative

Chapter Objectives

- Understand the importance of conducting evaluations
- Develop a strategy for goal and stakeholder-based evaluations
- Choose appropriate evaluation tools
- Make the best use of your results

Evaluation is the set of tasks related to gathering information from various sources in order to measure the effectiveness of your efforts in meeting the goals and objectives of your event. The standards set for the production of your event become the benchmarks for meaningful evaluation.

Case Study: The Tunnel's End

Years ago, I had the unique experience of traveling through the Siloam Tunnel in the ancient city of Jerusalem. Built in 700 BCE, the half-mile-long tunnel provided access to water supplied from a spring outside the city walls, representing the only source of water for the city if it were under siege. It also provided a secret escape route if the city walls were breached. We entered the tunnel from outside the Jerusalem walls and made our way through 1,000 meters of this burrowed opening cut through solid rock. Our tour guide told us that the tunnel was dug from both ends and met in the middle, a rather remarkable feat of engineering that must have included a bit of luck. As we journeyed through the dark tunnel, the water level gradually rose and at one point we were chin deep in nasty brown water. The walls and roof of the tunnel closed in on us at a point that the guide described as the meeting point of the workers from inside and outside the city walls. Besides a heightened level of nervousness that remained just on the control side of panic, I took one valuable lesson away from this adventure. As each group worked its way through the solid rock, their efforts at making a spacious opening were diminished. At the point that represented the end of each group's labor, the tunnel was at its smallest diameter.

This experience has repeatedly caused me to reflect on human nature in that we sometimes fail to maintain our motivation and initial level of productivity when we are near the end of a task. This lesson is important to the evaluation process, which inevitably takes place at the end of a rather demanding process of planning and presenting a special event. A commitment to quality, and to finishing the job, includes dedicating oneself to the process of evaluation.

Evaluation traditionally marks the end of your event and highlights the need to look back and review all aspects of your operations. It is also the beginning of the planning stages for your next event, requiring you to look forward aided by the information you have gathered. Evaluation creates a relationship between past and future that can be very influential in determining continued success. Evaluation is frequently given the least amount of attention by event organizers but can be the most critical element in determining the future success of your event and your organization. It requires a certain amount of maturity, both individually and as an organization, to adequately evaluate a program or event. Special events are time and energy intensive experiences. The initial reaction to the completion of an event is to get as far away as possible both physically and emotionally. Staff and volunteers need to recuperate from the long hours that are required during the actual presentation of the event. There must be a balance between the need for immediate feedback while it is still fresh in one's mind, and the benefit of stepping back and allowing for a wider perspective of the event that can only occur over time.

The goal of evaluation is to gather information regarding the quality of an experience that can then be used to make decisions regarding the planning and delivery of the event in the future.

Given the numerous aspects of any special event, the areas considered for evaluation must be well thought out and identified during the initial strategic planning of the event.

Likewise, there are many methods that can be employed to conduct an evaluation, again suggesting the need for prior planning. If the effort is going to be made to conduct an evaluation, it must be effective, realistic, and targeted toward gathering information that is deemed useful by the organization and the stakeholders.

Evaluation attempts to measure utility, identified as the usefulness of the efforts made in producing and delivering a special event. This type of research differs from scientific research in that the elements of validity, reliability, and generalizability might be secondary to the need for practicality and usefulness. Scientific research attempts to test or create theory based on data that can then be applied to a wider constituency. Event evaluation can certainly seek to do the same but is not limited by the constraints of these objectives. Event evaluation can be of a more limited scope and be applicable only to the event under consideration. Event evaluation is a form of feedback that helps to inform decision makers in making real-world assessments about the past performance and the future potential of their event.

Scientific research can also be a very valuable tool in the evaluation process, as information from other events that is gathered and interpreted can help to inform and establish the setting of standards and best practices for similar events. Empirical research also has the great quality of opening one's mind to perspectives and possibilities that might escape us during our daily routine. Research can change our view and allow for growth both individually and as an organization. An organization committed to learning and improvement benefits greatly from research. Evaluation is one method of research that can be of enormous value to your event and organization, as it creates an atmosphere of innovation, inquiry, creativity, and growth.

Setting Standards

Evaluation is not necessarily about judging the success or failure of an event, although these concepts might enter into and be considered during the process. Success or failure is really about meeting the objectives that support the goals of the event and is not usually an all-or-nothing proposition.

Prior to selecting a method of evaluation, a set of performance standards must be created for each element of the event that warrants evaluation. These standards are critical to understanding the outcomes of the event. Some standards are internal, such as recruitment of skilled volunteers or an increase in sponsorship support. Others may be external as a measurement of customer satisfaction, ticket sales, or public relations objectives.

A well-designed evaluation strategy identifies critical areas of performance, supports the development of realistic standards that identify success, and implements evaluation tools and techniques that effectively compare reported results to these standards.

Meeting or exceeding these standards should result in improved service delivery to customers, a reinforcement of the results of the SWOT analyses conducted at the onset of the process, and verification that the event matches the original intentions of the project. It is, generally speaking, a way to measure the effective and efficient use of the resources allocated to plan, produce, and deliver the event as determined by internal quality control standards and feedback garnered from participants and other stakeholders.

Developing an Evaluation Strategy

Evaluation procedures are confronted by the same limitations as the event it is designed to analyze; there are limited resources (time, money, materials, human capital) available to conduct the evaluation. Therefore, the evaluation process must have specific predetermined intentions. Both of these factors can be adequately addressed and managed if there is sufficient focus in the evaluation process. McNamara (1998) suggests considering the following questions in developing an evaluation procedure.[1]

What Is It That You Want to Be Able to Decide, Based on the Evaluation?

This question can be directed toward any aspect of the event that is perceived to need improvements or significant change for the future. Issues such as effective ticket pricing, improved traffic flow, improvements in the quality of entertainment, the effective role of concessions, determination of the length of the event, the optimum levels of sponsorship benefits, motivational factors for staff and volunteers, and more can be enhanced through timely feedback. It is important to prioritize the desired results so that resources are allocated that will guide the collection and analysis of data critical to the decision making process. The event history, as defined by previous evaluations, can help to determine potential areas for the reapportionment of resources.

Who Will Use the Information?

The formulation of the evaluation method and implementation of particular tools is greatly influenced by the anticipated audience that will receive, interpret, and act upon the findings. Is the evaluation an internal document for staff action, or is it shared with sponsors and other outside agencies that have a vested interest in the event? Are the results to be shared with the general public in order to serve the marketing and public relations objectives of the organization? These and other important questions must be raised in order to determine the direction to be taken in the evaluation planning process. A sophisticated organization may develop a multidirectional evaluation strategy for all of these reasons and more. For example, your organization may sense a need to improve the effectiveness of the volunteer training program. Information can be sought from the staff members that implemented the training program, from the volunteers who underwent the training, and from customers who were the recipients of volunteer services that were guided by the training process. All are valid sources of information regarding the training program, each representing a very different perspective on the program. The value of the information provided will be greatly influenced by the ability of the evaluators to ask the right questions of each group. The sharing of information would also benefit each of the participating groups in different ways and warrant a targeted report of the findings. A comparison of the trainer's impressions of the program with those of the volunteers or customers will also reveal interesting and useful insights.

What Information is Needed?

Having identified the affected parties in a particular situation, a consideration of the type of information that needs to be collected is the next logical step. The data must serve to answer the questions posed, or the levels of service desired, for specific groups that may include staff, volunteers, contractual employees, clients, general customers, demographic subgroups of participants, taxpayers, the media, and governmental leaders. The evaluation process is most effective if it is considered as an educational endeavor providing specific outcomes for particular groups. By adhering to this approach, evaluation can influence the planning process on several levels simultaneously. Some areas that may warrant evaluative analysis include demands and capacities of existing resources, changes to service standards, the delivery of information to various stakeholders (customers, vendors, contractual service providers), training procedures, perceptions, and practices impacting safety and security, marketing efforts, complaints and compliments, resource allocation and management, a review of organizational processes, strategies and systems, and customer satisfaction. Individual events with their particular challenges will dictate the exact nature of the evaluation strategy. It is useful to include the input from a diverse group of stakeholders in the initial formulation of the proposed evaluation strategy.

How Is the Information to Be Collected?

Through a thoughtful assessment of the objectives of the evaluation process, the formulation of a data-collection methodology and timetable can help to alleviate some of the post-event reluctance to conduct event evaluations. Much of the information needed to conduct the evaluation can be collected during the event. This requires the use of trained individuals, usually volunteers with supervision provided by a staff member, to interact with the groups to be surveyed in order to capture the necessary data. On-site data collection reduces the need for tedious post-event efforts, allowing for a less strenuous process of data interpretation and analysis. Some information, such as the overall satisfaction experienced by sponsors, vendors, and others, might have to be collected after the completion of the event in order to be an accurate representation of the entire experience. Much of the post-event data collection can be accomplished through the use of Internet-based surveys reducing staff time and allowing for an efficient compilation of data. Depending on the method of data collection and the desired level of information, either a *quantitative or qualitative* approach may be used.

Quantitative Data

Quantitative data is information represented by numerical, ordered results. This can include tools such as the *Likert Scale,* which typically ranks a response on a 1 to 5 continuum, indicating the strength of opinion of the interviewee regarding a particular topic. Other quantitative results include raw numerical data that describes demographic information such as age, gender, income, spending patterns, educational level, or any other information that can be represented by a number. Quantitative data generally seeks a limited amount of data from a relatively large number of people. Quantitative data must be recorded and tabulated to arrive at meaningful statistics that will aid the future decisions regarding your event. Quantitative information can be analyzed using simple mathematical analysis to determine measures of central tendency such as the *mean* or arithmetic average of all the scores in response to a question. The *mode*, or response that occurs most frequently, also identifies an element of central tendency. The *median* is a measure of central tendency that identifies the middlemost score in ranked results. Half the scores will have a higher value, and half will have a lower value. Various aspects of the event can be ranked in order of magnitude to determine the relative importance of particular aspects of the event as reported by various stakeholders.

Other important findings can be determined by measuring the variability or grouping of data as either closely packed or spread further around the mean or average score. This can be taken further to determine measures of variance and standard deviation, but you might want to call a doctor (a PhD)!

There are several issues that must be taken into consideration when conducting quantitative survey research. Typically, it is not possible to survey all the participants at an event. This is particularly true if the event extends over one or more days, has multiple entrances and exits, or attracts hundreds or thousands of people. In this case, it is advisable to collect data from a predetermined number of the participants on site. The motivation for this method is to collect a manageable amount of data from a percentage of the participants. This information is useful if it is a *representative sample* of the larger population of event attendees. The results from a properly determined sample will provide data that can be assumed to represent the larger group. This suggests that the information must not be biased by the methods of data collection. For example, if you surveyed only males or only people over the age of 55 at a family event, you would not have information that represented the entire group and therefore could not accurately draw any conclusions that were applicable to the entire family group. Likewise, if survey data is gathered at only one particular time of the day or only on one day of a weekend event, you will have biased results. The solution to this dilemma is to orchestrate a random-sample procedure for your event. Randomness suggests that all the attendees at the event had an equal chance of being selected for the survey. If the resources are available, you might provide surveys to individuals who enter the event at a certain interval, for example every tenth person who comes through the gate during your hours of operation. If this is too demanding, you can designate time frames known to be high traffic times throughout the event that will allow for the same level of random selection within an allowable time frame. While there is much discussion concerning the number of surveys needed to create a representative sample, it is agreed upon that too small a total will not yield the needed results. The reliability of the sample increases with the number of responses by minimizing responses that represent the outlying or extremities of the normal distribution curve. According to Hill et al.,

> "It is generally held in commercial research that a sample of 200 gives you adequate reliability for an overall measure of customer satisfaction, whether you have a population of 500 or 500,000."[2]

Qualitative Data

Qualitative data is generally considered as words that describe one's impressions, feelings, experiences, or opinions obtained through an interview, a detailed written account, through focus groups, or other means of discussing issues related to the event. Qualitative data intends to gather a great deal of in-depth data from a small number of participants. Qualitative results must be carefully read, coded, categorized, and analyzed in order to obtain manageable information.

Qualitative evaluations are time consuming and require more person-to-person contact, implying a need for well-trained interviewers in order for the exercise to be effective. A realistic assessment of the skills of your staff or the introduction of professionals to conduct this type of data collection should be considered. Qualitative information gathering is very valuable and helps to create a narrative description of your event that has many applications in the strategic-planning process. First person accounts are also valuable as marketing tool for future promotional activities.

Evaluation Methods

Evaluation methodologies can include goal-based evaluation, process-based evaluation, and outcome-based measures.

Goal-based evaluations. Goal-based evaluations consider the overall goals of the organization as well as the goals to be accomplished through the staging of your event. Goals can be classified as internal or operational if they address the means by which the organization accomplishes its mission. They are considered external, if the focus is on the effects of the event on those outside the planning and production process. Goals, as we know, lead to more specific objectives, standards, policies, and procedures that support and guide efforts toward the realization of them.

Process evauation. *Process evaluation* takes a particular look at how the event is managed, centering on the practices or procedures used to present the event. This can include decision-making processes, information-sharing practices, and other activities that are a part of the flow of the event. Typically this type of evaluation will identify best practices as well as inefficiencies in the delivery system.

Outcome-based evaluation. These procedures are gaining in popularity as they measure the effects of the event on particular stakeholders. Stakeholders might include paying customers, sponsors, or other external parties with an interest in the event. The benefits approach to recreational services is an example of an outcome based evaluative strategy. The effect of the event on internal customers, such as staff or volunteers, is also a valuable use of outcome based evaluation. Your own plan might incorporate strategies from all three approaches depending upon your evaluation needs and might include some of the following tools.

Data-Collection Tools

- **Pre/posttests** consist of a before-and-after analysis that can measure change. It can include a comparison of attitudes, preconceived notions, expectations, and beliefs, that might also allow for comparison to other events. This is effective for meeting the marketing goals of a sponsor for name/product recognition.
- **Logs or tally sheets** measure occurrences such as attendance, number of sales, product trials, or any other repetitive behaviors.
- **Rating sheets** provide for the numeric rating of services, attitudes, performances, and any other quantifiable information.
- **Interviews** represent a qualitative method of gaining additional insight through predetermined questions allowing for either limited or open ended responses. They provide for a more detailed analysis of subjective factors that might be representative of the event experience.
- **Surveys, questionnaires** are the most common means of obtaining quantifiable data in the least intrusive and yet most efficient manner. Surveys can be conducted in person, by mail, telephone, or electronically. These usually do not collect in-depth information.
- **Documentation review** consists of the evaluation of internal procedural methods, financial reports, and other organizational operations that may identify inefficiencies.

- **Focus groups** use small-group discussions in order to elicit information regarding preselected elements of the event.
- **Direct observation** guides trained individuals to observe or participate in event activities at a predescribed level in order to gather information regarding the experience of other participants.
- **Case studies** are detailed descriptions of the event that might include procedural observations, as well as accounts of the experience as provided through quantitative and qualitative data collected. This is a good way to tell the story of the event.

When Will the Results Be Needed?

A timetable for the collection and analysis of data must be determined so that the information can be effectively used in the planning process for subsequent events.

If the evaluative work is divided into manageable units driven by realistic deadlines, the process can be incorporated into the work schedule of staff members without a significant disruption of regularly scheduled responsibilities. If data is collected and analyzed but is not applied to the planning process in a timely fashion, the efforts might be wasted and the motivation for future data collection will be greatly reduced. This reflects on the initial premise that the evaluation process must have real-world applications. The information must be shared and acted upon in a meaningful way, or both motivation and credibility will be lost. The communication of the results to outside stakeholders is critical in helping them to make decisions concerning their continued or increased support of the event.

Analyzing and Implementing the Results

The primary motivation for conducting an evaluation is also the key to the analysis and implementation of the results. Information regarding the goals, processes, or outcomes of an event are sought in order to support past decisions and formulate new strategies. This suggests that all efforts at gathering data must be directly related to predetermined objectives that are seminal to the evaluation effort. Data must answer questions about, or provide insight into, issues that were prioritized and included in the list of evaluation topics. Evaluation strategies can include a combination of one or more methods of data collection that best serve the needs and abilities of your organization. If the reason for evaluation is to measure the effectiveness of the marketing campaign, efforts would be made to measure the outcomes of the marketing activities related to the event in a direct and goal-based manner.

The relative worth of data is determined by its relationship to existing knowledge or opinions regarding the areas under evaluation. The results of the evaluation can be compared to past data, to existing perceptions of the topics, to local or national standards, to anticipated outcomes, and to the stated objectives of that aspect of the event. The product of the evaluation process should be recorded in a manner that makes the results intelligible and accessible to respective audiences; staff, volunteers, sponsors, supporters, or governmental or corporate agencies. The results of the evaluation are then transformed into conclusions and recommendations that can be reported to the relevant parties. Different reports may be written for different audiences. Each audience might have different needs that are best met by reports that are custom designed to provide requested information in the most easily understood format. The reports can take the form of annual or quarterly reports, newsletters, web-based documents, media releases, public presentations, or a more formal evaluation plan.

The Evaluation Document

The formal evaluation plan, including the most recent evaluative results, then becomes an integral part of the strategic planning literature for the event. The recommendations put forth in the plan might be accompanied by, or be the catalyst for, action plans to incorporate the new information into the future operations of the event.

According to McNamara (1998) a well-devised evaluation plan should result in a document similar to Table 16.1.[3]

Table 16.1. Evaluation Plan

- Title page
- Table of contents
- Executive summary
- Purpose of the report
- Background of the event
  - Organizational description and history
  - Description of the event
  - Goals of the event
  - Outcomes and performance measures
  - Activities presented
  - Service delivery details
  - Staffing
- Evaluation goals
- Methodologies
  - Type of data collected
  - Data-collection procedures
  - Data-analysis procedures
  - Limitations of data
- Interpretations and conclusions supported by data
- Recommendations
- Appendices
  - Instruments used
  - Tabulated results
  - Narrative statements regarding evaluation process
  - Relevant case studies
  - Significant literature

Survey Use: What the Research Tells Us

Events present an interesting set of challenges in gathering meaningful data for evaluative purposes. Events, as we know, are not everyday occurrences. They are both infrequent and of a finite duration. The challenges associated with data collection are a very real obstacle to undertaking anything more than the collection of anecdotal impressions after an event. The following studies shed light on these challenges.

The survey method of collecting data from event visitors was studied by Smith and Schott (2004) in an attempt to evaluate issues concerning using this popular method during or after events. Several factors (See Table 16.2) were identified as shortcomings in conducting on site surveys:[4]

Table 16.2. Issues that Impact Participation in Surveys
Length of surveys
Opportunities to pre-test or pilot the survey
Effects on multi-performance events on survey response
Location and timing of survey administration
Effects of the atmosphere of the event
Human resources demands associated with the survey method

Survey obstacles also include the challenges of multi-entrance and exit point events and events with no physical boundaries such as street fairs and citywide celebrations. There is also a limited opportunity to administer surveys, as some events have defined starting and ending times that dictate traffic flow. Offsite surveys can eliminate this problem, but the issue of *memory decay*, not remembering important details after the event, comes into play the greater the time between the event experience and the survey. Attendees might be reluctant to participate in a survey as their motivation for attending is to have fun and escape daily routines. This can result in the perception that a survey is an intrusion into their event experience. The authors in this study documented a series of reasons why attendees refused to fill out a self-administered survey at three different events. The reasons included lack of interest, lack of time due to feeling rushed, and a desire to enter the venue for the event. Some cited other priorities such as watching the event, meeting other people, and the desire to visit concessions. Others mentioned the weather as the reason not to participate in the survey, while some had previously completed the survey, had language barriers, were not in the area to attend the event, or were actually working at the event.

Evaluation is a critical element for large-scale major events such as international festivals and global events such as the Olympics or the World Cup. An enormous amount of effort is required in the planning stages before a city is even considered as a possible site. Frequently, large sums of public funds and other resources must be allocated to the planning process. Event planners only get one chance to get it right. The post-event factors are equally important as changes can be made for future events and facilities that must have a useful life after the major event. It is for these and other reasons that large-scale events have drawn the attention of event researchers.

The Relationship of Events to the Tourism Industry

As early as 1984, the evaluation of the impact of hallmark events was being studied and reported upon.[5] Subsequently, researchers have also identified the need for the establishment of appropriate measures and standards for event evaluation (Getz, 1991, 1994, 1997). Carlsen, Getz, and Soutar (2001) identified the need for developing a standardized model for evaluating events. Shortcomings exist in both the post-event evaluation and the pre-event impact forecasting that is so important to large-scale, big-budget events. Carlsen et al.

embarked on a study of the current evaluation practices of event organizers by interviewing 55 event management industry experts regarding what practices they currently employ in event evaluation and what practices they feel should be included in a thorough event evaluation system. The following criteria were identified as being of importance (i.e., should be used) in the evaluation process and might provide some potentially interesting topics for evaluation at your local events. As mentioned earlier, local event evaluation must be grounded in the particular goals and objectives of your event. The following criteria might open your thinking to some new ideas and ways of promoting the value of your event. The researchers have identified the following criteria as critical to a thorough analysis of an event.

Pre-Event Evaluation Criteria

The elements of strategic planning in Table 16.3 should be identified and evaluated prior to initiating the event-planning process.

Table 16.3. Pre-Event Evaluation

Potential risk exposure for the organizing agency
Probability of success
Level of financial support needed
Event manager's capabilities
Potential number of visitors
Potential economic impact
Compatibility, capacity, and suitability of venues
Time of year of the event
Growth potential of the event
Expected level of local support
Potential regional benefits
Enhanced prestige for the local community
Potential community benefits
Benefits to host organization
Potential environmental impacts
Potential employment impacts
Fit with destination image
Potential for sponsorship
Potential for media impact
Catalyst for infrastructure development
Potential for links with other events
Regular staging in the location

Post-Event Evaluation Criteria

The more traditional measures of effectiveness or success that are accessible at the completion of the event are listed in Table 16.4.

Table 16.4. Post-Event Evaluation
Economic impact at the local level
Number of interstate and international visitors
Direct visitor expenditures
Financial results profit/loss
Problem-free operations
Sponsor satisfaction
Total attendance
Overnight visitors in area
Value of media coverage
Positive community attitudes
Employment creation
Cost-benefit analysis
Environmental impacts
Community sociocultural impacts
Yields per visitor
Infrastructure improvements
Urban renewal
Prestige
Image enhancement
Enhanced potential to host future events
Higher volunteerism and event expertise
Future use of purpose-built facilities

While these criteria represent the needs of major event organizations, many of these categories can provide insight into the evaluation needs of your local event. The authors identify the area of potential community benefits as being particularly important.[6]

Additional work is needed in developing methods of measurement that can quantify such concepts as community cohesion, community pride, improved health through participation, greater awareness of charities and causes, and the amount of funds raised by the event. There needs to be equal effort given to the evaluation of the costs associated with the presentation of events, extending beyond the financial realm, to issues such as traffic, inconvenience, overcrowding, increased crime, environmental issues, and other potential social problems associated with the event.

It is also useful to include a cost/benefit analysis that examines the tangible and intangible costs and benefits of the event. The *yield per visitor* measures the benefits to the host community including tangible and intangible benefits that is then quantified, usually in dollar amounts. These figures can subsequently be calculated to determine the net benefit of each visitor by dividing the benefits total by the number of attendees. This information can aid in determining the benefits of expanding the scope of the event including efforts at increasing attendance. This particular study concludes that more work is needed to develop standardized measures of event efficiencies and effectiveness.

Why Festivals Fail

Donald Getz, a pioneering leader in the evolution of the event management profession, conducted a study to discern why festivals fail. The motivation for this study was to explore the issues surrounding the topic, to help event managers avoid some of the pitfalls that lead to festival failure, and to aid in the strategic planning process. One hundred members of the International Festival and Event Association were surveyed regarding their understanding of the dynamics of event failure. Getz suggests that failure is a relative term, in that it is defined individually and reflects particular conditions and motivations for each case. Shutting down an event may be viewed either as a failure or as the result of changing community interests. Most respondents to his survey cited either the disappearance of a festival or the experience of serious problems with a festival during the past five years as an indication of failure on some level. Other major problems reported included festivals that stopped and were started up again unchanged, festivals that stopped and started with a new name or concept, festivals that were forced to change their location, festivals that were planned but never carried out, and festivals that experienced other serious problems causing major changes to their operation.

Festival failure was attributed to such diverse influences as

- poor weather,
- disgruntled merchants,
- lack of volunteers,
- lack of vision and management,
- riots,
- lack of future funding,
- banning of alcohol sales in public parks,
- incompetent event managers,
- fiscal mismanagement, and
- lack of adequate sponsorships.

The problems were ranked by respondents, with the most important internally based reasons for failure including inadequate marketing or promotion, lack of advanced or strategic planning, and inattention to program quality or service. External factors included the weather and competition from other events during the same time period. Many of the issues can be traced to resource-related shortcomings. Proper planning would probably result in a dynamic marketing plan that would attract new financial resources and produce robust gate receipts. Volunteers, sponsors, and other stakeholders must be identified and supported throughout the process. Getz tells us that predicting failure addresses the most obvious systemic problems but requires a concentrated effort to improve management in every dimension. He goes on to explain that a successful festival must become effective in securing and sustaining resources; the greater the uncertainty regarding resource availability and sustainability, the higher the chances for failure. The resource environment must be recognized and properly managed. Factors such as overdependence on a limited number of sources, control of resource consumption, effective resource acquisition and distribution, and initiating cooperative efforts with an increasing number of suppliers, all can help to support the changing environmental condition of your festival.[7]

Consider the group that carefully conceives an extraordinary event, dedicates innumerous hours to strategic planning, enacts a clever marketing campaign, but only experiences moderate success. Meanwhile, the "carnival comes to town" with the same rides, bad food, and sleazy atmosphere as last year, and they draw crowds in the thousands. Oftentimes our efforts miss the mark. We can lack an understanding of the environmental conditions that ultimately control success and failure. Survival in the biological sense is about competition for resources and adaptation to existing conditions. Organizations and events that are inflexible or inappropriately positioned within a community have a decreased chance of survival. Highly specialized organisms, such as the well-planned event, may have less of a chance of survival because of their inability to change. The carnival works every year because it is reliable; it might not be a high-quality experience, but it is predictable. If the carnival doesn't work in a community, it moves on and most likely does not return. It adapts to the environment by remaining flexible.

The challenge for a community event is to grow, to make changes, to continue to adapt to market forces but to also remain in close contact with the host community.

The Final Analysis

Effective evaluations lead to your organization making informed decisions concerning the continuation of your efforts to support a festival or special event. Information regarding customer satisfaction, operational effectiveness, local or regional economic impact, and other important issues must be carefully considered prior to the allocation of additional resources to a special event. At times, the decision to stop the future production of an event is the difficult but appropriate choice.

Discussion Questions

1. Identify three internal and three external standards for an event evaluation.
2. Which stakeholders might have an interest in the results of an event evaluation?
3. What areas might be included in the evaluation?
4. Differentiate between, and give an example of, quantitative and qualitative research methods.
5. What is a random sample? How might you achieve a random sample of event visitors?
6. Identify three types of data-collection tools.
7. What are reported to be reasons why individuals do not participate in a survey?
8. List five pre-event criteria that might be included in the evaluation process.
9. List five post-event criteria that might be included in the evaluation process.

1. MacNamara. Retrieved from www.mamagementhelp.org/evaluatn/fnl_eval.htm)
2. Hill, N., Brierley, J., & MacDougall, R. (2003). *How to measure customer satisfaction* (2nd ed.). Hampshire, England: Gower Publishing Limited, p. 33.
3. OP CIT. McNamara, p. 7–11.
4. Smith, K. (2004). There is only one chance to get it right: Challenges of surveying event visitors. In K. A. Smith, & C. Schott (Eds.), *New Zealand Tourism and Hospitality Research Conference* (pp. 386–397). Wellington New Zealand.
5. Ritchie, J. R. (1984). Assessing the impact of hallmark events: Conceptual and research issues. *Journal of Travel Research,23*(1) 2–11.
6. Carlsen, J., Getz, D., & Soutar, G. (2001). Event evaluation research. *Event Management,* Vol. 6, pp. 247–257.
7. Getz, D. (2002). Why events fail. *Event Management,* Vol. 7, pp. 209–219.

17

Professional Opportunities in Event Management

 Being the richest man in the cemetery doesn't matter to me. Going to bed at night saying we have done something wonderful, that's what matters to me.

Steve Jobs

Chapter Objectives

- Understand the various types of employment available in the profession
- Identify the criteria for a job to be considered a profession
- Delineate the process for securing a job in event management
- Identify the strengths and weaknesses of event management work

With the growth of the event industry as an integral component of commercial, non-profit and public organizations there is a demonstrated need for qualified individuals to meet the challenges of this important sector of the economy. This chapter will present information that can aid in the process of preparing for and securing a position in the field of event management.

There are a variety of job skills and positions required for event management offering the prospective employee many interesting choices for career paths. In addition to those who actually plan events, there are additional staff members who provide services like marketing, technology services, financial management, facility management, sponsorship development, volunteer coordination, various types of consultation, event security, insurance underwriting, food and beverage services, and outside sales. Depending on the size and scope of the organization, there may be as few as two or as many as one hundred or more individuals all contributing to successful event management.

The opportunities are further multiplied when one considers the many different types of organizations that provide events including meeting planners, wedding planners, conference staff, festival organizers, sporting event staff, travel event management, tourism destinations, and more. Within these diverse settings are both full and part time, seasonal and intern positions available for the right person. You might imagine that there will be a place for a well-prepared young entry-level professional in the field!

A further dichotomy exists when considering whether an organization is a *buyer* or a *seller* of event production services. This means that there are organizations that seek to stage events and are in the business of buying the necessary services to make events happen. And there are the sellers, or suppliers, that offer the services associated with venues, hospitality services, specialized services such as staging, sound reinforcement, and varying levels of consultation for successful event production. Oftentimes the suppliers are contractual service providers who will offer their resources and services to an event promoter for an agreed-upon fee for a specific period of time. Contract management is an important skill set for both buyers and providers of event management services.

A third category, slightly outside the buyer/seller configuration, is trade organizations that support event management professionals and their activities. Foremost in this field are organizations such as the International Festival and Events Association (IFEA) and the International Special Events Society (ISES). Each organization, as mentioned in previous chapters, provide a variety of services for both buyers and sellers of event-related goods and services. Overseas opportunities exist through organizations like www.eventindustryjobs.co.uk.

Planning for a Professional Career in Event Management

By the time you reach the age of seeking full-time employment, chances are you have attended hundreds of events of varying length and complexity. Generally speaking, most events provide us with many benefits that cause us to view these events as positive experiences. Positive experiences, it is commonly acknowledged, can have an impact on what types of decisions we make regarding a career path later in life. Whether it be music or sports or having a part-time job in a particular venue, we tend to reflect on these experiences when moving forward in life. It is important, therefore, prior to beginning a course of study or a serious job search effort, to reflect on your interest in this type of work. Experiencing an event as a visitor or client is, however, vastly different from working to make an event successful. An obvious example: it is usually enjoyable to attend a party at a friend's house or apartment; however, it is a different experience to plan and pay for your own party, safeguard your home during the event, and clean up after everyone leaves (and maybe apologizing to the neighbors in the morning). The initial experience of enjoying a festival or special event can certainly draw you in to wanting to work in these types of environments, but one must be realistic about the time and extensive and varied efforts required to be a successful event planner.

Before getting into the details of what it takes to be an event professional, it may be valuable to explore the idea of professions and professional behavior in a more general sense.

What Is a Profession?

The *Merriam Webster Dictionary* online version describes a profession as a) a calling requiring specialized knowledge and often long and intensive academic preparation; b) a principal calling, vocation, or employment; c) the whole body of persons engaged in a calling.[1] A profession is therefore different than an interest or passion about a particular activity. A profession moves beyond the initial or superficial attractiveness of an activity to taking very specific steps to gain both education and experience related to the activity.

Profession vs. Trade

Many fields of employment debate the differences between trades and professions. Historically, professions were considered to be academically founded vocations that were generally differentiated by the status the position held in society. Doctors and lawyers were in professions, while many other critical areas of employment were considered trades. Eventually other trades evolved and were considered professions like architects, dentists, nurses, and teachers. As the consumptive needs of societies have changed, certain service-related jobs were also considered professions including travel professionals, recreation professionals, and yes, event professionals.

A further analysis of the these jobs considered to be professions reveals common attributes. Professions usually have well-developed organizations that support the dissemination of information regarding the profession, provide opportunities for advanced education and training, establish standards of behavior, and provide a written code of behavior and ethics. Recreation, sport, event planning, travel and tourism, and social events all have professional or trade organizations associated with them. See the end of the chapter for a partial list of these types of organizations.

Is Event Management a Profession?

What is relevant in the dictionary definition provided above is that this type of employment requires a specialized knowledge and may require long and intensive academic preparation. As mentioned earlier in the text, the skills used in event production have existed for millennia but the development of courses of study is a fairly recent phenomenon. With the introduction of undergraduate majors, minors, and concentrations in event management and the codification of standards by organizations such as the International Festival and Events Association, we can confidently say that event planning/management is a bona fide profession in contemporary society. Certifications outside of academic programs are available through the IFEA, International Festival and Events Association and ISES, the International Special Event Society. Each of these well-founded organizations provides reputable and accessible educational materials that serve both the event professional and the greater public through the preparation and certification of well-trained event planners. It should be noted that there are many other organizations that claim to be institutes or learning centers for event management. Not all are useful or reputable, and caution should be exercised in making any financial commitment to these organizations.

The professionalization of the event planning occupation is captured in the sequential classification cited by Harris, in reference to an earlier work by Wilensky (1964), including the following progression:

- Stage 1: the emergence of a full-time occupation
- Stage 2: the establishment of a training school
- Stage 3: the founding of a professional organization
- Stage 4: political agitation directed toward the protection of the association by law
- Stage 5: the adoption of a formal code.[2]

The event industry can trace its development along the lines of this progression although there is no central organization or association that represents the entire industry. This is due in part to the wide variety of occupations that fit under the term *event planner,* each having a specific set of skills and expectations.

Further discussions by Harris (2004) cite a more pragmatic approach that calls for the event industry to exhibit a sense of social and professional responsibility and is then identified by society as a profession. This discussion leads to what Harris refers to as a "new commercialized version of professionalism" with an emphasis on accountability and profitability.[3] This is further delineated into three approaches that are characterized as a *trait approach,* a *functionalist approach,* and a *business approach.* From this, Harris offers a new model that incorporates a commercial vision, managerial skills, entrepreneurial skills, a code of conduct, shared interests, recognition by society, a reward system, and the provision of training and development. Harris concludes that "any definition of professionalism for the events industry will involve a complex process... that may be almost impossible to achieve."[4]

Table 17.1 is an outline of the principle considerations of the IFEA Industry Code of Professional Conduct and Ethics. In the full document there is evidence of the commitment of the organization to standards of conduct and specific expertise that support our understanding of event management as a true professional endeavor. For a complete reading of this document you can go to the IFEA website subsection on professional code of conduct (http://www.ifea.com/pdf/IFEA%20Industry%20Code%20of%20Professional%20 Conduct%20and%20Ethics.pdf)

The growth and popularity of this industry has been accompanied by an influx of event trainers/educators ranging from very well-established academic and commercial organizations as previously mentioned, to rather sketchy training programs, mostly online, that do not provide high levels of teaching or learning. One must realize that being good at event planning and having years of experience does not necessarily qualify an individual as an effective instructor in the acquisition of these skills. Teaching, like event planning, encompasses a specific set of skills that require specialized knowledge and exposure to academic settings wherein the concepts and practices can be analyzed and developed into a logical and effective curriculum. While there is no substitution for experience, it is by itself, not a substitution for pedagogy. Certification programs by reputable associations such as the IFEA *Certified Festival & Event Executive* program and the *New Professionals* program now identify a core curriculum addressing the areas of

- Sponsorship/sponsor service
- Administration and management
- Human resources
- Marketing and media relations
- Operations and risk management
- Non-sponsorship revenue programs

Entrance into the executive program calls for prerequisite years of experience, conference attendance, publications, speaking presentations and an assessment component.

Table 17.1. IFEA Industry Code of Professional Conduct and Ethics

Principle/Standard #1: Members shall ascribe to and promote the Mission and Ends of the International Festivals and Events Association

Principle/Standard #2: Members shall use any and all opportunities to improve the public's understanding of the role that festivals and events play in their community and in society.

Principle/Standard #3: Members shall assist in maintaining the integrity and competence of professionals in the festival and event industry.

Principle/Standard #4: Members shall embrace and promote the highest standards of human resource training and management.

Principle/Standard #5: Members shall practice and ensure the highest standards of safety and professionalism in the conduct of business affairs.

Principle/Standard #6: Members shall not engage in any conduct that involves legal fraud, commission of a crime, or violation of law.

Principle/Standard #7: Members shall represent and deliver their business commitments in an honest and complete manner. Members should avoid conflicts of interest that undermine the generally accepted business practices and ethical business conduct. Members shall make every reasonable effort to resolve business disputes with clients, other members, sponsors, and others in a fair and professional manner.

The National Recreation and Parks Association (NRPA), in cooperation with IFEA, has developed a two-year Event Management School offered through the association's professional development efforts at the Olgelby Resort and Conference Center in Wheeling, West Virginia. More information about this program can be found at http://www.nrpa.org/event-school/.

Professionalism is More than "Dressing Up"

Professionalism typically refers to an accepted standard of behavior in a chosen field. Professionalism has both connotative and denotative significance for the engaged professional. Denotation refers to the literal meaning of a word. Connotation signifies the associated ideas regarding the word that may evoke emotion, relevance or a slightly different interpretation of the word without totally abandoning the denoted understanding. For example, we might, if we are of a certain age, refer to something or someone as being "cool." The definition of cool (denotation) is either that of an adjective: at a fairly low temperature; a noun: a fairly low temperature, or as a verb: to become or cause to become less hot. When we refer to someone or something as cool, we are not necessarily taking their temperature but are referring to a certain set of qualities that makes them desirable or admired, unflappable, interesting, or out of the ordinary in a positive way. We can also refer to someone as cool who has not warmed up to their surroundings, as in being aloof. Again, not a reference to ambient temperatures. The Internet provides pages of connotations regarding the word cool. But spending any more of our time on these examples wouldn't be cool...

And so it is with professionalism. The definition of professionalism (denotation) according to Merriam Webster is

1. the conduct, aims, or qualities that characterize or mark a profession or a professional person
2. the following of a profession (as athletics) for gain or livelihood.[5]

The connotations of professionalism include the expectations regarding appropriate behavior that adhere to a set of standards that are accepted within the area under consideration.

Harris (2004), in the article entitled *Event Management: A New Profession*, presents an orderly investigation of the variables to be considered when determining the expectations associated with a profession. Harris cites Friedson (1994) in identifying three levels of consideration when discussing the term *professional*. The term is related to the individual, the organization, and the industry. In England, the definition is quite clear; a professional is one who has a minimum of a degree level qualification.[6] This includes the managerial class and specialized technical positions, which includes those who manage events.

How to Become a Professional

If we now have some idea of what a profession is and what it means to be professional, the next logical question might be, "How do I become an event professional?"

Professionalism is about skills and attitude. The skills associated with an event planner can be grouped into the three areas of management that are the focus of this text. These are skills that address the ability to manage human, financial, and physical resources. Each of these major areas of resource management lead to a very extensive subset of skills that encompass all the activities related to event management. This text is designed to expose you to these skills in a fairly detailed manner.

In a more general context, a professional event planner will need to have excellent customer service skills driven by a sense of empathy and understanding of what motivates others to seek the benefits of participation in planned special events. Communication skills, including oral and written public presentations, written technical reports and analyses, and the ability to develop effective marketing materials are necessities in this field.

Project management with all its associated skills of time management, team work, motivational and leadership skills, and the ability to delegate are valued traits in an event employee. Advanced computer skills and a strategic understanding of the use of social media will continue to be needed and will necessarily evolve quite rapidly in the next decade.

All of this must be seamlessly integrated in your ability to multitask, as the demands of event management vary from season to season, month to month, and certainly require the use of multiple skill sets during an actual event. This also suggests the ability to be a quick thinker and effective decision maker, particularly if combined with a broad sense of imagination and resourcefulness and a creative approach to problem solving. And did we mention that all of these skills and more must be implemented in time schedules with very tight deadlines...?

In addition to these cognitive abilities, there is a certain amount of physical demand that comes with the event industry. The lead-up hours to a special event and the actual hours and days during an event frequently extend well beyond the typical eight-hour day and forty-hour work week environment. You may work forty hours in one weekend during a two or three-day special event or festival. Physical strength and stamina are valued and appreciated by event coordinators when hiring new employees or taking on an intern during the busy season.

For the Student

Landing a position with an event company will depend on the experience you bring with you to a job interview. Due to the relationship between the skill sets needed for event management and the finality of the product, learning on the job is a sometimes necessary but risky proposition for an event company. What this means is that mistakes made in the planning of an event due to a lack of experience or focus will undoubtedly result in outcomes that can have a negative effect on the success of an event. It is not unlike a surgeon who needs a lot of practice before facing a real patient or event.

This presents the age-old dilemma for recent college graduates. The employer wants someone with experience, but you can't get any experience without working in the field. This is a real challenge, but is not fatal. Astute employers have come to appreciate the value of part-time experience, internships, and the value of volunteer activities that serve to build the skills of the potential employee. While some job descriptions call for a minimum of a college degree and several years of experience in the field, it is possible to substitute full-time experience with a series of part-time and volunteer experiences that approximate the requirements for the position. Sometimes the breadth of experiences attained in several part-time jobs and volunteer experiences actually provide the potential employer with a candidate whose skills are sufficiently developed for immediate and successful employment.

While you are in school, try to incorporate the following strategies into your personal strategic academic plan.

1. Spend some time reading event management job descriptions for the types of positions that you would like apply for at the end of your days in school.
2. Create a list of these job skills and choose courses that contain information and experiences that will help you to learn about and use these skills.
3. If your school has a major, minor, or concentration in event management, combine this with an appropriate course of study in recreation management, communication, hospitality and tourism management, marketing, or business.
4. Additional courses in organizational psychology, public relations, accounting, finance management, graphic design, and computer technologies would add to your tool kit.
5. Begin building your resume while you are in school. This idea cannot be overemphasized. Event management has become a popular field of study in the past few years, with hundreds of students completing degrees in order to find their dream jobs. What differentiates a viable candidate from the rest is the experience gained, the personal contacts developed, and the broader sense of the profession that emerges from extracurricular activities.

6. Find part-time or volunteer work that will provide you with experiences related to your career choice.
7. Apply for membership in a professional organization related to your career.
8. Commit the financial resources and time to attend state, regional, and national conferences in event management.
9. Subscribe to and read professional publications and subscribe to blogs, listserves, and other resources that relate to your professional aspirations.
10. Understand your place in the professional community. You will, by necessity, be starting at the bottom. You will be doing work and chores that you had not imagined that might cause you physical and emotional stress. Be humble, persevere, ask appropriate questions, excel at all tasks given, and don't forget to smile!

The Internship Experience

The role of an internship, oftentimes required for event management academic programs, can greatly enhance chances for landing a full-time position. Internships, like all things of value, must be properly planned for and allotted sufficient time to be developed in the most effective way. Some universities provide a one-semester seminar to help in the preparation and search for a suitable internship site. Others may have a detailed process for securing an internship without the support of a specific course. Ask questions about the policies and procedures concerning an internship at your institution long before it is time to enroll. Not having a plan is a plan for a less than optimum experience.

Understand the expectations of your department in terms of the number of hours and types of experiences and reporting procedures expected of your enrollment in an internship program. Ask other students who have completed a practicum or internship about their experiences. Start a chat room or webpage where you and your colleagues can discuss their internship experiences, but remember that nothing on the Internet is private these days.

As you research internship possibilities, determine locations that offer the types of programs and events that you could imagine yourself involved with in the future. Identify the benefits of each potential site in terms of geographic location, the possibility for hourly pay or a stipend, and the types of responsibilities that you would be offered at the site. Keep in mind that, although this is only an internship, it may also be your first full-time experience in the event industry.

Treat every aspect of this experience, from resume submission and phone interview, to the expected behaviors of the employees both on and off the job, as a real job experience. An internship can serve as a means of completing your degree, of obtaining needed and specific experience in the event industry, and as a lead up to continued employment with the company in a part time or full-time job after the completion of your weeks of interning.

Also keep in mind that many college graduates who are seeking full-time employment in a number of fields have voluntarily accepted internship positions, both paid and unpaid, after graduation in order to continue to develop their skills and marketability as an event professional and remain in contact with the event organization.

An internship should provide you with knowledge and on-the-job training that will help you to decide whether the demands of the profession are what you expected and whether event planning is a good fit for you. If you are committed to pursuing a career in this field, the internship should also help you to develop the professional contacts and continuing education opportunities to prepare you for competing for a place in the field. Finally, use your internship to develop a means of enlisting professionals as mentors. This may be your immediate supervisor at your internship or other professionals who are willing to help to develop your skills. By showing a respect for their time and a real appreciation for the information and guidance provided, this type of relationship can be beneficial for both the student and the mentor.

Transitioning from School to Work

What Makes for an Effective Resume?

There are numerous websites and guides for writing effective resumes that provide detailed and sometimes conflicting information concerning resume construction and content. If you are presently in school, it is a good practice to visit your career center to see what kind of advice they can provide. It can be disconcerting to hear so many diverse opinions about resumes. The best advice is to keep your resume real but be opportunistic in presenting any and all experiences that can demonstrate the skills needed for the sought-after position. It is also important to quantify (use numbers) to describe your experiences. Have you planned events for 10 people or 10,000 people? Both are important but suggest different skill levels.

A recent trend that might not be addressed in a class or at the career center is the growing practice of organizations using scanning technology to review resumes. Generally, there is a very large number of applicants for job openings, with many of the applicants not having sufficient education or experience to meet the minimum qualifications for the job. Human resource professionals have developed digital scanning techniques that search for keywords within a resume to help in the very time consuming process of determining viable candidates for further consideration in the hiring process.

Preparing a scannable resume requires new methods of presenting your materials. Because the resume will be "read" by an optical device, it is imperative that you do not confuse the optics with unnecessary visual clutter, and that you understand the capabilities and limitations of this type of process. The Purdue University online resume lab suggests the following strategies:

- Left justify the entire document.
- Avoid punctuation as much as possible.
- Avoid vertical and horizontal lines, graphics, and boxes.
- Do not fold or staple.
- Use only those abbreviations that are familiar with your field of study.
- Use fonts such as Times New Roman, New Century, Courier, or Helvetica.
- Font size should be between 10-12 pts.
- Avoid fancy font styles such as italics, underline, and shadows.
- Boldface and CAPITAL letters are acceptable provided that the letters do not touch each other.
- Provide white space between words.
- Avoid condensing the spaces between letters and lines.
- Keywords are the most important aspect of the scannable resume. It is advisable to create a paragraph where all the keywords are listed in order to be identified in the scan.

> ➤ Incorporating words that are commonly used within the industry and indicate your personal work skills increase the chances of having your resume read.[7]

These guidelines are explicitly for organizations that have indicated the use of scanning as a part of the sorting process. These practices should not, for the most part, be employed in a traditional resume. You may want to verify with the organization as to whether they will be using scanning technology as a part of their process. The best thing to do is to have a resume prepared in both formats so that you have an up-to-date and properly formatted resume ready for review.

The Job Search: Looking for Love in All the Right Places...

One important consideration when leaving school and entering the job market is to realize that it is a very competitive environment. Unless you are entering a family business, finding a job can be a long-term, somewhat stressful, and sometimes overwhelming proposition. The one consolation is that you are not alone.

Who Else is Looking for Your Job?

The abrupt changes in the economy in the past few years resulted in many individuals looking for new areas of employment. Positions once considered to be entry level are now being sought by people with years of experience. Others have settled for part-time work or jobs outside their field of expertise. This is not necessarily good news for graduating seniors. However, if a recently graduated student has accumulated sufficient experience *and* has mastered the newest technologies associated with design and marketing, the advantage may shift. A good example is the event planning company Red Frog (http://www.redfrogevents.com/) situated in Chicago but providing event management services in many locations. Older applicants may have extensive project management experience but may lack the current skills required in the ever-evolving field of event management.

Understand and capitalize on your strengths; identify and improve in your weakest areas, and you will be able to compete with the following groups seeking employment.

Event management students. With the growth of event management as an undergraduate program in many universities, the number of students identifying themselves as future event planners is growing annually.

Second career seekers. Due to the changes in economy mentioned earlier, there are those starting over with a vision of event management as an appropriate place to make use of long-developed management skills. These can include individuals with sales and marketing experience, hospitality industry backgrounds, project management, and customer service skills. These individuals may lack event specific skills but frequently can cite an extensive and very productive work history and a level of maturity and responsibility that can be seen as an advantage in a competitive job market.

Event workers seeking new positions. As in any multitiered industry, there are opportunities for movement both horizontally from one area of management to another and vertically to positions of higher responsibility and reward. Both cases create openings at various levels with event planning organizations, which might create opportunities for the new employees.

Internship extensions. In very competitive markets, individuals seek to retain internships beyond the requirements of their academic institutions. While this may provide little or no pay, the idea is that continuing the working relationship will add additional experience to a resume, will provide for additional contacts and networking opportunities in the profession, and can lead to being considered for any internal openings that might arise. In the best-case scenario, there might be a position created due to your indispensible contributions to the organization. This decision will often require finding a second job outside the time needed for the internship, which can be challenging. If you really want to be in the event industry, it might be worth the effort!

Where Can Jobs Be Found in the Industry?

The old-school technique for securing a job was to check the classified ads (in a newspaper or trade journal) and be ready to move to wherever a job might be available. While this can be a successful strategy, many individuals choose where they would like to live using geographic preference as a primary determinant in the job search. This process is explained in great detail in the book, *The Rise of The Leisure Class*, by Richard Florida. It would be wise for all students, particularly those pursuing careers in a creative industry such as event planning, to read and be familiar with the concepts provided in this insightful text.

Strategic Planning is Important

The Bureau of Labor Statistics provides very detailed information about hundreds of careers including those related to event planning and management. The link to 13-1121 Meeting, Convention, and Event Planners, http://www.bls.gov/oes/current/oes131121. htm#nat is a great place to begin to understand the event planning profession and to obtain information related to the industry profile including the number of reported positions in the profession, average hourly and salary wages, the highest concentration of positions by state and metropolitan area, and the salaries distribution by state. A quick study will show that nine out of ten top-paying metropolitan areas for event managers are on the east coast. But if you HAVE to live in the Rockies, there are localized pockets of good paying positions related to travel and tourism locales through the U.S.

In today's marketplace, the online advertising sources for job openings have become indispensible tools for creating an organized job search and obtaining detailed information about a particular job opening, and the sponsoring organization. The Google corporation has developed a program, *Google Alerts*, that provides a subscriber with periodic updates on keywords from various sources on the Internet. By providing keywords related to your job search, you may receive information that can help in your efforts to locate employment. As with virtually everything else on the Internet, problems exist with the reliability, accuracy and verifiability of the information provided. Simply put, there are varying levels of quality in the ever-expanding job search industry.

The U.S. Department of Labor identified this problem and sought to aid job seekers through the a program entitled "*Tools for American Job Seekers Challenge*" surveying over 16,000 job seekers as to their preferences for job seeking tools and sites provided on the Internet. The www.Careeronestop.org website is the result of this research providing reviews of over six hundred job seeking and career building tools in six critical areas. A review of the materials on this site will help in developing a strategic plan for managing your job search.

In addition to a review of the career sites offered online, it is very important, in fact absolutely critical, that one become familiar and conversant with the professional trade organizations related to your area of interest. This might include the national and international organizations related to event planning or a more focused interaction in areas such as meeting and convention planning, wedding planning, sport event planning, or community-based programming through a Chamber of Commerce or a parks and recreation agency. If you are drawn to a particular aspect of event planning, make the effort to connect with the appropriate organization that exists to provide professional development and networking opportunities.

The important thing to remember is you must be out there amongst those in the profession. Volunteer for events whenever possible, attend local regional and national conferences and workshops to increase your skills, build your resume, and socialize with professionals in the field. There is no substitute for personal relationships that are developed through this proactive approach to finding a rewarding position in this dynamic profession.

In addition to your physical presence, it is important to develop your virtual presence as a new professional. Your Facebook page can be an aid to your career or the worst thing you ever did, depending on the content of your site. Facebook is public, and how you represent yourself on this and other sites can impact your ability to get a job. It may not seem fair, but it is how things are these days. More importantly is to develop a professional persona through sites like Linkedin, which allows you to post professional details, your resume, references, and more in an acceptable format. You may also join groups within the site that allow for discussion of current topics in the profession, seek advice, and gain a presence with others in the field. An example on Linkedin is the *Who's Who in Events*, which provides a lively forum for all matters related to events and the event planning and management group.

A second site related specifically to event management careers is *EventJuice*, a British site that offers advice and information for event planners. http://eventjuice.co.uk/building-a-career-in-the-event-industry-part-2/.

In a recent online conversation, members of EventJuice reflected on their perspective regarding the best and worst aspects of their jobs.

The 10 Best Reasons to Work in Events

1. Making People Happy

Seeing guests enjoying themselves and getting great feedback, is in my opinion the most rewarding parts of working in events. When I used manage a venue, I organised personal events for local people, such as birthday parties, engagements, weddings, funerals, and christenings. These were really important events in their lives, so everybody at the venue worked their socks off to ensure that every part of each event exceeded expectations.

One event that springs to mind is a funeral that we organized. Funerals are obviously extremely sad occasions. But one of the best feelings in the world was after the funeral when Joe (the husband of the deceased) thanked me for our hard work and said that he literally couldn't have imagined the day going any better. I promise that being a part of something so special and important to someone is amazing!

2. Variety of the Job

Working in the event industry offers so much variety where most days are different.

3. Creativity

I particularly enjoy the creative parts involved in my job, such as coming up with ideas.

4. Travel

I've seen more parts of the UK through work than I ever have. Sure, I'm not relaxing whilst there, but you can still see quite a bit of a city when working.

5. Development

I really enjoy learning new things. I have found that working in events I am continually learning from the people around me, those I come across in the industry and from what I read.

6. Interaction With People (Clients, Suppliers, Participants, and the Media)

Working in events means that you'll have to deal with very different types of people—from a sales manager at a city centre five-star hotel to an instructor at an outdoor activity centre in the middle of nowhere—and you'll make some great friends.

7. Fun

Yes, it is. Not always, but most of the time.

8. Challenging

Fast-paced and an exciting environment where you're constantly dealing with difficult situations.

9. Visit Incredible Venues

I guess this one depends on the individual. Through work, I spend a lot of my time visiting beautiful hotels and venues in stunning settings, all over the country. I'm easily impressed by architecture, decor, and the stories that I'm told whilst walking around the buildings.

10. You Get To Experience Everything

A perk of working in events is being invited to many functions and parties, "familiarisation trips" where organisers experience venues and activities first hand.

The 10 Worst Reasons to Work in Events

1. Stressful

Thankfully my job isn't as stressful as others, but some people won't leave the office until 10:00 at night when working to tight deadlines set by their clients, or will hardly sleep in the build up to an event.

2. Dependent On Others

In the event industry, very few organizations are able to operate completely independently. The event industry is a network of event management companies, suppliers, venues, and people working together—relying on and influenced by each other. So if something happens to one, or there are changes in the external environment, such as the recession or a new trend this can result in a kind of domino effect—with some able to cope, and some smaller organisations not. For example, if a client decides not to book their annual event, this not only has an impact on the event organiser, but also on the suppliers and venues they use.

3. Competitive

Events is a highly competitive industry for jobs and business, where so many organisations offer identical services. One thing I really like about the business model of the company I work for, is that because it's an agency we don't own any kit, therefore we can't and don't copy others. If someone introduces something new to the market —if our companies are compatible and after testing, we can then offer it to our clients and they can run it, so nobody loses out and the client benefits from the experts running their part of the event—but recommended by a company they trust. Our position means that we can lead product developments with some of the suppliers we work with and trust.

4. Everyone Thinks They Can Do Your Job

Planning one birthday party is not the same as organizing and managing several different types of events, at different stages, at once. My dad is a perfect example. He works in demolition (and has worked extremely hard all of his life). I don't think I can remember him ever organizing an event; however, even he sometimes makes suggestions when I visit, such as "Hey, Mike, there's a bloke I know who owns a couple of quad bikes, I think you should give him a call." Now we would never just organize a quad biking event. "I noticed a nice place just outside of Bristol; it would be perfect for what you do." For what it's worth, it wasn't. Usually I just humor him and say, "I'll check it out," but I don't give my father tips on how to knock down a buildings, because I wouldn't have a clue.

Working in events, you'll find that once you tell someone what you do, everybody knows someone or something good(ish) for events and they'll start trying to think up solutions for you.

5. Disrupted Social Life

I don't know how they do it, but our suppliers spend most of their time on the road or on trains, working weekends and evenings (as well as weekdays), eating poorly, and not getting as much sleep as the rest of us. Be prepared for this.

6. Party Planner Label

By some, event management is not seen as a "proper" profession and should just be a hobby or an event should be organized in spare time. If those people were to sit in our office for a day or spend some time shadowing our suppliers, they would soon learn to appreciate the amount of work that goes into organizing event after event and how much knowledge, experience, and expertise an event organizer has.

7. Dealing With Difficult People

Just like it is lovely interacting with clients, participants, suppliers, and the media—sometimes it can be horrible.

8. No Testing – Only One Chance To Get It Right

An event is not a product. So unlike a product, where you can build a prototype to see what it looks like, feel it, and test to ensure that everything works properly before it's launched, there is that added pressure that you have to get it right first time around.

9. You Can't Please Everybody

Even though you and your client may be passionate about a project, you'll find that not everybody likes the same things or feels the same way about what you are doing, and people have different expectations (especially if you are not involved in setting the expectations in the first place). You may be asked to organise something for a really outgoing bunch of people but were not told about the really quiet person in the group who is easily embarrassed, or something could be happening in someone's life that troubles them at the time or it could just be as simple as the person is in a bad mood. You can't please everyone—done!

10. Sometimes Things Just Go Wrong

No matter how much planning you do, sometimes things just go wrong.[8]

Summary

The event management profession is in a constant state of evolution. There are myriad opportunities to become involved in organizing promoting and providing services to the delivery of event experiences. The opportunities for training and education include college and university programs, professional development organizations, internships, and on-the-job training. Securing a job in the profession requires a commitment to the opportunities you might find and the flexibility and maturity to build your career. It is a growth industry with room for dedicated young professionals who can grow along with the industry.

Review Questions

1. Define the term *professional.*
2. Define professionalism and describe how it applies to the event industry.
3. How has professionalism changed, according to Harris?
4. According to the Bureau of Labor Statistics website, where are the highest paying jobs in event management?
5. What is the impact of scanning on resume writing?

Useful Websites

www.ifea.com
www.ises.com
http://i-meet.com/public
http://institute-of-event-management.com/
www.eventindustryjobs.co.uk.

1. Retrieved from http://www.merriam-webster.com/dictionary/profession?show=0&t=1361815334
2. Harris. V. (2004). Event management a new profession? *Event Management*, Vol.9, pp. 103–109.
3. IBID 107.
4. IBID 108.
5. Retrieved from http://www.merriam-webster.com/dictionary/professionalism
6. Op. Cit. Harris, p. 104.
7. Retrieved from http://owl.english.purdue.edu/owl/resource/700/01/
8. Florida, Richard. *The rise of the creative class.* New York. Basic Books. 2002.

Index

SAGAMORE
P U B L I S H I N G

RELATED BOOKS AND JOURNALS

Recreation Programming
Designing and Staging Leisure Experiences
Sixth Edition
J. Robert Rossman
Barbara Elwood Schlatter

second edition
Supporting Individuals With
AUTISM SPECTRUM DISORDER
IN RECREATION
Phyllis Coyne   Ann Fullerton

HIGH PERFORMANCE AGENCIES
The Entrepreneurial Model for Public Parks, Recreation, and Tourism Organizations
PAUL A. GILBERT

SPRING 2014 • VOL 4 • ISSUE 1
JNEL
JOURNAL OF NONPROFIT EDUCATION AND LEADERSHIP
WKU.
Research Foundation, Inc.

BUY DIRECT & SAVE
MOST E-BOOKS 50% OFF PRINTED PRICE
INSTANT ACCESS | INSTANT SAVINGS

www.sagamorepublishing.com   1-800-327-5557